Writing Science Fiction and Fantasy

Writing Science Fiction and Fantasy

Edited by

Gardner Dozois, Tina Lee, Stanley Schmidt, Ian Randal Strock, and Sheila Williams

St. Martin's Griffin

New York

WRITING SCIENCE FICTION AND FANTASY. Copyright © 1991 by Davis Publications, Inc.
All rights reserved. Printed in the United States of America. No part of this book may be
used or reproduced in any manner whatsoever without written permission except in the
case of brief quotations embodied in critical articles or reviews. For information, address
St. Martin's Press, 175 Fifth Avenue, New York, N.Y. 10010.

Design by Erich Hobbing

Library of Congress Cataloging-in-Publication Data

Writing science fiction and fantasy / by the editors of Analog and
    Isaac Asimov's science fiction magazine, Gardner Dozois . . . [et
    al.].
        p.   cm.—(The writer's library)
    ISBN 0-312-08926-0
    1. Science fiction—Authorship.   2. Fantastic fiction—Authorship.
I. Dozois, Gardner R.   II. Analog.   III. Isaac Asimov's science
fiction magazine.   IV. Series: Writer's library (New York, N.Y.)
PN3377.5.S3W75   1991
808.3'876—dc20   90-26794

First St. Martin's Griffin Edition: April 1997

10   9   8   7   6   5   4   3

Contents

Part III
THE BUSINESS OF WRITING

Part IV
APPENDIX

Acknowledgments

Grateful acknowledgment is made to the following for their permission to reprint their copyrighted material:

"The Creation of Imaginary Worlds," by Poul Anderson, copyright © 1974 by Poul Anderson. Reprinted from *Science Fiction Today and Tomorrow*, edited by Reginald Bretnor, by permission of Scott Meredith Literary Agency, Inc.

The five articles by Isaac Asimov first appeared as editorials in *Isaac Asimov's Science Fiction Magazine: Revisions* (July 1982), copyright © 1982 by Davis Publications, Inc.; *Dialog* (April 1985), copyright © 1985 by Davis Publications, Inc.; *Writing for Young People* (July 1986), copyright © 1986 by Davis Publications, Inc.; *New Writers* (January 1987), copyright © 1986 by Davis Publications, Inc.; and *Plotting* (June 1989), copyright © 1989 by Davis Publications, Inc. All are reprinted by permission of the author.

"How to Build a Future," by John Barnes, copyright © 1990 by Davis Publications, Inc. First appeared in *Analog Science Fiction/Science Fact*. Reprinted by permission of Ashley Grayson, literary agent.

"The Creation of Imaginary Beings," by Hal Clement, copyright © 1974 by Hal Clement. Reprinted from *Science Fiction Today and Tomorrow*, edited by Reginald Bretnor, by permission of the author.

"Living the Future: You Are What You Eat," by Gardner Dozois, copyright © 1976 by the Science Fiction Writers of America. Reprinted from *Writing and Selling Science Fiction*, edited by the Science Fiction Writers of America, by permission of the author.

"On the Writing of Speculative Fiction," by Robert A. Heinlein, copyright © 1964 by Robert A. Heinlein. Reprinted from "How To, in Four Tricky Lessons," from *Of Worlds Beyond*, by permission of Blassingame-Spectrum Corp.

"Good Writing Is Not Enough," by Stanley Schmidt, copyright © 1986 by Writer's Digest Publications, Inc. First appeared in *The Secrets of Writing Popular Fiction*. Reprinted by permission of Scott Meredith Literary Agency, Inc.

"The Ideas that Wouldn't Die," by Stanley Schmidt, copyright © 1989 by Writer's Digest Publications, Inc. First appeared in *Writer's Digest*. Reprinted by permission of Scott Meredith Literary Agency, Inc.

"Authors vs. Editors," by Stanley Schmidt, copyright © 1990 by The Writer, Inc. First appeared (in somewhat different form) in *The Writer*. Reprinted by permission of Scott Meredith Literary Agency, Inc.

"Seeing Your Way to Better Stories," by Stanley Schmidt, copyright © 1990 by Writer's Digest Publications, Inc. First appeared (in somewhat different form) in *Writer's Digest*. Reprinted by permission of Scott Meredith Literary Agency, Inc.

Writing Science Fiction
and Fantasy

Introduction

As the editors of *Analog Science Fiction and Fact* and *Asimov's Science Fiction* magazines we see dozens of manuscripts every week from writers who would like us to buy and publish them. We would like to buy them, too; like every other editor, we are constantly searching for new talent. However, we receive so many submissions, and have so few pages in our magazines, that we simply cannot buy more than 1 or 2 percent of the stories we are offered. To sell us a story, you must make your manuscript stand out as *special* from at least 98 percent of the competition.

How can you do that? Many beginning writers ask us for criticism and advice, and those who don't ask would still like to get it. Regrettably, the volume of submissions makes it quite impossible for most editors to comment individually on submissions, except for those few that they *almost* want to publish.

We hope that this book will be the next best thing. Obviously it can't offer criticism of your manuscript, but it does offer a wealth of useful tips and insights from several well-known professionals in the field. Read them; strive to understand them and see how they apply to your own work; and you just may arrive a little sooner at the point where editors *want* to take your individual hand and help you over the hump.

This is not a "how-to" manual. It does not say, "Follow these steps, in this order, and you will become a best-selling author." Writing is too subtle and too competitive a business, and there are too many ways of doing it, for that to be possible. We have known hundreds of professional writers, and no two of them work

1

in quite the same way. Some of the authors in these pages may even seem to contradict each other, and for that we make no apologies. Science fiction and fantasy have become a very broad, diversified field. Different writers have different ideas about how to approach it, and even a single writer may find that what seems to be a general principle most of the time does not apply at all in a particular case. But it's a good idea to know the "rules" before you break them, if only so you will understand that you are doing something unusual—and why.

What we suggest is that you read *all* of these essays attentively and take from them what seems valuable for your goals. To build a writing career, you must find what works for *you* and then stick to it, no matter what anyone else says works for him or her.

But never forget that, in the final analysis, it is *readers* who decide what works and what doesn't.

Good luck!

—The Editors

Part I

STORYTELLING

On the Writing
of Speculative Fiction

ROBERT A. HEINLEIN

There are nine-and-sixty ways
Of constructing tribal lays
And every single one of them is right!
—RUDYARD KIPLING

There are at least two principal ways to write speculative fiction—
write about people, or write about gadgets. There are other ways;
consider Stapledon's *Last and First Men*, recall S. Fowler
Wright's *The World Below*. But the gadget story and the human-
interest story comprise most of the field. Most science fiction
stories are a mixture of the two types, but we will speak as if they
were distinct—at which point I will chuck the gadget story aside,
dust off my hands, and confine myself to the human-interest
story, that being the sort of story I myself write. I have nothing
against the gadget story—I read it and enjoy it—it's just not my
pidgin. I am told that this is a how-to-do-it symposium; I'll stick
to what I know how to do.

The editor suggested that I write on "Science Fiction in the
Slicks." I shan't do so because it is not a separate subject. Several

years ago Will F. Jenkins said to me, "I'll let you in on a secret, Bob. *Any* story—science fiction, or otherwise—if it is well written, can be sold to the slicks." Will himself has proved this, and so have many other writers—Wylie, Wells, Cloete, Doyle, Ertz, Noyes, many others. You may protest that these writers were able to sell science fiction to the high-pay markets because they were already well-known writers. It just ain't so, pal; on the contrary, they are well-known writers because they are skilled at their trade. When they have a science fiction story to write, they turn out a well-written story and it sells to a high-pay market. An editor of a successful magazine will bounce a poorly written story from a "name" writer just as quickly as one from an unknown. Perhaps he will write a long letter of explanation and suggestion, knowing as he does that writers are as touchy as white leghorns, but he will bounce it. At most, prominence of the author's name might decide a borderline case.

A short story stands a much better chance with the slicks if it is not more than five thousand words long. A human-interest story stands a better chance with the slicks than a gadget story does, because the human-interest story usually appeals to a wider audience than does a gadget story. But this does not rule out the gadget story. Consider "Note on Danger B" in a recent *Saturday Evening Post* and Wylie's "The Blunder," which appeared last year in *Collier's*.

Let us consider what a story is and how to write one. (Correction: how *I* write one—remember Mr. Kipling's comment!)

A story is an account that is not necessarily true but that is interesting to read.

There are three main plots for the human-interest story: boy-meets-girl, the Little Tailor, and the man-who-learned-better. Credit the last category to L. Ron Hubbard; I had thought for years that there were but two plots—he pointed out to me the third type.

Boy-meets-girl needs no definition. But don't disparage it. It reaches from the "Iliad" to John Taine's *Time Stream*. It's the greatest story of them all and has never been sufficiently exploited in science fiction. To be sure, it appears in most SF stories, but how often is it dragged in by the hair and how often is it the compelling and necessary element that creates and then solves the problem? It has great variety: boy-fails-to-meet-girl, boy-meets-girl-too-late, boy-meets-too-many-girls, boy-loses-girl, boy-and-girl-renounce-love-for-higher-purpose. Not science fiction? Here is a throw-away plot; you can have it free: elderly man meets very young girl; they discover that they are perfectly adapted to each other, perfectly in love, "soul mates." (Don't ask me how. It's up to you to make the thesis credible. If I'm going to have to write this story, I want to be paid for it.)

Now to make it a science fiction story. Time travel? Okay, what time theory—probable-times, classic theory, or what? Rejuvenation? Is this mating necessary to some greater end? Or vice versa? Or will you transcend the circumstances, as C. L. Moore did in that tragic masterpiece "Bright Illusion"?

I've used it twice as tragedy and shall probably use it again. Go ahead and use it yourself. I did not invent it; it is a great story that has been kicking around for centuries.

The Little Tailor—this is an omnibus for all stories about the little guy who becomes a big shot, or vice versa. The tag is from the fairy story. Examples: "Dick Whittington," all of the Alger books, *Little Caesar*, *Galactic Patrol* (but not *Grey Lensman*), *Mein Kampf*, David in the Old Testament. It is the success story or, in reverse, the story of tragic failure.

The man-who-learned-better; just what it sounds like—the story of a man who has one opinion, point of view, or evaluation at the beginning of the story, then acquires a new opinion or evaluation as a result of having his nose rubbed in some harsh facts. I had been writing this story for years before Hubbard pointed out to me the structure of it. Examples: my "Universe" and "Logic of Empire," Jack London's "South of the Slot," Dickens's, "A Christmas Carol."

The definition of a story as something interesting-but-not-necessarily-true is general enough to cover all writers, all stories—

even James Joyce, if you find his stuff interesting. (I don't!) For me, a story of the sort I want to write is still further limited to this recipe: a man finds himself in circumstances that create a problem for him. In coping with this problem, the man is changed in some fashion inside himself. The story is over when the inner change is complete—the external incidents may go on indefinitely.

People changing under stress:

> A lonely rich man learns comradeship in a hobo jungle.
> A milquetoast gets pushed too far and learns to fight.
> A strong man is crippled and has to adjust to it.
> A gossip learns to hold her tongue.
> A hard-boiled materialist gets acquainted with a ghost.
> A shrew is tamed.

This is the story of character, rather than incident. It's not everybody's dish, but for me it has more interest than the most overwhelming pure adventure story. It need not be unadventurous; the stress that produces the change in character can be wildly adventurous, and often is.

But what has all this to do with science fiction? A great deal! Much so-called science fiction is not about human beings and their problems, consisting instead of a fictionized framework, peopled by cardboard figures, on which is hung an essay about the Glorious Future of Technology. With due respect to Mr. Bellamy, *Looking Backward* is a perfect example of the fictionized essay. I've done it myself; "Solution Unsatisfactory" is a fictionized essay, written as such. Knowing that it would have to compete with real *story*, I used every device I could think of, some of them hardly admissible, to make it look like a story.

Another type of fiction alleged to be science fiction is the story laid in the future, or on another planet, or in another dimension, or such, which could just as well have happened on Fifth Avenue, in 1947. Change the costumes back to now, cut out the pseudo-scientific double-talk and the blaster guns and it turns out to be a straight adventure story, suitable, with appropriate facelifting, to any other pulp magazine on the newsstand.

There is another type of honest-to-goodness science fiction story that is not usually regarded as science fiction: the story of people dealing with contemporary science or technology. We do not ordinarily mean this sort of story when we say "science fiction"; what we do mean is the speculative story, the story embodying the notion "Just suppose—" or "What would happen if—." In the speculative science fiction story accepted science and established facts are extrapolated to produce a new situation, a new framework for human action. As a result of this new situation, new *human* problems are created—and our story is about how human beings cope with those new problems.

The story is *not* about the new situation; it is about coping with problems arising out of the new situation.

Let's gather up the bits and define the simon-pure science fiction story:

1. The conditions must be, in some respect, different from here-and-now, although the difference may lie only in an invention made in the course of the story.
2. The new conditions must be an essential part of the story.
3. The problem itself—the "plot"—must be a *human* problem.
4. The human problem must be one that is created by, or indispensably affected by, the new conditions.
5. And lastly, no established fact shall be violated, and, furthermore, when the story requires that a theory contrary to present accepted theory be used, the new theory should be rendered reasonably plausible and it must include and explain established facts as satisfactorily as the one the author saw fit to junk. It may be far-fetched, it may seem fantastic, but it must *not* be at variance with observed facts, i.e., if you are going to assume that the human race descended from Martians, then you've *got* to explain our apparent close relationship to terrestrial anthropoid apes as well.

Pardon me if I go on about this. I love to read science fiction, but violation of that last requirement gets me riled. Rocketships should not make banked turns on empty space the way airplanes bank their turns on air. Lizards can't cross-breed with humans. The term "space warp" does not mean anything without elaborate explanation.

Not everybody talking about heaven is going there—and there are a lot of people trying to write science fiction who haven't bothered to learn anything about science. Nor is there any excuse for them in these days of public libraries. You owe it to your readers (a) to bone up on the field of science you intend to introduce into your story; (b) unless you yourself are well-versed in that field, you should also persuade some expert in that field to read your story and criticize it before you offer it to an un-suspecting public. Unless you are willing to take this much trou-ble, please, *please* stick to a contemporary background you are familiar with. Paderewski had to practice; Sonja Henie still works on her school figures; a doctor puts in many weary years before they will let him operate—why should you be exempt from pre-paratory effort?

The simon-pure science fiction story—examples of human problems arising out of extrapolations of present science:

Biological warfare ruins the farm lands of the United States; how is Joe Doakes, a used-car dealer, to feed his family?

Interplanetary travel puts us in contact with a race able to read our thoughts; is the testimony of such beings admissible as evi-dence in a murder trial?

Men reach the Moon; what is the attitude of the Security Council of the United Nations? (Watch out for this one—and hold on to your hats!)

A complete technique for ectogenesis is developed; what is the effect on home, family, morals, religion? (Aldous Huxley left lots of this field unplowed—help yourself.)

And so on. I've limited myself to *my* notions about science fiction, but don't forget Mr. Kipling's comment. In any case it isn't necessary to know how—just go ahead and do it. Write what you like to read. If you have a yen for it, if you get a kick out of "Just imagine—," if you love to think up new worlds, then come on in, the water's fine and there is plenty of room.

But don't write to me to point out how I have violated my own rules in this story or that; I've violated all of them and I would much rather try a new story than defend an old one.

I'm told that these articles are supposed to be some use to the reader. I have a guilty feeling that all of the above may have been more for my amusement than for your edification. Therefore I shall chuck in as a bonus a group of practical, tested rules which, if followed meticulously, will prove rewarding to any writer.

I shall assume that you can type, that you know the accepted commercial format or can be trusted to look it up and follow it, and that you always use new ribbons and clean type. Also, that you can spell and punctuate and can use grammar well enough to get by. These things are merely the word-carpenter's sharp tools. He must add to them these business habits:

1. You must *write*.
2. You must *finish* what you start.
3. You must refrain from rewriting except to editorial order.
4. You must put it on the market.
5. You must keep it on the market until sold.

The above five rules really have more to do with how to write speculative fiction than anything said above them. But they are amazingly hard to follow—which is why there are so few professional writers and so many aspirants, and which is why I am not afraid to give away the racket! But, if you will follow them, it matters not how you write, you will find some editor somewhere, sometime, so unwary or so desperate for copy as to buy the worst old dog you, or I, or anybody else, can throw at him.

Living the Future:
You Are What You Eat

GARDNER DOZOIS

For a number of years I worked for the *Galaxy* group of magazines as a "slush pile" reader, evaluating the endless flow of unsolicited manuscripts—sometimes as many as a hundred a day—that come into a magazine or publishing house and end up heaped in filing cabinets or cardboard boxes: the slush pile. I read thousands of manuscripts then, and continued to do so later, as editor of *Asimov's Science Fiction*, from duds to instant classics to near misses to outright plagiarisms—and I'm here to tell you that, with the exception of those turned down because they were illiterate or indecipherable, most of the science fiction stories that came into the slush pile were rejected because they suffered from what I came to call the 1950 Syndrome.

You can easily recognize such material. It's A.D. 2653 and yet people drive around in gasoline-fueled automobiles with internal combustion engines, live in suburbia, shop in supermarkets, subscribe to the Book-of-the-Month Club, and mow the lawn every weekend. For amusement they go to the movies, dance, barbecue, or sit at home and watch television. Every man has a crewcut; he is a soldier called "Captain," "Major," or "Sarge," or a teacher called "Professor." Or he is a wealthy, self-

employed scientist who whips together world-saving devices out
of scrap metal and bailing wire in his basement workshop, in
which case he is called "Doc." More rarely is he a politician,
and referred to by his title—"Worldmaster Jones," "Coordinator
Grey"; or a bigwig white-collar businessman called "Mister An-
drews," or whatever, by everyone, including his children and
wife. No other professions exist. No women work except for an
occasional snappy, wise-cracking, gum-chewing girl reporter, and
this only until she marries the hero at the end of the story. The
only other women who exist are dumb younger sisters of the
hero, or the shy and sheltered daughters of atomic physicists with
basement workshops. There are no races: everyone is white, mid-
dle-class, American, middle-of-the-road. No one has ever heard
of homosexuality or drug addiction or pollution. People either
use thirty-year-old hipster slang ("cool," "you cats," "dig it") or
they all say "gosh" and "darn" a lot. Everyone is unflaggingly
and unquestionably patriotic. Everyone is smugly contented.
They are all the most trusting of optimists.

You recognize this world, don't you? In spite of the calendar
that reads A.D. 2653, it's certainly not the future. No. It's 1950.
Or rather, an oversimplified and prettied-up version of 1950,
distilled by the popular imagination from years of *Ozzie and
Harriet*, *Father Knows Best*, and *Leave It to Beaver*. In an age
that's seen Jonestown, the Iran-Contra scam, MTV, the Chal-
lenger disaster, the advent of the home computer, weather satellites, microsurgery, Teenage Mutant Ninja Turtles, and the
crumbling of the Berlin Wall, it's hardly credible as the Past, let
alone the Future.

And yet, stories reeking of the Syndrome turn up over and
over again in the slush pile.

Why?

Well, after all, science fiction is pretty easy to write, isn't it?
It's just a matter of using fancy names—just change the names,
apply a thin layer of technologese and jargon, right? Say "helicar"
instead of car, "helipad" instead of driveway, "tri-vid" instead of
television, "feelies" (or "smellies," or "grabbies") instead of mov-

ies. Better still, use the word "space" as a prefix for everything: spacesuit, spacegun, spacehelmet, spacehouse, spacedog, spacecow. . . . Right? Just change the names and you can write a confession-magazine love story, a cowboy story, a gothic, or a nurse novel, and sell it as science fiction. Right?

Wrong.

There's no better way to ensure that your story will not sell. Stories deeply tainted by the 1950 Syndrome are not science fiction; they do not do what science fiction should do—they are swindles. They are thin and transparent frauds that are almost automatically rejected by nearly every SF editor in the business. Even the most routine hack space opera demands and delivers more. They are the duds, the unsalable lowest denominator of the slush pile.

Why do people of intelligence and talent turn out Syndrome stories when they first try their hand at writing science fiction?

Because of tunnel-vision. Because they know no better. Because they have not learned to unleash, discipline, and control their imaginations. Because they simply have not been taught to look at a future society as a *real, self-consistent, and organic thing.*

It works like this: a layman decides to write SF, and immediately starts to grope for a science-fictional idea. He reaches down into his subconscious, the well of creativity, and the first thing he hits is the vast harvest of concepts and assumptions and ideas he's gleaned over the years from all the bad comic books and horror movies and television shows that have been labeled Science Fiction. A moment's rational reflection should tell him that if the idea/image were floating about in the easily accessible part of the mind, it has probably been used to death in print years before—why else would it be such common property as to show up in the mind of someone with only the most casual of contacts with the genre? But he does not so reflect, because he's being mentally lazy, and so off the story goes. Like General MacArthur, it will return.

Thus, the layman, the one unfamiliar with the genre. But even the more habitual science fiction reader may fare no better. In fact, he is often more susceptible to the Syndrome, and may well be worse off than the layman—in addition to comics and the visual media, he must also cope with the sediment laid down by years of reading bad pulp space opera. This is why, twenty-five years or more after they've ceased to be commercially viable, the same old stock SF gimmicks, cousin-german to the 1950 Syndrome stories, continue to march needlessly across editorial desks: vast Galactic Empires and the intrepid secret agents who single-handedly overthrow them; Bug-Eyed Monsters who lust after beautiful ladies; interstellar armadas banging away at each other so unimaginatively that you can almost hear the sails flapping. Stories wherein, in Harry Harrison's words, "Bright young things voyage out from Earth in miraculous ships that get anywhere in a flash, to alien planets with oxygen atmospheres where exotically-shaped aliens talk colloquial English and think exactly like their American counterparts. . . ." Kurt Vonnegut's Eliot Rosewater complains that science fiction writers "write about Earthlings all the time, and they're all Americans. Practically nobody on Earth is an American." Damon Knight asks, "Where is the space hero who is an Indian from India, or a black African, or a Maylay or a Chinese, or—all right, let's not ask too much—where is the hero who is Italian?"

Why aren't there different kinds of people and different ways of thought out among the stars? Why is the future 1950? Why doesn't anything *new* happen in these stories? Because bad fiction perpetuates itself, and stifles the imagination that might otherwise revitalize or replace it.

To write good SF today, you must go beyond all that. You must push further and harder, reach down deeper into your own mind until you break through into the strange and terrible country wherein live your own dreams, your own ideas and images, your own nightmares. You must reject easy answers, soggy and chewed-out questions, facile images that come too automatically to the fingertips. You must reject all the clichés that falsely masquerade as genre, skirt by the dead and burnt-out shells of what were once viable fictional structures.

You must come upon the future as if you'd just discovered it; you must look at it with new eyes. You must make it a real place, then visit and explore it.

The first step is a philosophical—almost a mystical—one; an act of faith, an exercise of will. You must retool your mind. You must teach your eyes to see. One of the premier values of science fiction as literature is that it enables us to look at ourselves through alien eyes. It enables us, as do few other forms of art, to see not only what is, but, submerged in it, what has been, and what will be: to perceive the linkages, the connections, the web of cause-and-effect that holds the world together. The *interdependence* of things. Today this is sometimes called "thinking ecologically," but SF writers knew about it long before ecology became fashionable, knew that in the long run (and sometimes the short) everything affects everything else, that Heisenberg's Principle can also be applied to people and to society.

This mental retooling is vital—I cannot emphasize its importance too much, especially for someone not well-read in the genre. It is the first step, and the biggest one; without it there is no way to proceed, no way to get there from here. Science fiction deals, or should deal, with *change*; and change, with all its subtle causes and consequences, is a thing that's seldom dealt with in mainstream fiction, which usually presupposes an eternal and unchanging present, which usually assumes that people and the lives they lead are pretty much the same down through the ages, that motives and passions and goals and desires and fears are interchangeable from generation to generation.

But that simply is not true. The present is neither eternal nor unchanging. Human society is a process, ever in motion; it is coming from somewhere, it is going someplace else. It was not the same then as now, nor will it ever be so again. We are not our parents; our children will not be us. The past was not 1990 with horses; the future will not be 1990 with chrome. THINGS CHANGE!

Everything changes: this is the central philosophic vision of good science fiction; if you cannot adjust to it, cannot believe it, cannot *feel* it and see it in everything around you and in yourself, then you're wasting your time trying to write the stuff.

Nothing is simple. Everything changes. Things connect.

You are what you eat.

And want, and do, and think, and fear, and dream.

You live in an organic surround, an interlocking and interdependent gestalt made up of thousands of factors and combinations thereof: cultural, technological, biological, psychological, historical, environmental. For all practical purposes, you *are* that surround; if the things that make up that surround are altered, then you will be altered with them.

This is why imagination, although it's vital, is not by itself enough. One must have the vision to see the connections, and the sense to make them consistent. Much science fiction has failed on these grounds. Jules Verne predicted much of our present technology, but described it as working with a Victorian economy and society without working any change on that society *at all*; as a result, he is much less germane today than Wells, who knew better. If everything connects, then no social change, no technological innovation, takes place in tidy isolation.

Fictionally, this means that one postulate will spawn a host of others. If you have a world where everyone teleports, you can't have massive traffic jams; if everyone's a telepath, no one needs telephones; if everyone's part of a Group Mind, no one needs separate bedrooms. If all are blind, why do they need neon signs? If all have blasters, why do they need swords?

Alfred Bester, in *The Stars My Destination*, postulates that teleportation is a common ability—and the social ramifications of that one fact are endless: if you can teleport, and you don't like it where you are, why stay? Why live in cities at all? Why suffer night when you can follow the sun around the world? Why endure cold when you can teleport to the tropics? Why work when you can teleport to the scene of a natural disaster and loot and get away before the police catch you? And if the police do catch you, how are they going to hang on to you if you can teleport out of prison? What happens to the entertainment business when anyone can go anywhere? How do you keep a teleporting burglar out of your house? And in *The Demolished Man*, Bester does the same with telepathy: how can you keep a secret, get away with sharp business practices, lie, commit murder? The factors must add up, and the books must be balanced.

If you are writing about a near-future society, you must be careful of what Arthur C. Clarke has called a "failure of nerves" in prediction. Often a writer will present as a daringly possible innovation something that has already been developed and is in use; or worse, depict an advanced society that is less technologically sophisticated than the present. You are in trouble if your fictional tomorrow is already yesterday. One perfectly awful example of this was the slush pile story wherein the myopic women of the future had to choose between wearing "ugly eyeglasses" or "stumbling nearsighted through life"—it's the twenty-first century, and they haven't even heard of contact lenses! Conversely, it isn't enough to let your imagination run wild—you must not contradict what is presently known to be known unless you can explain why, and unless your explanation is plausible enough to suspend belief at least while the story is being read. The books must balance.

To write good SF, then, you must learn to perceive the hidden relationships that most do not; to pinpoint the trends just emerging in the present that might become prominent in the future, and to extrapolate logically their results in fictional terms, in terms of what they mean to *people*.

For practice, examine our own society and try to see it as a time traveler or a Martian might. It has come from somewhere, it is going somewhere else. There is a reason for everything, and a history behind every reason, right down to the design of the chairs on which you sit. Do you live in an apartment house? If so, then it's possible the building originally was a private house later cut up into apartments, and *that* explains the odd angle of the living room wall, or the blank window in the hall, or why you have to walk through what is now the bedroom to get to the bathroom. Slums turn into high-society districts, then back into slums. A hundred years ago, the street where you live might have been a swamp; a hundred years from now, it might be a swamp again, or a radioactive crater, or the lowest level in a two-mile-high city, or preserved in Lucite as a memorial to the quaint glories of the past.

And these are just the details of your physical environment. There are countless more, affecting the way you act and think and talk and dress and eat, who you think you are and how you feel about it. The world only seems static because we are too short-lived to see it change. If we could speed up time, condense eons into seconds, we would see mountains flow like water and fish learn to walk.

So your fictional future must be at least as complex as the present, or give the impression that it is. Practically speaking, you'll probably use only a relatively small percentage of these details in any one story—after all, your characters will not come in contact with *everything*—but you must still work the other details out; they must still be present in potential, or you will constantly stumble over contradictions and mistakes. Even if the reader never has occasion to learn in the course of a story that the city was overrun by the Vandarians two decades ago and that everyone paints himself blue on Sunday as a consequence, still the *author* must know that they do, and *the characters in the story must know it, too*. Your society should be worked out in detail and depth, in wonders and warts, monuments and pay toilets. If you thump it, it must ring sound, not hollow.

Remember: the most important changes are not always the biggest or the most obvious. For example, one current theory blames much of the worldwide postwar population explosion on the adoption by backward villages of "technologies" such as the separation of well and latrine, and the use of wire mesh for doors and windows—things that drastically dropped the infant mortality rate. Much of the confusion in this area comes from a misunderstanding of what technology is, what society is, and how they affect us. Is technology a computer or a condom, a hydrogen bomb or a flint ax, a rocketship or a fliptop can? Does it affect your life more by putting you out of work through automation, or by killing the mosquitoes in the marsh behind your house, or by poisoning the air, or by providing you with eyeglasses if you are myopic? Is society the Gutenberg Bible or a nudity taboo, the jury system or the Eleusinian mysteries?

Remember that science fiction depicts not only new technologies and societal trends and their effects, but also how they cause people to react *to each other*.

Be careful with emotional emphasis, with how your characters *feel* about the things making up their lives. Even if their everyday appurtenances would to us be wondrous beyond belief, to them they would be mundane. This is a detail commonly gotten wrong in much SF, especially in some of the stories of the thirties and forties which tended to become worshipful hymns to the wonders of future technology. We don't sit in awe of our television sets, after all, even though in some ways their effect on us has been much more profound than the early prognosticators ever imagined. Conversely, what is commonplace to us may someday seem remarkable and romantic to our remote descendants. Robert Heinlein, Larry Niven, and others have postulated that the people of the future, used to spaceships and supersonic shuttles, will nevertheless be aghast to think of the ordinary commuter of today going to work in the family car—no radar, no ballistic computer, no gyrostabilizers, no regulated traffic pattern; everything done by muscle power and guesswork. Who would ever dare to trade places with him? James Tiptree, Jr., has a beautiful story bit in which a highly advanced alien is staggering around the rush-hour traffic in Washington, D.C., taking deep breaths of the smog and saying things like "How primal. How unspoiled. Such peace!" It all depends on your context.

Be aware that wild factors can upset the most impeccably logical timetables. Hardly anyone foresaw the incredible acceleration of technological advance since WWII, or the mass cultural/psychological nervous breakdown of the late sixties. If your fictional scenario is exceedingly neat and tidy, perhaps you'd better throw in some wild factors, mess it up a little, make it more like the confusion in which we usually live.

If you are imagining a world that has degenerated into barbarism, that world must still be self-consistent, and cultural cause-and-effect must still hold true. If you have no electricity, you have no electric lights; no needle and thread, you cannot sew; no plows, you cannot turn the ground.

Remember that our descendants won't be us in chrome helmets and Spandex—the working out of that proposition has produced some of the most worthwhile SF ever. The people who populate the worlds of Jack Vance, Ursula K. Le Guin, Robert Silverberg, Samuel R. Delany, Gene Wolfe, Joanna Russ, Philip K. Dick, Brian Aldiss, Damon Knight, Kate Wilhelm, Frederik Pohl, and many others, are creatures of their own times, formed by those times in thought and spirit and habit. Isaac Asimov's people in *The Caves of Steel*, who so suffer from agoraphobia that they never leave their enclosed cities or see the sun; the Urbmon dwellers of Robert Silverberg's *The World Inside*, who have not only learned to live with conditions of extreme overcrowding, but who have come to find them desirable and spiritually satisfying; Jack Vance's Sirenese, who never show their naked faces from birth to death—who indicate their status by the type of mask they wear, and communicate with each other by playing appropriate passages on a bewildering variety of musical instruments. These are not familiar people, people we know. They are different kinds of people, and when we meet them we feel the shock of recognition—part fear, part amazement, part joy.

And like all literature, science fiction should entertain as well as enlighten. The most profound Heavy Thinking, the most intricate preplanning, the most germane social criticism, is useless and untenable if you have no story to tell, and no real people to tell it about.

One of your major narrative problems will be to get across to the reader an enormous amount of background material without gumming up the story's flow. There are as many solutions to this particular problem as there are writers. Some prefer to explain little or nothing directly—to tell the story as if it had been written by someone in the future for his contemporaries—and let the reader sort things out by implication and from context. One of the best examples of this technique is *Murder in Millennium VI*, by Curme Gray, a book that actually fulfills an ideal most writers only give lip service to: it explains *none* of the highly complicated far future background—the reader must figure out or intuit what is happening page by page, on the fly, or he's lost. Similarly, many writers like Felix Gotschalk also delight in plunging right into a story at full speed—"Who would have ever thought that men could alter the speed of the earth—and by such an obvious method as reverse photosynthesis?"—and letting the reader catch up if he can. James Tiptree, Jr., once said her preferred narrative technique was to "Start from the end and preferably 5,000 feet underground on a dark day and then DON'T TELL THEM." Many authors have achieved some remarkably successful results and striking effects in using this technique, but of course the danger here is that the writer will give the reader so little to go on that the reader will give up in bafflement. *Murder in Millennium VI*, for instance, is about as accessible and pellucid as a brick, and as a result it was not much of a commercial success.

One of the popular techniques is to introduce an outsider into your society as an observer, who will then learn about the society as the story progresses; the reader will learn also through his eyes (cf. *When the Sleeper Awakes* and *The Left Hand of Darkness*). Its major drawback is the plausibility of the observer—sometimes he tends to be something of a rabbit-out-of-a-hat, popping up out of nowhere with only the most tenuous of justifications.

Or you can couch the story as a fictionalized historical analysis from a viewpoint of a future *ahead* of the story's time; or, in a variant, write your story as an open-ended testament or memoir addressed to an unknown future audience, by an isolated survivor of an atomic war, for instance. Either of these approaches justifies the narrator's explanation of much that *his* audience wouldn't know (as well as *yours*) either directly in the narration or through "scholarly" footnotes, interpolations, introductions, afterwords, appendices. But this tends to make your story dry and talky, so encrusted with pseudoscholarly baggage that it has trouble moving.

Or the material can be conveyed through the omniscient author technique, or through interrelations of characters, or in any of a half-dozen other ways. You will learn in time which is best for you, how much to tell, how much to imply, how much to conceal—or you may make up a new technique. It may be a technical bottleneck at first, but you must at all costs resist the temptation to break through it by having your characters explain at length to each other things they should logically already know: "As you know, Frank, we are all androids, and must recharge our powerpacks every four hours or die. . . ." *That's probably the most common beginner's mistake on the books.*

Be careful with language, both in dialogue and in narration. Alexei Panshin says, "The future equivalent of 'damn,' expressed in present terms, is 'damn.' " But at the same time, it cannot be denied that many authors have had a great deal of success in working future slang and "alien" technology believably into their stories. Clearly, however, this isn't a knack every writer has, not even every writer of talent, and you must be clearheaded and ruthless in your appraisal of whether you possess it or not. You can't afford to fool yourself, or you will wreck the mood and believability of your stories again and again with language that sounds wrong or even ludicrous. You may even end up writing what James Blish has labeled "Call a rabbit a smeerp" stories:

"They *look* like rabbits, but if you call them smeerps, that makes it science fiction."

Beware of the Star Trek Syndrome: creating stories that are unabashed duplicates of the Roman Empire and Nazi Germany. This is another prime example of mental laziness, since such societies are untenable on at least two grounds: one, that in spite of the time-honored proverb, history does *not* repeat itself, not in cozy one-to-one analogues anyway; and two, that such societies are drawn not from historically accurate sources, but from grossly distorted popular simplifications. The Roman Empire was vastly more complex, contradictory, surprising, and multifaceted than the simplistic version we get from television, movies, and bad historical novels. And the people who inhabited it were as different from us as any citizens of A.D. 2100 are likely to be. In fact, the Old Egyptians and the Old Romans would be more alien to us than most authors' Martians.

Finally, remember that there is no such thing as THE future, only many different possible futures.

Science fiction is not easy to write. It is often beyond the capabilities even of authors of talent and intelligence, because those qualities are not enough unless they are combined with a certain kind of imagination, perception, and mental flexibility. So think it over. Appraise yourself carefully and with scrupulous self-honesty. You might not be capable of writing good science fiction, and if so, face up to it.

If, however, this is what you really want to write, and you feel at least potentially capable of meeting the special challenges it presents, then take heart: the task is not as impossible as it may appear. Few professional science fiction writers are geniuses, after all, and yet most have managed to cope. The biggest hurdle is the already-discussed psychological reorientation. After that, after you have trained your mind and your hands to the task, it is mostly a straightforward matter of learning your craft—and like any craft, it becomes easier with practice.

There are a few things you can do to make it more likely that you will succeed: first, and perhaps most important, if you are going to try to write science fiction, then for God's sake, READ it. Get an idea of what the present State of the Art is, of which magazines and anthologies are buying what. Another advantage of actively reading SF is that you'll save yourself a great deal of time and anguish on the road to becoming a selling writer. How? Because you will know better—you'll know *beforehand* that such-and-such is a worn-out cliché. And most of all: *if you don't enjoy reading science fiction, you're wasting your time trying to write it.*

Have as many inputs and interests as possible: most SF writers read copiously and catholically, and this greatly enriches their work. Anything and everything can be grist for your mill: science, anthropology, psychology, poetry, mythology. You need a good, working layman's knowledge of what's presently considered technologically possible or impossible, and at least a vague idea of why. There are many good popular science books available—some written by SF writers: Isaac Asimov, Arthur C. Clarke, Ben Bova—and you'll find that many experts, both scientists and teachers, are willing to assist you with advice and information if you're polite in asking for it. You'll also need to keep up with the constant flow of new ideas, so subscribe to some of the less technical scientific journals, like *Science News* and *Scientific American*.

Another helpful hint: science fiction is a friendly field. Established authors will frequently be willing to share their expertise with you, give you tips, point out pitfalls; genre editors are often willing to work extensively with you to renovate your story, sometimes spending much more time on it than is commercially justifiable.

And if none of the above lessens your trepidation, consider this: there is a joy to this business of creating worlds that eventually almost becomes its own reward.

Try it now. Try out your new legs, and see how well you walk.

Think yourself into the future, your future world. Think yourself into the skin of someone who lives there, and look around through his eyes. Remember to examine what it is you see with suspicion; sniff it carefully to see if it fits. Well, then, what *do* you see from the window in this world of the future? Do you see slender but sky-scraping Fäerie towers, elevated roadways winding among the building tops, clouds of small family helicopters drifting from one landing platform to another?

The hell you do! That's a 1940 version of 1970, remembered by a thousand paperback covers—as a vision of 2100, it's as inappropriate as a windmill in Times Square. You're not tapping anything worthwhile, you're still accepting easy answers, if that's what you see from your window. For that matter, should there be a window? In 2100? Suppose you're living in a plug-in modular apartment, close to the core, or in an inflatable rubber pyramid, or in a clear plastic fishbowl house, or 20 stories underground— would you have a window? a TV repeater screen? a hologram tank? a moving 3-D mural? a pornographic picture? a blank wall? What? What do *you* see there?

Now turn and look into your mirror (mirror?), there in the future. Are you a human being, a cyborg, an artificial brain-body environment, a mobile extensor for a computer, a chimera, or a mutated chimpanzee? Are you man, woman, hermaphrodite, neuter? Do you have extra limbs, organs, senses? Do you dye your skin? Have phosphorescent inlays of bone and jewels? Aesthetically-arranged patterns of multiple eyes? Do you have a morbid fear of ceilings? Are you sexually aroused by the color orange? Are you a devout Robbinsite? Is your building heated by fusion, by solar screens, by power broadcast from a black hole? Do you work as a plastic-eater, neurosis peddler, an algae-skimmer? Do you work? Do you go to the gene-reel for recreation, or are you one of those who believe that a self-inflicted lobotomy is the highest form of sensuality?

Professor J. B. S. Haldane once said: "The Universe is not only queerer than we imagine—it is queerer than we *can* imagine."

Nevertheless, we must try. To write good science fiction, we must make the attempt somehow to reason and intuit our way to a vision that is at least somewhat as complex as reality. We shall fail, inevitably, but perhaps in time we shall learn how to fail somewhat less totally.

And meanwhile, it's fun to try.

Plotting

ISAAC ASIMOV

Every once in awhile, an article about me appears in a newspaper, usually in the form of an interview. I don't go looking for these things, because I hate the hassle of being photographed (which, these days, invariably goes with interviews) and I hate the risk of being misquoted or misinterpreted.

Nevertheless, I can't always turn these things down because I'm not really a misanthrope, and because I do like to talk about myself. (Oh, you noticed?)

As a result of one such interview, an article about me appeared in the *Miami Herald* of 20 August 1988. It was a long article and quite favorable (the headline read "The Amazing Asimov") and it had very few inaccuracies in it. It did quote me, to be sure, as saying that my book *The Sensuous Dirty Old Man* was "nauseating." That is wrong. I said that the books it satirized, *The Sensuous Woman* and *The Sensuous Man*, were nauseating. *My* book was funny.

It also quoted me as saying that I considered "Nightfall" to be my best story. I don't, not by a long shot. I said it was my "best-known" story, a different thing altogether.

Usually any reporter who interviews me is willing to let it go at that, but the *Miami Herald* reporter was more enterprising. She asked questions of my dear wife, Janet, and of my brother,

Stan, who's a vice-president at the Long Island *Newsday*. Both said nice things, but then they both like me.

However, she also consulted someone who teaches a course in science fiction at Rutgers University. Her name is Julia Sullivan, and I don't think I know her, though it is clear from what she is quoted as saying that she is a woman of luminous intelligence and impeccable taste.

She praised my clarity and wit, for instance, but I'm used to that. The thing is, she is also quoted as saying about me that "he surprises me. Sometimes I think he's written himself out, and then he comes up with something really good. . . . He has the greatest mind for plot of any science fiction writer."

That's nice!

I can't recall anyone praising me for my plots before, and so, of course, it got me to thinking about the whole process of plotting.

A plot is an outline of the events of a story. You might say, for instance, "There's this prince, see? His father has recently died and his mother has married his uncle, who becomes the new king. This upsets the prince, who hoped to be king himself and who doesn't like the uncle anyway. Then he hears that the ghost of his dead father has been seen—"

The first thing you have to understand is that a plot is not a story, any more than a skeleton is a living animal. It's simply a guide to the writer, in the same way that a skeleton is a guide to a paleontologist as to what a long-extinct animal must have looked like. The paleontologist has to fill in the organs, muscles, skin, etc. all around the skeleton, and that's not feasible except for a trained person. Hence, if you give the plot of *Hamlet* to a nonwriter, that will *not* help him produce *Hamlet* or anything even readable.

Well, then, how do you go about building a story around the plot?

1. You can, if you wish, make the plot so detailed and so complex that you don't have to do much in the way of "building."

Events follow one another in rapid succession and the reader (or viewer) is hurried from one suspense-filled situation to another. You get this at a low level in comic strips and in the old movie serials of the silent days. This is recognized as being suitable mainly for children, who don't mind being rushed along without regard for logic or realism or any form of subtlety. In fact children are apt to be annoyed with anything that impedes the bare bones of the plot, so that a few minutes of love interest is denounced as "mush." Of course, if it is done well enough, you have something like *Raiders of the Lost Ark*, which I enjoyed tremendously, even if there were parts that made no sense at all.

2. You can go to the other extreme, if you wish, and virtually eliminate the plot. There need be no sense of connected events. You might simply have a series of vignettes as in Woody Allen's *Radio Days*. Or you might tell a story that is designed merely to create a mood or evoke an emotion or illuminate a facet of the human condition. This, too, is not for everyone, although, done well, it is satisfying to the sophisticated end of the reader (or viewer) spectrum. The less-sophisticated may complain that the story is not a story and ask "But what does it *mean?*" or "What happened?" The plotless story is rather like free verse, or abstract art, or atonal music. Something is given up that most people imagine to be inseparable from the art form, but which, if done well (and my goodness, is it hard to do it well), transcends the form and gives enormous satisfaction to those who can follow the writer into the more rarefied realms of the art.

3. What pleases the great middle—people who are not children or semi-literate adults, but who are not cultivated esthetes, either—are stories that have distinct plots, plots that are filled-out successfully, one way or another, with non-plot elements of various types. I'll mention a few.

3.a. You can use the plot as a way of bringing in humor or satire. Read books by P. G. Wodehouse, or Mark Twain's *Tom Sawyer*, or Charles Dickens's *Nicholas Nickleby*.

3.b. You can use the plot to develop an insight into the characters of the individuals who people the story. The great literary giants, such as Homer, Shakespeare, Goethe, Tolstoy, Dostoyevsky, do this supremely well. Since human beings and their relationships with each other and with the universe are far more complex and unpredictable than are simple events, the ability to deal with "characterization" successfully is often used as a way of defining "great literature."

3.c. You can use the plot to develop ideas. The individuals who people the story may champion alternate views of life and the universe, and the struggle may be one in which each side tries to persuade or force the other into adopting its own world-view. To do this properly, each side must present its view (ostensibly to each other, but really to the reader) and the reader must be enticed into favoring one side or another so that he can feel suspense over which side will win. Done perfectly, the two opposing views should represent not white and black, but two grays of slightly different shades so that the reader cannot make a clear-cut decision but must *think* and come to conclusions of his own. I go into greater detail on this version than on the other two, because this is what *I* do.

There are many other ways of dealing with plot, but the important thing to remember is that they are not necessarily mutually exclusive. A humorous novel can be full of quite serious ideas and develop interesting characters, for instance.

On the other hand, writers can, more or less deliberately, sacrifice some elements of plot build-ups in their anxiety to do, *in great detail*, what it is they want to do. I am so intent on presenting my opposing ideas, for instance, that I make no serious attempt to characterize brilliantly or to drench the tale in humor. As a result, much is made of my "cardboard characters" and I am frequently accused of being "talky." But these accusations usually come from critics who don't see (or perhaps lack the intelligence to see) what it is that I am trying to do.

But I'm sure that this is not what Ms. Sullivan meant when she said I had "the greatest mind for plot."

I rather think she means that my stories (especially my novels) have very complicated plots that hang together and have no loose ends, that don't get in the way of the ideas I present in my stories, and that are not obscured by those ideas, either.

Now, how is that done?

I wish I could tell you. All I'm aware of is that it takes a great deal of hard thinking, and that between the thinking and the writing that I must do, there is little time for me to do anything else. Fortunately, I both think and write very quickly and with almost no dithering, so I can get a great deal done.

Which brings me to another part of the interview. The reporter speaks of my apartment as "filled with eclectic, utilitarian furniture chosen more for comfort than for style, much like Asimov's wardrobe. For a recent speaking engagement, he wore a Western tie, a too-big jacket, and a striped shirt with the kind of long wide collar that was popular in the 1970s."

She's absolutely right. As far as style is concerned, I'm a shambles. It doesn't bother me, though. To learn to live and dress with full attention to style would require hours upon umpteen hours of thought, of education, of decision-making, and so on. And that takes time I don't want to subtract from my writing.

What would *you* rather have? Asimov, the prolific writer, or Asimov, the fashion-plate? I warn you. You can't have them both.

Dialog

ISAAC ASIMOV

Most stories deal with people, and one of the surefire activities
of people is that of talking and of making conversation. It follows
that in most stories there is dialog. Sometimes stories are largely
dialog; my own stories almost always are. For that reason, when
I think of the art of writing (which isn't often, I must admit) I
tend to think of dialog.

In the Romantic period of literature in the first part of the
nineteenth century, the style of dialog tended to be elaborate and
adorned. Authors used their full vocabulary and had their characters speak ornately.

I remember when I was very young and first read Charles
Dickens's *Nicholas Nickleby*. How I loved the conversation. The
funny passages were very funny to me, though I had trouble with
John Browdie's thick Yorkshire accent (something his beloved
Matilda, brought up under similar conditions, lacked, for some
reason). What I loved even more, though, was the ornamenta-
tion—the way everyone "spoke like a book."

Thus, consider the scene in which Nicholas Nickleby confronts
his villainous Uncle Ralph. Nicholas's virtuous and beautiful
sister, Kate, who has been listening to Ralph's false version of
events, which make out Nicholas to have been doing wrong, cries
out wildly to her brother, "Refute these calumnies . . ."

Of course, I had to look up "refute" and "calumny" in the dictionary, but that meant I had learned two useful words. I also had never heard any seventeen-year-old girl of my acquaintance use those words, but that just showed me how superior the characters in the book were, and that filled me with satisfaction.

It's easy to laugh at the books of that era and to point out that no one *really* talks that way. But then, do you suppose people in Shakespeare's time went around casually speaking in iambic pentameter?

Still, don't you want literature to improve on nature? Sure you do. When you go to the movies, the hero and heroine don't look like the people you see in the streets, do they? Of course not. They look like movie stars. The characters in fiction are better-looking, stronger, braver, more ingenious and clever than anyone you are likely to meet, so why shouldn't they speak better, too?

And yet there are values in realism—in making people look, and sound, and act like real people.

For instance, back in 1919, some of the players on the pennant-winning Chicago White Sox were accused of accepting money from gamblers to throw the World Series (the so-called "Black Sox scandal") and were barred from baseball for life as a result. At the trial, a young lad is supposed to have followed his idol, the greatest of the accused, Shoeless Joe Jackson, and to have cried out in anguish, "Say it ain't so, Joe."

That is a deathless cry that can't be tampered with. It is unthinkable to have the boy say, "Refute these calumnies, Joseph," even though that's what he means. Any writer who tried to improve matters in that fashion would, and should, be lynched at once. I doubt that anyone would, or should, even change it to "Say it isn't so, Joe."

For that matter, you couldn't possibly have had Kate Nickleby cry out to her brother, "Say it ain't so, Nick."

Of course, during much of history most people were illiterate and the reading of books was very much confined to the few who were educated and scholarly. Such books of fiction as existed were supposed to "improve the mind" or risk being regarded as works of the devil.

It was only gradually, as mass education began to flourish, that books began to deal with ordinary people. Of course, Shakespeare had his clowns and Dickens had his Sam Wellers, and in both cases, dialog was used that mangled the English language to some extent—but that was intended as humor. The audience was expected to laugh uproariously at these representatives of the lower classes.

As far as I know, the first book that was written entirely and seriously in substandard English and which was a great work of literature nevertheless (or even, possibly, to some extent *because* of it) was Mark Twain's *Huckleberry Finn*, which was published in 1884. Huck Finn is himself the narrator, and he is made to speak as an uneducated backwoods boy *would* speak—if he happened to be a literary genius. That is, Twain used the dialect of an uneducated boy, but he put together sentences and paragraphs like a master.

The book was extremely popular when it came out because its realism made it incredibly effective—but it was also extremely controversial, as all sorts of fatheads inveighed against it because it didn't use proper English.

And yet, even so, Mark Twain had to draw the line, too, as did all writers until the present generation.

People, all sorts of people, use vulgarisms as a matter of course. I remember my days in the Army when it was impossible to hear a single sentence in which the common word for sexual intercourse was not used as an all-purpose adjective. Later, after I had gotten out of the Army, I lived on a street along which young boys and girls walked to the local junior high school in the morning, and back again in the evening, and their shouted conversations brought back memories of my barracks days with nauseating clarity.

Yet could writers reproduce that aspect of common speech? Of course not. For that reason, Huck Finn was always saying that something was "blamed" annoying, "blamed" this, "blamed" that. You can bet that the *least* he was really saying was "damned."

A whole set of euphemisms was developed and placed in the mouths of characters who wouldn't, in real life, have been caught dead saying them. Think of all the "dad-blameds," and "gol-darneds," and "consarneds" we have seen in print and heard in the movies. To be sure, youngsters say them as a matter of caution, for they would probably be punished (if of "good family") by their parents if caught using the terms they had heard said parents use. (Don't let your hearts bleed for the kids, for when they grow up they will beat up *their* kids for the same crime.)

For the last few decades, however, it has become permissible to use all the vulgarisms freely and many writers have availed themselves of the new freedom to lend an air of further realism to their dialog. What's more, they are apt to resent bitterly any suggestion that this habit be modified or that some nonvulgar expression be substituted.

In fact, one sees a curious reversal now. A writer must withstand a certain criticism if he does *not* make use of said vulgarisms.

Once when I read a series of letters by science fiction writers in which such terms were used freely and frequently, I wrote a response that made what seemed to me to be an obvious point. In it, I said something like this:

> Ordinary people, who are not well educated and who lack a large working vocabulary, are limited in their ability to lend force to their statements. In their search for force, they must therefore make use of vulgarisms which serve, through their shock value, but which, through overuse, quickly lose whatever force they have, so that the purpose of the use is defeated.
>
> Writers, on the other hand, have (it is to be presumed) the full and magnificent vocabulary of the English language at their disposal. They can say anything they want with whatever intensity of invective they require in a thousand different ways without ever once deviating from full respectability of utterance. They have,

therefore, no need to trespass upon the usages of the ignorant and forlorn, and to steal their tattered expressions as substitutes for the language of Shakespeare and Milton.

All I got for my pains were a few comments to the effect that there must be something seriously wrong with me.

Nevertheless, it is my contention that dialog is realistic when, and only when, it reflects the situation as you describe it and when it produces the effect you wish to produce.

At rather rare intervals, I will make use of dialect. I will have someone speak as a Brooklyn-bred person would (that is, as I myself do, in my hours of ease), or insert Yiddishisms here and there, if it serves a purpose. I may even try to make up a dialect, as I did in *Foundation's Edge*, if it plays an important part in the development of the story.

Mostly, however, I do not.

The characters in my stories (almost without exception) are pictured as being well educated and highly intelligent. It is natural, therefore, for them to make use of a wide vocabulary and to speak precisely and grammatically, even though I try not to fall into the ornateness of the Romantic era.

And, as a matter of quixotic principle, I try to avoid expletives, even mild ones, when I can.—But other writers, of course, may do as they please.

Afterword: There is a top-ranking science fiction writer who seems constitutionally incapable of not using vulgarisms, even when this makes serious trouble for him with important businessmen he is dealing with. I once tried to make peace on his behalf by saying, "When he says to you—— —— ——, that's just his way of saying, 'Hello, how are you?' " The person I was talking to, however, refused to be appeased.

You and Your Characters

JAMES PATRICK KELLY

Once I admitted to myself that I had the raging hunger to write, I gobbled up every book on the subject I could find. I still have most of them; I've just gathered fourteen and stacked them beside my computer monitor for inspiration. Each has a chapter on characterization. If you're looking for technical jargon, have I got some used books for you!

It seems that there are all kinds of characters: developing characters, static characters, round characters, flat characters, cardboard characters (oh, are there cardboard characters!), viewpoint characters, sympathetic characters, unsympathetic characters, stock characters, confidantes, foils, spear carriers, narrators, protagonists, antagonists. But that's not all; characters can play many roles. There are flat, sympathetic, static confidantes, like the unnamed first-person narrator in H. G. Wells's "The Time Machine." Or developing, flat, unsympathetic antagonists, like HAL in *2001, A Space Odyssey*. Still with me?

Recently I've been teaching my daughter Maura to ski, a skill described by a language every bit as arcane as that of characterization. To execute the stem turn, for example, you must learn to unweight, sideslip, and reset the edges of your uphill and downhill skis. Suppose I were to ski alongside of you as you write your next story, shrieking instructions. "Okay now, drop a little description here, shoulders downhill, unweight the uphill ski . . . now use your foil to set your edges, sideslip, that's it, keep your spear carriers nice and flat . . . no, *no!* Slow down! *Tell, don't show!*" You'd get so flustered trying to follow directions that you'd end up face down in the snow. No one can tell you how to ski—or write—until you've already tried it and taken some falls. You should open a how-to book like this only after a hard day of *doing*, when you're sitting with your feet propped in front of a crackling fire and figuring out what went wrong, how to make it better tomorrow.

Although the vocabulary of characterization is important, it also can get in your way. In fact, even if you were to memorize all of the definitions, your next move would be to forget them as soon as possible. I don't worry about who's round and who's flat when I'm working on a story; I'm too busy trying not to slam into the trees. The way to master technique is by writing, not by reading. You need to load the fundamental concepts of the craft into your intuition, where they can do the most good, rather than into your consciousness, where they can only distract you. Internalize, internalize!

Having said that, there's one suggestion I can offer before you launch yourself onto fiction's slippery slopes. Nothing startling, nothing abstruse—just a little trick that works for me. Why don't you try it before we sort through the nomenclature?

In my opinion, the best way to write believable stories is to pretend that each character is you.

The operative word here is *pretend*. You couldn't possibly be your characters, since you exist in different worlds. There are no wizards or vampires in your neighborhood and you'll probably never get into orbit, more's the pity. The life histories you create for these imaginary people will necessarily be different from your own. You'll have to pretend to be both male and female, young and old, good and evil. Yet no matter how far a story leads away from your own experience, or even from the familiar precincts of reality, you must strive to put yourself in your character's place.

Imagining you are your characters can help keep you from reproducing the cast of plot-driven robots that traditionally has clunked through our genre. Take, for example, the bore. Chances are you wouldn't dream of lecturing people in a casual conversation and you look for the exits when some bore does start to pontificate. Yet characters in badly written SF are always dumping information on each other in order to advance the story. Or consider the plot convert, who spends most of the story thwarting the hero until a moment of blinding revelation. A conversion follows that makes St. Paul's on the road to Damascus seem half-hearted, so that the writer can present us with an ending as tidy as a military school bunkroom. In my experience, people admit they're wrong grudgingly, if at all. Yet another example is the damn fool. Why is it that when some bloodthirsty creature clearly threatens the planetary exploration team, some damn fool always wanders off and gets himself killed? Would *you* leave the safety of the spaceship? Of course not! However, the damn fools do every time; otherwise there'd be no story.

All right, you know better than to make such basic mistakes. So then why does every character have to be you? Can't you draw from your circle of friends and acquaintances? Your Aunt Mary? George Bush? Yes, by all means. Many writers base characters on real people who are not themselves. I know I have. However, I do not fool myself into imagining that I've captured my real life models in words. Maybe I can make my characters act just like people I've met or read about. If I'm lucky, I might even have the benefit of having heard my models explain why they did what they did. But most people live the unexamined life that Plato warned us of; their insight into their own motivations is limited. Besides, human behavior is overdetermined. We have more than one reason for doing just about everything we do. When the real-life murderer confesses, "I killed him because of this," he's oversimplifying. What he should say is, "I killed him because of this and this and this and especially *that*, which I had

no way of knowing." Journalists report confessions; when readers
want simple truth, they buy a newspaper. But readers also crave
more complex truth. When they seek a literary experience that
maps the often bewildering convolutions of their own inner lives,
they buy *Asimov's*. As a fiction writer, your job is to sift through
an array of possible motivations—some logical, many not—and
present only the ones that make the most story sense to you. The
way to do that is not to ask "What would make one man kill
another?" Unless you're a telepath, the answer to that question
will always be unknowable. Better to ask "What would make me
kill someone?"

While I believe that this unblinking self-examination is absolutely necessary, I realize that it can be very disturbing. You
want to be liked and would much prefer to present your best side
to the world. However, fiction is not public relations. We all
have dark impulses that we've been taught to hide, perhaps even
to deny; to be a writer you must unlearn some of the lessons of
civilization. Nobody takes seriously a story in which the good
guys are all saints and the bad guys are the spawn of hell. Saints
can have their bad days and even monsters love their moms.
Increasing the level of moral ambiguity usually enhances a character's believability. Only psychopaths do wrong for the fun of
it. Most of the evil in the world is perpetrated by people like you
and me—the very people you want to characterize. Sometimes
we do it out of malice; sometimes we're merely selfish or lazy;
often as not we think we're doing the right thing. In any event,
you have to be brave enough to portray your own ugliness in
order to create memorable characters.

I know that some will resist this advice. Why go to all the
trouble of putting yourself into stories, stretching your moral
imagination to the breaking point, perhaps scaring the hell out
of yourself in the process? In the May 1985 issue of *Asimov's*,
the great Isaac Asimov himself stirred up a controversy when he
published a polemical essay called "The Little Tin God of Characterization." Isaac's thesis was that because of the unique nature
of science fiction, characterization is not as important as getting

the ideas right. "I do what I can, but I've got my limits, and if I have to settle for less than 100 percent, I just make sure that I remember where the science fictional bottom line is. Not characterization, not style, not poetic metaphor—but idea. Anything else I will skimp on if I have to. Not idea." Throughout the history of the genre, others have made similar arguments for the supremacy of idea over characterization. In fact, if there ever was a war between the humanists and the cyberpunks of my generation (a dubious proposition), it was fought over this very issue. You'll find any number of published, award-winning writers who will "skimp" at times on characterization while they dazzle us with the brilliance of their ideas. In fact, some writers, myself among them, actually have been taken to task for attempting to write the science fiction novel of character—an oxymoron, to some sensibilities. So whom should you believe?

First of all, as Isaac and others were quick to point out, character and idea are not mutually exclusive. Moreover, few are gifted with the extrapolative genius of an Asimov. The rest of us, beginners especially, must work as hard at characterization as we do on our ideas in order to maintain the suspension of disbelief that readers demand. When a wonky idea, a wooden character, or even an incoherent sentence cause readers to realize they're reading *fiction*, the writer has lost the game. And there are certain standards of characterization below which even the hardest of hard science fiction writers dare not descend. There is, however, an even-more-telling objection to those who maintain that brilliant ideas can carry mundane characters.

The quality of speculation is directly related to the quality of characterization. Readers presented with a new reality, whether it is a generation starship, an alien planet, or a magic kingdom, apply certain tests of credibility. How long could a closed system in outer space be self-supporting? Could a world without metals support a technological civilization? What would keep the wizards from taking over everything? Although questions about infrastructure, of political and social organization, may be the first to occur, readers eventually will ask another, equally crucial question before disbelief is completely suspended. Does the fictive world support the diversity of human life that we see in the real world? It makes no difference that the shiny mag-lev trains run on time if the riders are all middle-aged white American males in three-piece suits. A richly imagined world inhabited by manikins is inherently less believable than the same world would be if it teemed with well-drawn characters who are truly citizens of their alternate reality. In my opinion, this is one reason why some of the classic writers of science fiction are now so painful to read. E. E. "Doc" Smith's work is still chock-full of intricate speculation, but who can take his characters—especially his women—seriously? It's not only bad art, it's bad extrapolation. The science fiction character is the reader's guide to the ideas of the story. If she doesn't belong, nobody will trust her; if she isn't real, no one will believe her. Even the writer who aspires to write idea stories skimps on characterization at her peril.

The problem with this whole debate is that it makes the questionable assumption that we can yank characters out of their natural environment of plot and setting to analyze them. It's like expecting to learn something about the ethology of rainbow trout by watching the one you've just caught as it flops and gasps on the hot deck of your fishing boat. Or as Henry James said, "What is character but the determination of incident? What is incident but the illustration of character?" Character, plot, setting, theme, idea, and style are inextricably bound; all must stand or fall together.

So yes, it's necessary to work at characterization, no matter what your ambitions in the genre are. And since your technique will be better if it's intuitive rather than self-conscious, it may help to try to imagine that you are your characters. However, as we have seen, writers and critics have developed a common language over the years so that they could talk to one another about this subject. Time now for some vocabulary drill. Don't worry; there's no pop quiz at the end of this chapter. You don't have to memorize the list in order to write well. However, whether or not you can define these terms, eventually you must come to understand them.

Antagonist: a.k.a. "the bad guy," but better thought of as the opponent of the protagonist or central character. The action of a story arises from conflict between the antagonist and protagonist, as in Baum's *The Wonderful Wizard of Oz*, with its struggle between the Wicked Witch of the West and Dorothy. The antagonist need not be a person at all but may be an animal, an inanimate object, or even nature itself. For example, the antagonist in Tom Godwin's story "The Cold Equations" is outer space.

Cardboard character: a stereotype, manikin, drone, or otherwise uninteresting simulacrum passing for a real character. Cardboard is what you use when—for whatever reason—you fail to put yourself into your characters. It is the only pejorative I've included in this list. The utopia of Edward Bellamy's didactic "idea" novel *Looking Backward* is entirely populated with right-thinking men and women of cardboard.

Confidante: someone in whom the central character confides, thus revealing her personality. Once again, that someone need not be a person. In Robert Heinlein's *The Door into Summer* the central character, Dan Davis, continually confides his plans and feelings to his cat Pete.

Developing character: a character who changes over the course of the story. The central character is often, but not always, a developing character. However, it's crucial that the action of the story causes some character to change. When I attended the Clarion Writers' Workshop, Damon Knight used to write "Who cares?" at the end of stories in which no one develops—a characteristically terse criticism that I found devastating. A tour de force of developing characterization is Louis Sacchetti, the protagonist of Thomas Disch's *Camp Concentration*, who is infected with a disease that makes him a genius.

Flat character: someone who is characterized by one or two traits. "Flat" and "round" were terms first proposed by E. M. Forster in his *Aspects of the Novel*, and they often are misapplied by modern critics. Flat is especially corrupted when used as a synonym for cardboard; in Forster's usage, flat is not a derogatory term. Rather, it describes a character who can be summed up in a sentence. Gollum from *The Lord of the Rings* is a wonderful character who is absolutely flat in that his character is determined by his obsession with the recovery of the ring, "his precious." Every story needs some flat characters, and many successful stories, for instance, Charles Dickens's A *Christmas Carol*, have nothing but flat characters.

Foil: someone whose character contrasts to that of the protagonist, thus throwing it into sharp relief. In Connie Willis's "The Last of the Winnebagos," Katie Powell serves as a foil to the protagonist David McCombe. Katie chases after David to expiate her guilt over killing one of the last surviving dogs on Earth, while David runs away from Katie and from admitting to himself that he, too, is responsible for the dog's death.

Narrator: the fictional storyteller. When the narrator is involved in the action of the story, she's called a first-person narrator. The sentence "I watched the triceratops eat my purse" is narrated in first person. When the narrator stands outside the story, she is usually taken to be the implied author. "Persephone watched as the triceratops ate her purse" is narrated in third person, presumably by the writer. Narrators can either be reliable or unreliable. For example, in *Gulliver's Travels*, Gulliver narrates his own story: "I began last week to permit my wife to sit at dinner with me, at the farthest end of a long table, and to answer (but with the utmost brevity) the few questions I ask her." However, he is so credulous at the start and misanthropic at the end that we know enough not to take everything he tells us seriously. Since he is unreliable, we must read between his lines to discover Jonathan Swift's intent. On the other hand, we have every reason to trust the third-person narration in "Nightfall";

the implied storyteller, Isaac Asimov, means exactly what he says. The vast majority of author-as-narrator stories are told reliably. Indeed, a story in which the implied writer appears to be unreliable usually is scorned as a "reader cheater." However, there have been interesting experiments in unreliable third-person narration. The implied Bruce Sterling in "Dori Bangs" makes clear that he is unreliable in pursuit of higher truth. This is all very complicated, I know. We'll talk more about narrators when we get to viewpoint characters.

Protagonist: the central character, or the one whose name comes to mind when you ask the question "Whose story is this?" A story ought to have just one protagonist but a novel can have several, as in Kate Wilhelm's multigenerational novel of the Sumner family, *Where Late the Sweet Birds Sang*.

Round character: one who is complex and perhaps even contradictory. E. M. Forster (see flat character) put it succinctly, "The test of a round character is whether it is capable of surprising in a convincing way." If a flat character can be summed up in a sentence or two, a round character probably would take an essay. For example, Genly Ai in *The Left Hand of Darkness* is one of Ursula Le Guin's many round characters.

Spear carriers: minor characters who provide verisimilitude. They must necessarily be flat, since they rarely are named or described in any detail. They tend to run in crowds; in movies these are the folks who make up the "cast of thousands." The dim-witted population of Earth in C. M. Kornbluth "The Marching Morons" are spear carriers.

Static character: a character who does not develop. Most characters in a story should be static, so as not to distract from the significant changes you will be depicting in the central character. Static, however, most certainly does not mean boring. In Shirley Jackson's "The Lottery," all of the characters except for the scapegoat, Tessie Hutchinson, are static.

Stock character: a.k.a. stereotype, but actually a special kind of flat character who is instantly recognizable to most readers, as in the brave starship captain or the troubled teen or the ruthless businessperson. In the hands of a clumsy writer, the stock character never rises above the cardboard stereotype, which is unfortunate. Even as clichés encapsulate a kernel of truth, so do stock characters reflect aspects of real people. Courage is required of military personnel; people in business act ruthlessly at times in order to survive in that Darwinian world. In his collection of short stories, *Fancies and Goodnights,* John Collier demonstrates how to bring stock characters to life—he's particularly good with devils.

Sympathetic character: one whose motivations readers can understand and whose feelings they can comfortably share. This is the kind of character of whom naive readers will say "I could identify with her." The protagonist is often, but not always, sympathetic. Note that a sympathetic character need not be a good person. In George Orwell's *1984,* despite the fact that he betrays Julia and his own values by embracing Big Brother, Winston Smith remains a sympathetic character.

Unsympathetic character: one whose motivations are suspect and whose feelings make us uncomfortable. The boundary between sympathetic and unsympathetic characterization is necessarily ill defined. The protagonist of Lucius Shepard's "Black Coral," an ugly American named Prince, is definitely not sympathetic, nor is he intended to be. However, once he brings destruction down on himself, we feel sorry for him. The central irony of this story is that the punishment Prince receives is to become a sympathetic character.

Viewpoint character: the focus of narration, the person or persons through whom we experience the story. One kind of viewpoint character is the first-person narrator. Here's Mitchell Courtenay, the first-person viewpoint character of Pohl and Kornbluth's *The Space Merchants:* "As I dressed that morning I ran over in my mind the long list of statistics, evasions and exaggerations that they would expect in my report." When author herself acts as narrator, she usually chooses to tell the story in the third person, limiting herself to the perspective of one character. While she is in his point of view, she has access to his thoughts and memories but not to those of anyone else, as in "The View from Venus," by Karen Joy Fowler: "Linda knows, of course, that the gorgeous male waiting for her, holding the elevator door open with his left hand, cannot be moving into apartment 201." A well-written third-person viewpoint can be so seductive that it appears that the viewpoint character is, in fact, the narrator; the implied author seems to disappear. However, the invisible author must continue to be reliable even if the viewpoint character is an unreliable focus on the action of the story. John Kessel's *Good News from Outer Space* has several limited third-person viewpoint characters—some fairly reliable, some less so. Kessel maintains consistency of point of view by switching only at the chapter breaks. It's also possible to have no viewpoint character at all, as when an omniscient author sees through everyone's eyes. In "Day Million" Frederik Pohl not only tells us what all of his characters think but also what his imaginary readers are thinking as they read his story!

There is one bit of advice that I most certainly will not give you. It says in some of the how-to-write books here in my collection that when you create characters, you must "Show, don't tell." This pernicious commandment charges you always to dramatize the personalities of your characters rather than to explain or comment on them. So instead of simply informing us that "Balthazsar was a reckless man," you must send him over Niagara Falls in a barrel. Don't believe it!

A short story is not a play. The playwright can enter the consciousness of his characters only with great difficulty, through awkward devices like the soliloquy or the aside. Almost all fiction, however, starts inside someone's head; readers expect to have complete access to the thoughts and feelings of at least one character. Although our inner life is not inherently dramatic, it is the stuff of superior fiction. Daniel Keyes's "Flowers for Algernon" for example, is told almost entirely in the form of journal entries; there are relatively few scenes. Yet Charlie Gordon is one of the more memorable characters of science fiction. This is because, happily, telling can be showing. A character like Charlie dramatizes himself when he describes what he thinks and feels or when he interprets the actions of other people.

There is also the problem of limited resources. You would be squandering precious story time were you to allow each and every member of the crew of the starship to act out his reasons for choosing space service. Showing should be reserved only for very important persons. Feel free to tell readers exactly why your spear carriers are restless.

Finally, as a science fiction writer, you usually have the dual challenge of creating both character and context. In order to place your imaginary people in their imaginary world, it may at times be necessary to come right out and explain that your heroine is a girlygirl, an underperson, "cat-derived, though human in outward shape," and that this has everything to do with the fact that she falls hopelessly in love with a human lord of the Instrumentality and then never tells him. Or at least Cordwainer Smith thought so when he wrote "The Ballad of Lost C'Mell."

This is not to say that such tools of dramatic characterization as dialogue, action, and reaction are not essential. Rather it is to warn that "Show, don't tell" ought not be carved on the foundation stone of your house of fiction.

Before you turn the page to the next chapter, one last tip on characterization: remember that when you make a new world, the people in it must necessarily be the crown of your creation.

Seeing Your Way
to Better Stories

STANLEY SCHMIDT

The first time I met Kelly Freas, the renowned science fiction artist, he had just published a series of posters to promote interest in and support for the space program. The entire series was displayed on walls throughout the house, and Kelly was asking all the guests at a party which posters they thought most effective. He found a fascinating pattern in the results. "Verbally oriented" people always picked the one showing a moon rocket, three ghostly sailing ships, and the phrase, "Suppose Isabella had said *no* . . ." "Visually oriented" people always picked the one with no words, just a picture of a rocket "hatching" from an Earth-like egg.

Writers, by the nature of their work, tend to be "verbally oriented." But they would do well to realize that many of their readers are less so. Most readers do not pick up a novel or short story to admire the author's cleverness in turning a phrase, but to experience vicariously something they cannot experience directly. Your job as a writer is to make your reader *forget* that he or she is reading and give him or her the illusion of *being* in the story, seeing and hearing and smelling and feeling what's happening to your characters. Hence the oft-repeated dictum: "Show, don't tell."

What, exactly, does that mean? I've found that the most important key to making a reader see a scene vividly is that the *author* must see it clearly to be able to convey the illusion to someone else. And one of the best pieces of advice I can give a writer suffering from a tendency to tell rather than show is this: *try telling it as a play.*

All the World's a Stage

Telling rather than showing breaks down into several specific types of faults: describing character rather than showing it through dialogue and action; directly disclosing thoughts of nonviewpoint characters; summarizing dialogue as indirect discourse instead of quoting it directly; speaking in generalities rather than specifics. All of these things tend to distance the reader from the scene and reduce the illusion of being a part of it.

In a play you *can't* do those things. Except for a few special cases of unusual structure, like the Stage Manager in Thornton Wilder's *Our Town* or Sakini in John Patrick's *The Teahouse of the August Moon*, there is nobody on a stage to *tell* you what kinds of people the characters are. The only way you can find out is by watching what they do and listening to what they say to one another. And they say and do *specific* things, which the playwright must spell out. So if you've written a scene for a story in which you have told too much that you could have shown, a good way to force yourself to find specific ways to solve the problem is to recast the scene as a play—and then translate the result back into story form.

Let's see how it works in a hypothetical snippet of a badly written story:

Ralph stepped nervously into Commissioner Reed's office. It was clearly the office of a career bureaucrat, and Ralph could see

at a glance that Reed was the kind of bureaucrat who did everything by the book and disliked anything that threatened to deviate
from it. But the fate of California depended on Ralph's convincing
him in the next few minutes that he *had* to deviate from the book.

Reed already had Ralph's dossier in front of him and seemed
to be reading the crucial article. He looked up and greeted Ralph
with a few words of perfunctory small talk. Then he said, "So
what you're saying in your paper is that you're sure the Big One
is coming in six months, but you know a way to make it less
destructive?"

"That's right," Ralph replied nervously, trying to collect his
thoughts and brace his confidence for the confrontation to come.

"But your cure," Reed grated, "is going to cost the taxpayers a
lot of money. Right?"

"I'm afraid so," Ralph admitted as apologetically as if it were
his fault. He drew himself up and said firmly, "But if we let the
earthquake go its own way, it will cost a lot more."

"How much money?" the bureaucrat demanded.

How does this go wrong? Let me count the ways. We are told
that Ralph is nervous, but we are left on our own to picture how
this affects his behavior. It would be better to do it the other way
around: show us how he acts and let us conclude for ourselves
that he is nervous. We are told that Reed is marked by his office
and his personal appearance as a career bureaucrat who can't
stand things that don't fit standard procedure, but we're not shown
a single piece of evidence to justify Ralph's sizing him up that
way. Their conversation begins with "a few words of perfunctory
small talk," but again we're left to guess what they are—whereas
if they were *quoted*, they themselves could provide some of the
character clues that we haven't been given in any other way.
Once Ralph and Reed get down to business, every speech is
described by an adverb or worse, and the author seems determined
to find a new synonym for "said" every time anybody opens his
mouth.

Now try it as a scene of a play:

(*We see an office lined with glass-fronted bookcases, locked and filled with leather-bound volumes. A single desk sits in the middle of the room, its top empty except for a telephone and a folder containing several papers. REED, a slightly built, tight-lipped man of fifty or so, with a few strands of greasy black hair combed haphazardly across his pate, is frowning through thick, rimless glasses at the top paper in the folder. RALPH enters through the door and walks to the desk, checking his belt buckle and smoothing his hair down with quick little motions as he goes. When he reaches the desk he stops, shifting his weight back and forth from one foot to the other. Reed looks up at him, not lifting his head but simply peering over the tops of his lenses. Ralph avoids meeting his eyes directly.*)

REED: Hmph. So you're Tambori.

RALPH: Yes, sir.

REED: And what you're saying here (*he taps the paper*) is that you're sure the Big One is coming in six months, but you know a way to make it less destructive?

RALPH: That's right.

REED: But your cure is going to cost the taxpayers a lot of money. Right?

RALPH: I'm afraid so. (*He straightens up and looks Reed in the eye.*) But if we let the earthquake go its own way, it will cost a lot more.

REED: How much money?

A few things still have to be described, of course. Furniture and other fixed features of the physical setting can't speak for themselves; human beings can and should. The theater audience will see what the scene looks like by looking at it, but the stage manager has to be told how to set it up for them. The actors need some suggestions—such as Ralph's avoiding Reed's eyes and Reed's peering over the top of his glasses while keeping the rest of himself aimed at his desk—of how to convey their personalities and states of mind. But the way people talk is conveyed simply by what they say and how they say it. The adverbs and "said-bookisms" are gone. There is no place for them on the stage—and there's seldom a need to put them back in when you translate it back to a story:

> There was nothing in the room except some cases of musty books and a single wooden desk, and the desk was bare except for a telephone and a folder containing a few papers. Reed, a slightly built, tight-lipped man of fifty or so with a few strands of greasy black hair combed haphazardly across his pate, seemed to be studying the top paper intently through thick, rimless glasses. He was frowning, and Ralph shifted his weight back and forth from one foot to the other as he waited for the commissioner to speak.
>
> When he finally looked up, he didn't lift his head but simply peered at Ralph over the tops of his lenses. "Hmph. So you're Tambori."
>
> "Yes, sir."
>
> "And what you're saying here"—he tapped the paper—"is that you're sure the Big One is coming in six months, but you know a way to make it less destructive?"
>
> "That's right."
>
> "But your cure is going to cost the taxpayers a lot of money. Right?"
>
> "I'm afraid so." Ralph drew himself up and looked Reed in the eye. "But if we let the earthquake go its own way, it will cost a lot more."
>
> Reed scowled. "How much money?"

Notice that not only are the adverbs and strained synonyms for "said" gone, but even the word *said* itself is seldom necessary. As on the stage, once the audience or readers have been given a *picture* of the characters and setting, they can fill in for themselves such details as who's speaking and in what tone of voice. On the printed page, where they can't physically see and hear who's speaking, they may need an occasional reminder—but with only two characters "onstage," this can be provided easily and unobtrusively by an occasional reference to something else one of the speakers is doing, like, "Reed scowled."

There is still room on the printed page for an occasional direct reference to the viewpoint character's thoughts, but even those can often be avoided. The original reference to how important this meeting is seemed unnecessary in the revision because that would have already been hinted at in earlier scenes, and the reason for its importance quickly becomes apparent in the dialogue of this one. The very existence of a viewpoint character is perhaps the most essential difference between a story and a play, but it's not as big a difference as it first seems. In a play, *everybody* is revealed only through his words and deeds. In a story, *one* character is known more directly—but even he, and through him the reader, remains an audience for everyone else.

As the writer, you, too, see much of the action from an audience's viewpoint. But this can work to your advantage: if you visualize your characters and their doings clearly enough, all you have to do is watch what they do and write it down.

Setting the Stage

There are, of course, a number of important differences between a play and a story. One is that the reader does not actually see the stage, so you as storyteller have to create it in his mind— and you want him to feel as if he's *in* the scene, not looking at it from section 6, row 5, seat 2. I've been talking about "seeing" and "watching" and "visualizing," but those are really a metaphorical shorthand for "perceiving and experiencing." Seeing is perhaps our most vivid and detailed sense, but much of the fullness of the world comes from the fact that it is only one of several. Poul Anderson, probably best known as a science fiction writer but highly regarded in several other genres as well, has said that in setting a scene, he consciously tries to appeal to at least three of the reader's senses. Consider the following, for example, the fourth paragraph of a scene in Anderson's novel *The People of the Wind:*

By then they were strolling in the garden. Rosebushes and cherry trees might almost have been growing on Terra; Esperance was a prize among colony planets. The sun Pax was still above the horizon, now at midsummer, but leveled mellow beams across an old brick wall. The air was warm, blithe with birdsong, sweet with green odors that drifted in from the countryside. A car or two caught the light, high above; but Fleurville was not big enough for its traffic noise to be heard this far from the centrum.

This brief paragraph plants not only visual images, but sounds, smells, the feeling of warmth, and even tactile sensations in the mind of the reader, with just a few words each. The phrase "old brick wall" alone tickles at least three senses for any reader who has ever seen and smelled and felt one. When your story is set in a place similar to ones the reader has experienced, a word or two like *rosebushes* can trigger a great deal of imagery. If the setting is not likely to be familiar to the reader, as often happens in science fiction, fantasy, and historical novels, the writer can take less for granted and may have to work harder, and even use more words, to give the scene enough depth to draw the reader in. Even then, though, careful *choice* of the words is often preferable to using vast numbers of them. Anderson has a special knack for bringing alien worlds to life by giving things found there the sorts of instantly evocative names that human colonists might coin for them:

Further down a slope lay sheds, barns, and mews. The whole could not be seen at once from the ground, because Ythrian trees grew among the buildings: braidbark, copperwood, gaunt lightningrod, jewelleaf which sheened beneath the moon and by day would shimmer iridescent.

No reader of *The People of the Wind* has ever seen a braidbark, copperwood, or jewelleaf—but every reader gets an instant *picture* from each one-word name, complete with overtones like suggestions of texture. No reader gets exactly the same picture that the author had, but that's not important. What is important is that each gets *a* picture, suitable as a setting for the action and substantial enough for verisimilitude.

The Viewpoint Character

These days, most successful fiction is told as if seen through the eyes (and other senses) of a single character, called the viewpoint character. The viewpoint character may not be the same through an entire story, particularly a long and complex one; but each scene, at least, is experienced by the reader as it is experienced by *one* of the participants. This means, for example, that a passage like this one won't work:

> Astonished, Elmer looked at Esmerelda standing in the doorway. He'd never expected to see her again, and he didn't know whether he should invite her in or throw her out. There was no doubt in her mind, though. She'd come back for revenge, and she could hardly wait.

It's true that people used to write that way, but most readers and writers have become so used to the greater vividness and immediacy of narration from a single clearly defined viewpoint that "omniscient" storytelling now seems remote, artificial, and confusing. The word *astonished,* and the description of Elmer's thoughts and feelings, solidly establish him as the viewpoint character. Telling what is in Esmerelda's thoughts seems to do the same for her. The reader is left disoriented, unable to feel a part of the scene because his or her perceptions seem to keep jumping randomly around the room. If Elmer is the viewpoint character, with whom the reader is to identify for the duration, he has no way of knowing what's in Esmerelda's mind—except as it's suggested by her external appearance and actions. The last two sentences, for example, might be replaced by:

She smiled, but there was an odd quirk to her lips, and she looked more directly into his eyes than she had ever done before. "Aren't you going to invite me in?" she asked.

"Uh . . . sure." Only as she stepped across the threshold did he notice the slight bulge under her jacket that could only be a shoulder holster.

Tell it that way and the reader never leaves Elmer's head—and may feel a shiver along with him, without being *told* to.

Beyond the simple technical requirement of *consistency* within your chosen viewpoint, you need to *understand* how your viewpoint character thinks and feels. If your heroine has been a private detective for ten years, she's not going to react to things in the same way as if she's been a nun for ten years. A nun who became one out of deep religious conviction may be very different from one who entered an order to hide from the secular world. This is why you're often advised to construct biographies for your important characters: because what happened to them *before* the story will profoundly influence how they see and react to events *during* the story. One important thing to remember, though, is that hardly anybody is either a villain or an idiot in his or her own eyes. Everybody's actions make sense—from his or her own point of view. As a writer, you must understand that point of view and convey it sympathetically, no matter how much you may personally disagree with it. In fact, a good exercise for broadening your range of characters is to set out deliberately to write sympathetically about a character you personally find distasteful.

The Rest of the Cast

At first glance, it may seem self-contradictory to talk about seeing the story through the eyes of characters other than the viewpoint character. The reader normally doesn't—but the author should.

The reason is simple: if you don't, your other characters will tend to act in the way most convenient for *you*, rather than in the way that makes the most sense for *them*. Since the driving force of a story is conflict, often among characters, the critical points in a plot are likely to involve two or more characters flung together in a situation in which each of them has to make a decision. (Should Elmer try to throw Esmerelda out, or should he scream, or should he try to reason with her? Does she really want to do something as drastic as killing him, or will that mess her life up even more than it already is?) In the real world, if the decision is about something that matters to both parties, they're both likely to invest a good deal of mental and/or emotional energy in deciding what to do—and upon reflection, it often happens that the best course a person can choose is *not* the first one that might spring to mind. In fiction, all too often a writer is determined to have the hero or heroine's life go a certain way, and so has the other characters do things that will steer it in that direction. The result often bears an uncomfortable resemblance to cardboard puppets—with the strings showing.

Negative examples are easy to find; we've all read or watched too many war stories and westerns in which the bad guys were just plain *bad*, with never a thought for whether they would actually have any reason to do the specific things they did. For a positive example, you might look at *Forest of the Night*, a first novel by Marti Steussy, about human colonists on a harsh planet whose native inhabitants include creatures called "tigers" for their superficial resemblance to their terrestrial namesakes. In the early part of the book, the resemblance seems to go even deeper, as several incidents occur in which tigers are seen to attack humans, sometimes killing or injuring them, sometimes leaving them unharmed. In the hands of a less careful writer, this could easily have been another of those tedious tales of humans under siege by alien predators who are nothing more than mindless killing machines. But Steussy's tigers are actually highly intelligent, and there's a very specific reason for every one of the mysterious features of the "attacks." You don't find out what those reasons are until much later in the book—but the reason the book makes sense is that *she* thought those incidents through from the *tigers'* point of view before writing them, even though she first *described* them only as seen by the humans.

Occasionally a writer will explicitly show an incident from more than one viewpoint in the finished story. This happens repeatedly in T. Coraghessan Boyle's recent novel *World's End*, chronicling the interwoven histories of two families living in the Hudson Valley between the seventeenth and twentieth centuries and retelling many key incidents from the viewpoint of everybody involved. Unless you have a very special reason for doing this, though, it's usually better to think each part of the story through from each important character's viewpoint, but then *tell* it only once, from that viewpoint which is most effective for that scene. To minimize the risk of reader confusion, it's also best not to change viewpoint even when you change scene unless there is a particularly good reason to do so—and virtually never *within* a scene.

Epilogue

Several of the most useful skills you can have as a fiction writer are nothing more than looking at the substance of the story in the right ways: through the eyes of an imagined audience; through more than one sense; from *inside* the viewpoint character; and through the eyes of characters *other* than the viewpoint character. All but the first of these may be thought of as secondary skills for the act of translating the play back to story form. But the basis of the whole process is that initial step of visualizing the action in dramatic form.

When I first mentioned this idea to an actor and playwright friend, he said, "Good idea—but I'd take it a little further. Tell them to write it not only as a play, but as a play *without parenthetical instructions to the actors on how to say their lines.*" That may sound extreme to a fiction writer used to relying heavily on adjectives and adverbs—but if you think about it, that's how Shakespeare did it.

And look where it got him.

Turtles All the Way Down

JANE YOLEN

The famous philosopher Will James had just finished giving a lecture on the solar system in Cambridge, Massachusetts, when he was approached by an elderly admirer. She was shaking her head and her umbrella and looking very stern.

"Mr. James," she admonished him, "I am shocked by your notion that we live on a ball rotating around the sun. That is patently absurd."

Politely, James waited, inclining his head toward her.

"We live on a crust of earth on the back of a giant turtle," the grande dame announced.

James, ever gentle, asked, "If your . . . um . . . theory is correct, madame, what does this turtle stand upon?"

"The first turtle stands on the back of a second far larger turtle, of course," the old woman replied.

James lifted his hand. "Ah, madame, but what does this *second* turtle stand upon?"

The dowager's eyes were bright. She laughed triumphantly, "It's no use, Mr. James—it's turtles all the way down!"

And so it is with writing fantasy—whether books for adults or children, whether a plot revolving around elves or unicorns or

travel through time or angels stalking the earth or Chinese dragons
having tea with detectives. Each book stands on the back of story.
And as the old lady in Cambridge would agree, it's no use—it's
story all the way down.

The writing of fantasy relies on that relationship, thrives on
the ironies of a modern intelligence at work on the old tales, is
enhanced by the juxtaposition of what-we-know-now and what-
we-once-believed. Making fantasy stories is *sciamachy*, or boxing
with shadows. Old shadows. Devious shadows. Wily shadows.
Weird shadows. Our own shadows.

Writer as the Careful Observer

Since the creating of fantasy worlds, which contains universes,
is built on the sturdy crust of story, the first important rule is that
one needs to be sure of one's roots. Socrates said about allegories
and myths that:

> He is not to be envied who has to invent them; much labor and
> ingenuity will be required of him; and when he has once begun,
> he must go on and rehabilitate centaurs and chimeras dire. Gor-
> gons and winged steeds flow in apace, and numberless other
> inconceivable and portentous monsters. And if he is sceptical
> about them, and would fain reduce them one after another to
> the rules of probability, this sort of crude philosophy will take up
> all his time.

In other words, do your research and believe in your mon-
strocities—at least as long as you are writing of them. Otherwise
your skepticism will translate into condescension on the pages
and alienate readers.

It is difficult enough to make believable what is not, in broad
daylight, believable: the seelie court alive and well in Minneapolis, water rats and moles conversing and messing about in
boats, a furry-footed manikin out to save the world by tossing
away a magic ring, a boy pulling a sword from a stone and thus

becoming a king, a young man fighting his shadow self for possession of power, a young woman calling her dark sister out of
a mirror, a world in which dragons can be ridden through time
and alternate space. The writer of such stories must know something, then, about the seelie court, about the habits of water rats
and moles, about his own furry-footed manikin's geneology,
about all the things that will bolster belief. Belief by the author,
belief by the reader.

Background, then, is important. The landscape of the world
must be carefully limned. Sometimes, as in Emma Bull's *War
for the Oaks*, the place is real and the author lives there. Still,
as well as Bull knows Minneapolis, she had to research material
on the seelie or elvin court. Sometimes the author takes a trip
to the place, as Ellen Kushner did for her novel *Thomas the
Rhymer*, striding across the Eildon Hills of Scotland, avoiding
cowpats and taking notes. As I did for *The Dragon's Boy*, scouting
the Glastonbury marshes for duckweed and frogbit and bright-
yellow kingcup and the white clusters of milk parsley, my wildflower book in hand. Sometimes the research is done in libraries
only, as Susan Shwartz did for her fantasy novels about the Silk
Roads. But in fantasy, outer landscape reflects inner landscape.
The hills and mountains must be true, whether they are based
on actual places like Minneapolis or Scotland or England or
China—or are made up analog fashion, from places in the author's mind. All of the fantasy authors I know own research
volumes on wildlife, wildflowers, insects, birds. *Peterson's Guides*
have a use Roger Tory Peterson never intended, perhaps, but
they are useful all the same.

Analog fashion. By that I mean if you are not using the city
of Minneapolis or the actual Eildon Hills or the fenland around
Glastonbury with the tor mounding up over the quaking land,
but rather a construct of your own, it needs to have some sort of
referent in real life. Writers need to be observers first.

If you have never seen a mountain, I mean really *looked* at
one, don't put a mountain in your fantasy land. If you have not
studied a wildflower and noted that certain types grow in marshy

places, others in drier scrub, then don't pepper your fantastic
landscape with red and blue *catch-me-nevers* or *beggar-my-neigh-
bors* or whatever you decide to call them. You are sure to describe
a hothouse variety where only a scraggle-rooted one will do. And
don't send seabirds sailing over mountaintops, or water pippits
stalking up rock slides. Look hard at the real world and then look
slightly askance. That is how you make your fantasy analog. As
Emily Dickinson advised in one wise little poem, "Tell all the
truth/but tell it slant." Fantasy looks at the world through slotted
eyes.

So, too, the creatures of a fantastic world need careful observation. If you intend to use elves, for example, don't rely on
Tolkien or any other modern writer's elves. Go back to source.
You will find that elves are not the cute, pointy-eared, fur-loin-
clothed critters that modern comic books would have us believe.
Rather, according to older lore gleaned from such books as Kath-
erine Briggs's *The Fairies in English Tradition and Literature* or
her *An Encyclopedia of Fairies*, they are amoral, they are lovers
of tidyness, and they set high value on courtesy and respect, and
yet "honesty means nothing to (them). They consider they have
right to whatever they need or fancy, including . . . human
beings themselves." Or if you want to put dragons in your story,
find out as much about the difference between Western and
Eastern dragons as a start, and then decide if your dragons *could*
exist. (Would they, for example, need hollow bones like large
birds?) If you wish Wotan or Coyote or Manannan MacLir to
come striding into your fantasy, go back to source to get the
descriptions of clothing, speech patterns, and the color of mist
that wraps around the god. If you decide to depart from source,
at least *you will know what you are departing from.* The dilution
of modern mythologies comes from writers who think that a
Dungeons and Dragons manual is prime source material or that
they can know all about Hercules from watching B movies and
learning what the acronym SHAZAM stands for.

So the writer as careful observer comes first. If the writer creates
what Eleanor Cameron calls "the compelling power of place,"

building up the fantasy world or the real world in which the fantastic takes place with a wealth of corroborating details, the reader will *have* to believe in the place. If the place is real enough, then the fantasy creatures and characters—dragon or elf lord or one-eyed god or the devil himself—will stride across that landscape leaving footprints that sink down into the mud. And if those creatures are also compelling, having taken root in the old lore and been brought forward in literary time by the carefully observing author, those footprints in the mud can be taken out, dried, and mounted on the wall.

Writer as Vatic Voice

The vatic voice is the prophetic or inspired or oracular voice. Nowhere in writing is this voice used as narrative so well as in the literature of the fantastic. Fantasy is dreamer's history and often it is the dreamer's voice, the bard afire with the word of God, *vates*.

The voice of fantasy pipes through the writer down strange new-yet-old valleys wild. There is nothing tame in the world of faerie. Tendrils of green lianas crawl across the paths. Invisible beasts call from behind dark trees. The world is moonlit, a chiaroscuro world where light and dark are in constant play. But the calling is not one voice, the piping not one single tone. One might almost name three: the oracle, the schoolboy, and the fool.

The oracular voice speaks in a metaphoric mode, from hollow caves, out of swirling mists of perfumed, drugging smoke, in riddles and gnomic utterances. It sings with the bardic full chest tones. This is the sound of the high fantasy novel. Three who do it to perfection are J. R. R. Tolkien, Ursula Le Guin, and Patricia McKillip. Others include Robin McKinley, Meredith Ann Pierce, and Lloyd Alexander. It is no coincidence that riddles play an important role in their books.

There is the riddle of the ring poem in the beginning of *The Lord of the Rings* that binds the three books (really four, counting *The Hobbit*) with as fierce a power as the rings bind the characters who dare put them on.

And in Le Guin's *The Wizard of Earthsea*, the riddles Ged, the young master wizard, must ask himself, have to do with shadow and substance, good and evil, light and dark. He is told by the Master Wizard:

> This sorcery is not a game we play for pleasure or for praise. Think of this: that every word, every act of our Art is said and is done for good or for evil. Before you speak or do you must know the price that is to pay!

Ged answers, driven by shame: "How am I to know these things when you teach me nothing?" His finding the right answers to the riddles of his master's teachings are, of course, the basic thrust of the book.

Patricia McKillip uses the riddle itself as the main metaphor for her entire trilogy. In *The Riddle Master of Hed*, the riddle is the key to Morgon's self-knowledge. As he says, "The stricture according to the Riddle-Masters at Caithnard is this: 'Answer the unanswered riddle!' So I do." And he spends the rest of the three volumes trying to learn to temper his passion for unriddling with wisdom, compassion, and an understanding (inherent in all great fantasy novels) that *magic has consequences.*

The oracular tones are the full *basso profundo* of fantasy dialects, the ground bass on which the melodies of the others overswell. The words are sometimes archaic—elven, sorcery, stricture. Sometimes they are fanciful, Latinate, sonorous. There is frequent use of alliterations: "a *ring* to *rule* them"; "*pleasure* or for *praise.*" And the sentences, like chants, often end on that full stop, the strong stress syllable that reminds one of a knell rung on a full set of bells. One can declaim high fantasy, sing out whole paragraphs, even chapters. I expect that if they were set to music, it would be Beethoven, full and echoing, melodic, resonant, touching deep into the most private places of the heart.

The schoolboy voice is more securely set in the here and now. While fantasy figures bend and bow around it, the voice remains childlike, innocent, a sensible commentary on the imaginary. Ray Bradbury, E. Nesbit, C. S. Lewis, Diana Wynne Jones, and Natalie Babbit reign supreme here. The voice speaking in ordinary tones about the extraordinary recall us to our humanity in the midst of the fantastic.

Listen to the way a Nesbit child reacts when first coming upon a psammead, a creature that has "eyes on long horns like a snail's eyes . . . a tubby body . . . shaped like a spider's and covered with thick soft fur . . . and . . . hands and feet like a monkey's." She says: "What on earth is it? . . . Shall we take it home?" which seems eminently childlike and sensible.

And while in C. S. Lewis's Narnia wars and witches are raging, the voice of a very real British schoolboy, Eustace, meeting the elegant and marvelous talking mouse Reepicheep, who has just bowed and kissed Lucy's hand, remonstrates:

> "Ugh, take it away," wailed Eustace. "I hate mice. And I never could bear performing animals. They're silly and vulgar and—and sentimental."

Two schoolchildren's reactions to marvels: opposite, apposite, and very real.

And when Winnie Foster in Babbit's *Tuck Everlasting* first hears the strange story of the Tucks and their water of everlasting life, she thinks not about the unbelievability of their history but rather about the humanity that confronts her:

> It was the strangest story Winnie had ever heard. She soon suspected they had never told it before, except to each other—that she was their first real audience; for they gathered around her like children at their mother's knee, each trying to claim her attention, and sometimes they all talked at once, and interrupted each other in their eagerness.

There, quite simply, is the key to the schoolboy voice. The child in this kind of fantasy takes over the role of the adult, shepherding the fantastic creatures through their paces, guiding, guarding—even when frightfully afraid—for this world belongs *to* the child, this world in which magic has slipped through. And it is not the magic itself that is startling, because children expect that kind of magic to occur, but the vulnerability of the creatures of magic who are sad in their magnificence and, in Eustace's words, sometimes "silly and vulgar and—and sentimental." The child responds to this vulnerability by becoming both more child-like and yet adult, a paradox seen whenever a child plays house, giving advice and taking it at one and the same time.

These are the middle tones, carrying the tunes so familiar to us, dancing in and out of the fantastic as a Bach fugue does, using a simple tune made more complex by its interweaving; plain, unelaborated except where the fantastic itself is concerned, it is the everydayness of the language that reveals when set against the extraordinary. Natalie Babbit does this brilliantly, eschewing the fanciful for the ordinary in the opening of *Tuck Everlasting.* She reports with a painter's eye, and that report becomes the metaphor for the book:

> The first week of August hangs at the very top of summer, the top of the live-long year, like the highest seat of a Ferris wheel when it pauses in its turning. The weeks that come before are only a climb from balmy spring, and those that follow a drop to the chill of autumn, but the first week of August is motionless, and hot. It is curiously silent, too, with blank white dawns and glaring moons, and sunsets smeared with too much color. Often at night there is lightning, but it quivers all alone. There is no thunder, no relieving rain. These are strange and breathless days, the dog days, when people are led to do things they are sure to be sorry for after.

The third voice, high and piercing, full of ridiculous trills and anachronisms, ludicrous and punning, is the voice of the fool. But don't be guiled by it. Underneath the pratfalls and the bul-

bous-nose mask, behind the wild shrieks and the shaking of slap-
sticks, lie deep, serious thoughts. As Montaigne says in his *Essays*,
attributing it to Cato the Elder, "Wise men have more to learn
of fools than fools of wise men."

Examples of this voice are Lewis Carroll, Sid Fleischman,
Norton Juster, Terry Pratchett, Esther Friesner, and Craig Shaw
Gardner. Like a comic opera by Mozart, there are wild, sweet
melodies hidden amid the silliness, and you would be a fool
indeed to miss them.

When Lewis Carroll invented his Mad Teaparty, he little knew
that it would serve generations of English teachers and writers as
well as children. Listen:

> "You should say what you mean," the March Hare went on.
>
> "I do," Alice hastily replied, "at least—at least I mean what I
> say—that's the same thing, you know."
>
> "Not the same thing a bit!" said the Hatter. "Why, you might
> just as well say 'I see what I eat' is the same thing as 'I eat what
> I see'!"
>
> "You might just as well say," added the March Hare, "that 'I
> like what I get' is the same thing as 'I get what I like'!"
>
> "You might just as well say," added the Dormouse, which
> seemed to be talking in its sleep, "that 'I breathe when I sleep' is
> the same thing as 'I sleep when I breathe'!"
>
> "It *is* the same thing with you," said the Hatter. . . .

That is not just straight silliness. The applicability to everyday
life is so fierce in *Alice in Wonderland* that I wish to remind you
of the time of Watergate in this country when the following
phrases—and more—were lifted from the *Alice* books by col-
umnists, commentators, essayists, and editorialists and used to
explain politics:

> "I told you butter wouldn't suit the works"
> "Believing six impossible things before breakfast"
> "Sentence first, verdict after"
> "Curiouser and curiouser"

Sid Fleischman's humor is regional, hyperbolic, and anything but casual. The silliness is unrelieved, or so it seems. But Fleischman is a traditionalist when it comes to humor, and he knows well how to disguise pain with the puttynose, to teach us wisdom with a wisecrack.

In *Chancy and the Grand Rascal*, my favorite of his many books, Chancy, who is so skinny he'd "have to stand twice to throw a shadow," goes through a series of picaresque adventures in order to find his family because "kin belonged together, didn't they?" And when a wicked man is described as "gander-necked . . . with a nose like a stick," the absurdity of it sets the tone and character with economy and grace. We laugh, but we are properly fearful, too.

Norton Juster's *The Phantom Tollbooth* is not just a book-long play on words, although at times it may seem so:

> "If you please," said Milo [speaking to King Azaz the Un-abridged] ". . . . your palace is beautiful."
>
> "Exquisite," corrected the duke.
>
> "Lovely," counseled the minister.
>
> "Handsome," recommended the count.
>
> "Pretty," hinted the earl.
>
> "Charming," submitted the undersecretary.
>
> "SILENCE," suggested the king. "Now young man, what can you do to entertain us? Sing songs? Tell stories? Compose sonnets? Juggle plates? Do tumbling tricks? Which is it?"
>
> "I can't do any of those things," admitted Milo.
>
> "What an ordinary little boy," commented the king. "Why my cabinet members can do all sorts of things. The duke here can make mountains out of molehills. The minister splits hairs. The count makes hay while the sun shines. The earl leaves no stone unturned. And the undersecretary," he finished ominously, "hangs by a thread. Can't you do anything at all?"

That is a hymn to language, our use and misuse of it that William Safire, Russell Baker, and Edwin Newman would envy. But it is also story—not Sunday editorial polemic.

In the end, of course, the voice of fantasy is not a particular dialect at all—not the oracle, the schoolboy, the fool. There is a much older voice that lies in back of them all—the storyteller's voice—bridging the gap of history, singing to us out of the mists of time, telling truths.

As the Maori people say when beginning a tale:

> The breath of life,
> The spirit of life,
> The word of life,
> It flies to you and you and you,
> Always the word.

If the fantasy story does not have that breath of life, whether it uses the words of the oracle, the schoolboy, or the fool, it does not deserve to live and will lie, stillborn, on the pages of a dust-covered book.

Writer as Visionary

It surprises no one that writers of realistic fiction write about the society in which they live, that their stories reflect current thinking, and that fictional accounts of child abuse or women's rights or nuclear issues are published in the decade of public awareness and social legislation. But fantasy authors are just as mired in society as authors of realistic work are, though their work is like the wicked queen's magic mirror that does not always give back the expected answer.

For example, Charles Kingsley's *Water Babies* is a picture of the underbelly of English society in the nineteenth century, but the plight of poor chimney sweeps is only the mirror's first casting. What Kingsley didn't realize was that later readings would judge his anti-black, anti-Jewish, and anti-Catholic attitudes, which are only slightly disguised in the book, rather more harshly than he ajudged the rich-poor dichotomy. Rudyard Kipling's otherwise brilliant *The Jungle Books* is marred by jingoism. *Mary Poppins* and *Dr. Doolittle* share a cultural bias against peoples of color. *Charlie and the Chocolate Factory* in its first printing showed the Oompa-loompahs with skin "almost black" because they are "Pygmies . . . imported directly from Africa," as if they were so much yardgoods. In later printings of the book the little workers in Willy Wonka's factory have been transmogrified into a different color and a different place of origin.

What is easy to see with these examples is that fantasy books deal with issues (consciously or unconsciously, in a good light or in a bad) as thoroughly as realistic fiction, but *one step removed*. For example, Randall Jarrell's book *The Bat Poet* is about the artist in society, Le Guin's *Tehanu* about woman's power, Patricia Wrightson's *A Little Fear* about active old age, my *Sister Light, Sister Dark* about the integration of personality as well as the inaccuracies of history.

But it is the phrase *one step removed* that is the most important. Fantasy fiction, by its very nature, takes us out of the real world. Sometimes it takes us to another world altogether: Demar, Middle Earth, Narnia, Earthsea, Prydain, the Dales. Sometimes it changes the world we know in subtle ways, such as showing us the "little people" who live behind the walls of our houses and "borrow" things. Or that in a very real barn, but out of our hearing and sight, a pig and a spider hold long, special conversations. Sometimes a book of fantasy travels us between planets (*A Wrinkle in Time*), between worlds (the *Oz* books), or between times (*A Connecticut Yankee in King Arthur's Court*), or the traveler himself is from somewhere else, such as Nesbit's psammead or Bull's pucca or Diana Wynne Jones's goon.

By taking that one step away from the actual world, the writer of fantasy can allow the reader to pretend that the book is not talking about the everyday, the mundane, the real society when indeed it is. It is a convention all agree to. A mask. In eighteenth-century Venice, when masked balls were common, it became a convention that a person who wished to go about the street and be treated as if he were disguised needed only to wear a pin in the shape of a mask on his lapel. Thus accoutred, he was considered masked and could act out any part he wished without fear of shame or retribution or recognition.

So fantasy novels go capped and belled into literary society, saying in effect: this is not the real world we are talking of, this is of course faerie, make-believe, where bicolored rock pythons speak, where little girls converse with packs of cards, where boys become kings by drawing swords from stones, and where caped counts can suck the blood of beautiful women in order to live forever.

Children who read fantasy *may* be beguiled, because they *may* not totally understand the conventions. They mistake the pin for the real. They write to Maurice Sendak and ask for directions to the place where the Wild Things live. They believe in Narnia and Middle Earth and Prydain and Demar, and for them these worlds *may* become even more real than the every day. After all, when we write about such places we must adhere to three very persuasive laws: first, that the fantasy world have identifiable and workable laws underpinning it. (Lloyd Alexander says that "Underneath the gossamer is pre-stressed concrete.") Second, that there is a hero or heroine who often is lost, unlikely, powerless at first or second glance, or unrecognized and therefore easy for the reader to identify with. And third, that in a fantasy novel things always end justly—though not always happily. Come to think of it, adults also are beguiled—at least for the length of the book—that such things are so because of those three laws.

Therefore, it is important that writers of fantasy be aware of the moral underpinnings of their work. Lloyd Alexander wrote, "Fantasy, by its power to move us so deeply, to dramatize, even melodramatize, morality, can be one of the most effective means of establishing a capacity for adult values." Thus the writer of a fantasy novel must have a vision of the world, must be a visionary.

Of course, there is this to be understood about writing any kind of novel: the novelist knows very little about what she or he is doing at the start. We learn more as events, characters, and landscape take form. Every plunge into a new novel is a parallel adventure—for the hero and the novelist. Like our fictional counterparts, we take a journey into the unknown. We authors are Joseph Campbell's definition of the hero: "A hero ventures forth from the world of common day into a region of supernatural wonder: fabulous forces are there encountered and a decisive victory is won; the hero comes back with the power to bestow boons on his fellow man." We venture forth from our writing rooms—the *world of common day* into the *supernatural wonder* of the story. We encounter *supernatural forces* like slippery words, monstrous, unwieldy plots. *The decisive victory* won is the book completed. And after all, there is only one letter difference between the words *boon* and *book*, which we bestow on readers everywhere.

Once we understand the vision, it is our basic charge that we must write all stops out to make that vision sing. It is, after all, what fantasy does best, has done always. Turtles all the way down.

Learning to Write Comedy

or

Why It's Impossible and How to Do It

CONNIE WILLIS

Writing comedy is a real pain, made more painful by two persistent myths. The first is that writing comedy is a hoot, something people do for fun when they've written too much serious stuff, and that the main problem is to stop laughing so hard you can't type. While reading comedy may be an amusing experience, writing it is the same pain in the neck as any other kind of writing, only more so. It's a lot like ballet—on stage it's all pink tulle and graceful lifts, but in practice it's mostly sweat, corns, and ripped ligaments. Ditto comedy, especially the corn part.

The second myth (which apparently *everybody* believes) is that comedy can't be analyzed, that looking at it too closely kills it. This ridiculous notion seems to have evolved from the deadly results of attempting to explain a joke, though it does not take into account the fact that the reason the joke had to be explained in the first place was that it wasn't funny.

Wherever these myths came from, they're just not true. The Marx Brothers, those supposedly spontaneous crazies, used to write the scripts for their movies and then take them on the road to try out the humor on an audience, revise and rework the routines, polish up the jokes, and look for dead spots. It didn't kill their comedy, did it? And you didn't notice Harpo collapsed in (silent) mirth at his own jokes, did you? No, he was too busy cutting off people's ties and handing people his leg.

There's no step-by-step method for writing humorous fiction (Step 4: Insert clever wordplay every sixth line) and no easily learned formula. It's not possible to be taught to write comedy— I doubt if it's possible to be *taught* to write anything—but that doesn't mean you can't learn. And the way to learn to write comedy is to watch and read comedies and analyze what you're watching and reading.

I need to explain something before we go any farther. To my mind, writing comic science fiction is no different from writing any other kind of comedy. Actually, I don't see any difference between writing any kind of science fiction and writing anything else, an attitude that has gotten me in trouble from time to time. I will be using some examples from science fiction stories, but I believe firmly that if you want to learn to write something, you should study the masters, and the masters, to my way of thinking, are Shakespeare, Mark Twain, P. G. Wodehouse, and Jerome K. Jerome. Jerome's *Three Men in a Boat* is possibly the funniest book ever written, Mark Twain was a comic genius, Wodehouse devoted his entire career to comedy, and Shakespeare knows everything. Which is why I use them as examples along with science fiction writers.

After you've read a bunch of comedy, you'll see that why it's funny (if it is funny) is due largely to the comic bag of tricks the writer uses and has nothing to do with the situation at hand.

Hollywood has never figured this out. They constantly make the mistake of thinking that the only thing required for a comedy is a funny situation. "Let's have Chevy Chase slip and fall in the mud," they say, or "Let's have Dolly Parton and Meryl Streep play twins." You've all seen these movies.

A funny situation is never enough, mostly because there is no such thing as a *comic* situation. The situations that occur in comedies are the exact same situations that occur in dramas. And tragedies. And TV cop shows. And Shakespeare. He used to, in fact, use the same plots for his comedies and tragedies. His star-crossed lovers in *Romeo and Juliet*, where no one was laughing, appear again as Bottom/Pyramus and Flute/Thisbe in *A Midsummer Night's Dream* and the hopeless twits Hero and Claudio in *Much Ado About Nothing*.

People fail to communicate, quarrel, get arrested for crimes they didn't commit, get lost, run for political office, search for gold, die, and all of this can be either high drama or low comedy. It all depends on the techniques used. These techniques range from high satire to low burlesque, with all sorts of wordplay and high jinks in between. And the most important technique of comedy is language.

No, that's not stating it strongly enough. Language is the life blood of comedy. Serious prose can get by if it is merely serviceable and moderately clear. Comic prose can't. It must be perfectly clear, and consistently amusing besides.

Everyone's heard jokes badly told: "So then St. Peter said to the farmer's daughter, 'I was talking to the duck,'—no, wait. That isn't how it goes. Anyway, it was something to do with a duck . . . or was it a turkey?" If the setup for the joke isn't perfectly clear, the point will be missed completely. And a great deal of comic writing depends not on punchlines but on conjuring up a funny picture in the reader's mind, and here language is everything.

In *Roughing It*, Mark Twain describes how a camel had eaten his overcoat:

> . . . after he was done figuring on it as an article of apparel, he began to contemplate it as an article of diet. He put his foot on it, and lifted one of the sleeves out with his teeth, and chewed

and chewed at it, gradually taking it in, and all the while opening and closing his eyes in a kind of religious ecstasy, as if he had never tasted anything as good as an overcoat in his life. Then he smacked his lips once or twice, and reached after the other sleeve. Next he tried the velvet collar, and smiled a smile of contentment that it was plain to see that he regarded that as the daintiest thing about an overcoat. The tails went next, along with some percussion caps and cough candy, and some fig paste from Constantinople.

Jerome K. Jerome's *Three Men in a Boat,* having forgotten their can opener, try to open a tin of pineapple:

> Then Harris tried to open the tin with a pocket knife, and broke the knife and cut himself badly; and George tried a pair of scissors, and the scissors flew up, and nearly put his eye out. While they were dressing their wounds, I tried to make a hole in the thing with the spiky end of the hitcher, and the hitcher slipped and jerked me out between the boat and the bank into two feet of muddy water, and the tin rolled over, uninjured, and broke a teacup.

As in all writing, the detail work is everything. Comic writing has to be specific, using those minor, telling details that make us see the whole picture clearly.

But language is not only essential to comedy, it's fun, and writers indulge in all sorts of extravagances of language just for the heck of it, as when Ron Goulart is relating the Martians' explanation of why Mars was in the middle of a depression:

> Instead of . . . building up comforting supplies of zugbeams, or what we would call deathrays, he had foolishly poured the taxpayers' money into Yerb, which is something like our social security. ("The Yes-Men of Venus")

Comedy writing uses all sorts of linguistic special effects, from Wodehouse's creative comparisons:

. . . he sat motionless, his soul seething within him like a Welsh rabbit at the height of its fever. ("Tangled Hearts")

to Carol Emshwiller's unusual descriptions:

. . . and one looks like Wanda Landowska, and two look like versions of the young Frank Sinatra while another looks like the elderly version. ("As If")

to Jerome K. Jerome's surprising metaphors:

I never see a steam launch but I feel I should like to lure it to a lonely part of the river, and there in the silence and the solitude, strangle it. (*Three Men in a Boat*)

to Shakespeare's complicated wordplay:

MESSENGER: I see, lady, the gentleman is not in your books.
BEATRICE: No; an he were, I would burn my study.
(*Much Ado About Nothing*)

Which brings us to the pun. Most people groan at them, some feel they are a powerful argument for the reinstatement of capital punishment, and some are, unfortunately, addicted to them.

I take sort of a middle position on puns. Hanging seems too severe. Say five years to life. They are a true form of wordplay— I mean, Shakespeare used them—and they make wonderful titles, but they should be as clever as possible and should never be expected to carry a story all by themselves.

Neither should funny names and words, though they can be a lot of fun. Wodehouse delights in naming his characters things like Psmith ("the p is silent, as in *pshrimp*") and the Empress of Blandings (a pig) and his settings Towcester Abbey (pronounced Toaster), and Shakespeare got a lot of mileage out of Dogberry's inability to use the right word:

DOGBERRY: Our watch, sir, have indeed comprehended two aspicious persons, and we would have them this morning examined before your worship.

LEONATO: Take their examination yourself and bring it to me. I am now in great haste, as it may appear unto you.

DOGBERRY: It shall be suffigance.

(*Much Ado About Nothing*)

But Shakespeare didn't try to write *Much Ado About Nothing* without lots of other kinds of comic writing, and without the "merry war" between Beatrice and Benedick. They never met without there being "a skirmish of wit between them," and their dialogue, unlike puns and silly names, does carry the story.

Characters in comedy, like Dorothy Sayers's Lord Peter Wimsey, love to talk piffle. They love to talk, period. And they do. Wodehouse's Bertie Wooster novels are one long, astonishing monologue, an assault on the ears and good sense, and Heinlein, though not usually thought of as a writer of comedy, had several narrators who were talkative, smart, and witty, including Kip Russell in *Have Spacesuit, Will Travel*:

> . . . I stacked a pyramid of Skyway Soap on each end of the fountain and every cake was accompanied by a spiel for good old Skyway, the soap that washes cleaner, is packed with vitamins, and improves your chances of Heaven, not to mention its rich creamy lather, finer ingredients, and refusal to take the Fifth Amendment.

Characters in comedy don't just talk, they expound and chatter and banter and orate and prattle, bringing far more energy and enthusiasm to their conversations than is probably necessary, with the delightful result that their dialogue ranges from rambling—

> She was a good soul—had a glass eye and used to lend it to old Miss Wagner, that hadn't any, to receive company in; it warn't big enough, and when Miss Wagner warn't noticing, it would get twisted around in the socket, and look up, maybe, or out to one side, and every which way, while t' other one was looking as straight ahead as a spyglass. Grown people didn't mind it, but it most always made the children cry. (*Roughing It* by Mark Twain)

to witty:

BEATRICE: I wonder that you will still be talking, Signior Benedick. Nobody marks you.

BENEDICK: What, my dear Lady Disdain? Are you yet living?

BEATRICE: Is it possible Disdain should die while she has such meet food to feed it as Signior Benedick?

(*Much Ado About Nothing*)

to unfriendly:

"Hullo, aged relative," I began, as suavely as I could manage.

"Hullo to you, you young blot on Western civilization," she responded.

(*The Catnappers*, by P. G. Wodehouse)

to thickheaded, as when William S. Hart attempts to explain that they are dealing with the undead in Howard Waldrop's "*Der Untergant des Abendlandesmenschen*":

". . . er, ah, vampires . . ."

"You mean," asked Billy, "like Theda Bara?"

You will notice that the above contains a joke, which brings us to another matter.

A lot of people have the idea that writing humorous fiction is just writing a series of jokes. For awhile in science fiction there were a number of short short stories called Ferdinand Feghoots (after the hero of R. Bretnor's versions of this sub-subgenre). The story would at first appear to be a science fiction story, complete with characters and a plot (one of my favorites, which I suppose is not strictly a Feghoot, since it's by Damon Knight, was about a vegetable vampire that sucked the juice out of celery and carrots), but when you got to the end of the story, you realized you had been had and the last line was actually a punchline, or even worse, a pun (in the case of the veggy vampire, they drove a steak through his heart), and the whole story had been nothing more than a very long joke. The Ferdinand Feghoots received a great deal of criticism, although I always sort of liked them, and some editors refused to buy them. They still pop up now and then, and the editors still refuse to buy them.

The problem with the Feghoots (besides the awfulness of some of the puns) was that the story was not a story. It was merely a setup. These setups were ingenious and often very funny, but with a joke, the only thing that matters is the punchline, and the setup is nothing more than a means of getting to it.

Comedy writing means jokes, certainly. And setups, and word-play and banter and funny names and clever dialogue, but it also tells a story that exists for its own sake and makes the reader laugh not just at the gags but at the world the writer has created.

This world is frequently an exaggerated version of our own—as Jerome says, "a really quite likely story, founded, to a certain extent, on an all but true episode, which had actually happened in a modified degree some years ago." Exaggeration is a staple of comic fiction, the turning up of the volume on the truth to point out the humor inherent in it.

When Harris, one of the *Three Men in a Boat*, goes into Hampton Court Maze, he doesn't just get lost, he manages to lose an entire squad of people along with him, "people who had given up all hope of ever getting in or out, or of ever seeing their home and friends again," and when the keeper finally comes to rescue them, *he* gets lost, too.

Mark Twain is, of course, the master of exaggeration:

> In the space of one hundred and seventy-six years the Lower Mississippi has shortened itself two hundred and forty-two miles. That is an average of a trifle over one mile and a third per year. Therefore, any calm person, who is not blind or idiotic, can see that in the old Colitic Silurian Period, just a million years ago next November, the Lower Mississippi River was upward of one million three hundred thousand miles long, and stuck out over the Gulf of Mexico like a fishing rod. (*Life on the Mississippi*)

The creation of exaggerated worlds, "if this goes on . . . ," is science fiction's natural domain, and many of the best comedies in science fiction are biting satires.

In "Stable Strategies for Middle Management," Eileen Gunn exaggerates the tendencies already in the business world to a point where corporate types undergo bioengineering to actually become the insects they already resemble. Tom Disch's "The Santa Claus Compromise" tells the story of what happened when the last disenfranchised group, the five-year-olds, were given their civil rights, and Gordon Dickson's "Computers Don't Argue" is a classic cautionary tale.

There are moments when Damon Knight doesn't even seem to be exaggerating in "The Big Pat Boom," a story in which he relates what happened when the aliens came to earth on vacation and the only souvenir they were interested in was the cowpat. His tale of the ensuing opportunism, greed, and general silliness seems entirely plausible.

The flip side of exaggeration is of course understatement, the turning down (or even off) of the volume. Great effects can be achieved by leaving out details and downplaying what might be gleefully described.

Understatement is the equivalent of the deadpan delivery of a comedian. Benedick proposes to Beatrice: "Come and I will have thee, but by this light I take thee for pity," and Beatrice (who is as crazy about him as he is about her) answers, "I would not deny you, but by this good day, I yield upon great persuasion, and partly to save your life, for I was told you were in a consumption."

Even though Bertie Wooster's adventures frequently involve shinnying down drainpipes, stealing cow creamers, and perching on top of chiffoniers, Wodehouse never raises his voice:

> I sat up in bed with that rather unpleasant feeling you get sometimes that you're going to die in about five minutes. (*The Code of the Woosters*)

After Jerome's Harris has gotten his group thoroughly lost, he gets out his map again:

> but the sight of it only infuriated the mob, and they told him to go and curl his hair with it. Harris said that he couldn't help feeling that, to a certain extent, he had become unpopular.

Sometimes Jerome not only understates, he omits, as in the battle of the pineapple tin:

> Then we all got mad. We took that tin out on the bank, and Harris went up into a field and got a big sharp stone, and I went back into the boat and brought out the mast, and George held the tin and Harris held the sharp end of his stone against the top of it, and I took the mast and poised it high up in the air, and gathered up all my strength and brought it down.
>
> It was George's straw hat that saved his life that day. He keeps that hat now (what is left of it), and, of a winter's evening, when the pipes are lit and the boys are telling stretchers about the dangers they have passed through, George brings it down and shows it round, and the stirring tale is told anew, with fresh exaggerations every time.
>
> Harris got off with merely a flesh wound.

Harris may be exaggerating, but Jerome is leaving it strictly to our imaginations, and it's much funnier than any description he possibly could have given us.

Both exaggeration and understatement are funny because of their inappropriateness to the situation, the unexpectedness of the writer's response to what is happening, and it is this that is the essence of comedy.

It refuses to take things seriously—or rather, it refuses to take the same things as the rest of the world takes seriously, seriously. "Nick and Jane were glad that they had gone to see the end of the world because it gave them something special to talk about at Mike and Ruby's party," Silverberg writes in "When We Went to See the End of the World," and we think "That's *not* funny," which of course is exactly why it is.

Comedy refuses to be awed by anything, it takes all the wrong things seriously, it turns ideas and attitudes on their heads, and it makes connections where there obviously aren't any. All of this is called divergent thinking and is what Gracie Allen made a career out of. And Wodehouse:

"Tell me, Egbert," he said, "who would a tall, thin chap be?"
Colonel Wedge replied truly enough that he might be anyone—
except of course, a short, stout chap.

(Full Moon)

The reader is led to expect one thing and gets another. Oscar
Wilde is the acknowledged king of deceiving you into thinking
you know what he plans to say. Aphorisms like "A man cannot
be too careful in the choice of his enemies" and "The only way
to get rid of a temptation is to yield to it" are brilliant examples
of ruined expectations, and oddly enough, instead of being disappointed or angry at being deceived, we laugh at the incongruity.

And at the underlying truth, as when Mark Twain talks about
"all the modern inconveniences," and says solemnly, "It could
probably be shown by facts and figures that there is no distinctly
native American criminal class except Congress." *(Pudd'nhead
Wilson's New Calendar)*

Comedy is in this sense very much like mysteries. It deals in
misdirection, in playing on our assumptions and then using them
against us. Sentences start out going one direction and end up
going another—

> BENEDICK: I will live in thy heart, die in thy lap, and be buried
> in thy eyes, and moreover, I will go with thee to thy uncle's.

—and words appear in sentences where you *never* expected them
to be:

> Our electric pads have rendered the hot water bottle obsolete.
> Three speeds . . . Autumn Glow, Spring Warmth, and Mae
> West. *(Ring for Jeeves*, by P. G. Wodehouse)

Divergent thinking is not so much a comic technique as a skewed
way of looking at the world, a slightly off-center perspective science fiction has always had.

Only in science fiction could you find Howard Waldrop's "The
Night of the Cooters," in which H. G. Wells's Martians make
the mistake of landing in Texas, where men are men and the

sheriff won't put up with any nonsense, or Alfred Bester's "Will You Wait?" in which a man can't even sell his soul to the devil because of bureaucratic red tape.

In Robert Sheckley's "Pilgrimage to Earth," the hero, tired of his logical life, goes to Earth to find love. When he asks one of the locals where true love can be found:

> "Walk uptown two blocks," the little man said briskly. "Can't miss it. Tell 'em Joe sent you."

Divergent thinking permeates comedy, from Shakespeare to R. A. Lafferty's "The Hole on the Corner" and Fredric Brown's "Puppet Show," and is the very essence of comedy. It is also nearly impossible to describe. Individual lines can't convey it, and many very funny comedies have almost no funny lines at all. The humor comes from the entire piece, from a sort of over-joke that infuses the whole story and has a cumulative effect that is impossible to describe in an article like this. I'm not even sure exactly how it's accomplished, either, though it has something to do with running jokes and the ringing of unexpected changes on the same theme and cappers.

A capper is one final joke, the one that sends the reader over the edge. It's not necessarily the funniest joke in the piece, but that one last straw that breaks the camel's back. In movies and plays, people will frequently smile or giggle intermittently throughout a scene and then burst out loudly at the end. They are not really laughing at the capper. They are laughing at the cumulative effect of the entire scene, which somehow the capper has summed up.

After Harris's trials and tribulations in the maze, he describes how the old keeper finally came and let them out:

> Harris said he thought it was a very fine maze, so far as he was a judge, and we agreed that we would try to get George to go into it, on our way back.

These lines are not nearly as funny here as they are when reading *Three Men in a Boat,* which is why articles like this on how to write comedy are ultimately doomed. It may also be another reason why that dissection-equals-death myth persists.

Which is why what I said at the beginning of this article holds— if you want to learn to write comedy, you have to read it and watch it, not in little snips like this, but the real stuff.

Go read *Much Ado About Nothing*, *Three Men in a Boat*, and all the P. G. Wodehouse you can get your hands on. Read Mark Twain's *Life on the Mississippi* and *Roughing It* and *The Innocents Abroad*. Read Ron Goulart, Tom Disch, and Eileen Gunn, Kim Stanley Robinson's "Escape from Kathmandu," Damon Knight's "The Big Pat Boom" and "ERIPMAV," Asimov's "The Up-to-Date Sorceror," and Shirley Jackson's "One Ordinary Day, with Peanuts." Read R. A. Lafferty and Robert Sheckley and Carol Emshwiller and both Freds (Brown and Pohl) and Howard Waldrop.

And pay attention. Try to see how the writers do whatever it is they are doing. It won't kill the comedy. I had to read all of this stuff again for this article. It was still funny. And the part in *Three Men in a Boat* where Harris tries to sing a comic song reduced me, as it always does, to helpless laughter.

Part II

IDEAS
AND FOUNDATIONS

Good Writing Is Not Enough

STANLEY SCHMIDT

Only a month after it appeared in *Analog* in mid-December 1985, S. C. Sykes's short story "Rockabye Baby" was well on its way to nomination for a Nebula, one of the two most prestigious awards in science fiction. It also had been picked up for a "Best of the Year" anthology, and was doing quite nicely in *Analog*'s own annual reader poll. Another story attracting much favorable comment in that poll (it was our readers' favorite short story of the forty-two we published last year) and elsewhere was Stephen L. Burns's "A Touch Beyond" (January 1985). "A Touch Beyond" was a first sale; "Rockabye Baby," a second. Editors do buy, and successfully publish, stories from new writers.

Yet, a magazine like *Analog* receives so many submissions that it has room for only one or two percent of them. Many stories are rejected not because of anything conspicuously *wrong* with them, but simply because nothing sufficiently *special* about them makes them stand out from ninety-eight percent of the competition.

What makes stories like "Rockabye Baby" and "A Touch Beyond" stand out? How can you make *your* stories do the same?

The key words are *imagination, discipline*—and the first word in "science fiction."

What about writing? It's important, but *good writing is not enough*. Oh, it *can* be. If your writing is truly extraordinary, you may breathe enough new life into an old idea to make something fresh and commanding of it. "Rockabye Baby" deals with a paraplegic faced with the opportunity to have his nervous system restored to normal—at the price of all his present memories. The idea of nerve regeneration is not new to science fiction, but the vividness with which Sykes makes the reader feel what it's like to be handicapped—and what memories really mean—makes the story unforgettable. "Emergence," by David R. Palmer (another highly successful first story, which we published in January 1981), brings some novel twists to the global holocaust and superman themes—such as minimal use of nuclear weapons to trigger biological ones, and a plausible way for a natural epidemic to produce a new "species"—but the basic ideas behind the story are among the oldest in science fiction. The story draws most of its impact from a remarkably vivid portrayal of an exceptionally memorable character. Palmer dared to tell his story through the journal of an eleven-year-old girl, trapped alone in an underground shelter after the war, who doesn't yet realize just how special she is. Her personality is so unusual, engaging and wide-ranging, and every word so carefully chosen, that when Palmer complained that a routine copy-editing change of a single word was "out of character," there was no question that he was right.

Few stories can pull that off. What I see more often are stories that are competently written—but little more—and don't *say* very much. They lack content—*ideas*. Science fiction requires two sets of skills: writing, and imagining in that special way that makes speculations both plausible and integral to the story. I want to concentrate on that second set of skills. Too many writers try to get by on good writing alone, without developing the *other* tools of their trade.

Adam and Eve, Revisited

To write science fiction, you must first understand what it is. Watching movies is not enough; most "science fiction" in movies and television is not science fiction at all, by the standards of *written* science fiction. If you haven't read many science fiction books and magazines, you should—both to get a feel for what it takes to write them, and to avoid rehashing worn-out ideas. (Ben Bova, my predecessor at *Analog*, warned me that I'd get several tories a month involving a man and woman who find themselves alone on an unnamed planet and turn out to be Adam and Eve. I quickly learned to recognize these stories on the first page.)*

Science fiction is fiction in which:

At least one speculative idea is *integral* to the story.

Whatever science the story uses is *plausible* in the light of known science.

What do these criteria mean? "Rockabye Baby" is very much a "people" story; you may not even realize it's science fiction until you're halfway through it—but its final impact depends completely on its characters' having the option of the nerve-regeneration process. In "Emergence," the speculative ideas on which the story depends are a war that wipes out most of humanity and a new kind of human being that supersedes *Homo sapiens*. In Marc Stiegler's "Petals of Rose" (November 1981, and yet another memorable story by a writer with only one previous sale), humans must cooperate on a long-range project with beings whose adult lives are one-day frenzies of intensely concentrated activity. In "A Touch Beyond," Stephen Burns extrapolates the well-known "phantom limb" effect experienced by amputees to imagine a kind of surgery done telekinetically by surgeons who have sacrificed their physical hands; the story focuses on the other sacrifices such a surgeon is forced to make in exchange for his special ability.

*See "The Ideas that Wouldn't Die," p. 200.

As demonstrated in these examples, an idea being "integral" to a story means that you can't remove the speculation without destroying the whole story. This does *not* mean that stories must contain a lot of talk about science or technology—or that the presence of such talk automatically makes the stories science fiction. The movie *Star Wars* is full of "science fictional" hardware and trappings, but at heart it's a western. Replace the spaceships and light sabers with horses and six-guns, and you can tell essentially the same story in the Old West. In contrast, Daniel Keyes's *Flowers for Algernon* (or the movie *Charly*) contains almost *no* science fictional gimmickry or jargon, yet it is quite clearly science fiction. It is a story first and foremost of what goes on in a particular human being's mind; the speculative element— the one that makes *Flowers* a science fiction story in its comfortably contemporary setting—is the operation that increases Charlie Gordon's intelligence. The book does not go into much detail about the operation—but *everything that happens to Charlie grows directly out of it.* Remove the operation and nothing remains of the story. You might still tell a story about Charlie Gordon, but it would not be even remotely *this* story. And it certainly wouldn't be science fiction.

The plausibility of that speculation is also important. What can and can't happen in a particular setting is determined by scientific laws, primarily those of physics, chemistry, and astronomy; there is strong evidence that these laws apply everywhere in the universe. Others, such as the principles of earthly biology, are special applications of the more general laws of physics and chemistry. You must reckon with them if you're writing about life on Earth, but physics and chemistry may lead to quite different biologies elsewhere (such as the silicon-based organisms in Stanley G. Weinbaum's classic short story, "A Martian Odyssey").

To tell a plausible story about a situation covered by known scientific laws, you must know what those laws say and how they apply to your imagined situation. You will not, for example, write about enormous spiders running around eating people: a spider of such a size could not support its own weight.

Original Sins

For another example, my first two novels, *The Sins of the Fathers* and *Lifeboat Earth*, form a single large story in which humans must escape an explosion of our galaxy's core by accepting the aid of mysterious aliens who offer to move Earth bodily to another galaxy. The *story* is about *people* and what happens to their lives—but the changes in their lives are all consequences of the core explosion and planet-moving. In writing *Lifeboat Earth*, I had to make such calculations as the apparent position and brightness of the sun at various stages of the Earth's journey and how much the ground appeared to tilt as a result of acceleration. It got so involved that I bought a programmable calculator and developed some fairly exotic programs that will probably never be used again.

"But I can't do that," you may say. "You're talking about *calculation*, and I'm a writer, not a mathematician." Sorry; you *must* do that, to the extent that you can, and get help when you need it. You don't have to be a professional scientist or engineer; few stories need as much background calculation as *Lifeboat Earth*. But if you want to write real science fiction, and not fantasy or westerns with spaceships, you must check the consequences of your assumptions and see whether they work and what side effects they have.

How can you develop solid scientific backgrounds if you're not a scientist? Learn all you can about everything. Take courses—but don't depend on them. Learn to teach yourself. Read widely. Basic physics, chemistry, astronomy, and biology are essential. Virtually anything else will sooner or later prove useful: geology, psychology, anthropology, history, linguistics—the more the merrier. Use *recent* books, and don't stop there. These fields change rapidly (astronomy has changed more in the last twenty years than in the preceding four hundred.) Watch the tip of the iceberg, at least, in magazines like *Scientific American* and *New Scientist*. All this reading serves not only as a safeguard against unworkable story ideas, but also as a source of good ones. Knowing where the present limits of knowledge are will suggest what lies beyond.

No matter how thorough your basic education, you'll run into questions for which it has no ready answers. Things like "How long does a radio message take to get from Earth to Titan?" or "How high can a Piper Cherokee fly on a planet with ninety percent of the gravity and eighty percent of the atmospheric pressure of Earth?" Sometimes you can evade such questions by setting up your story in such a way that the exact numbers aren't critical. But if you do give (or imply) numbers, make sure they're consistent, because readers *love* to catch authors in mistakes. Learning about all kinds of things is part of the fun of writing science fiction; but since you also want to make money at it, you can't afford to spend too much time answering simple questions. So it pays to develop good library skills, covering not only encyclopedias and card files but also the semipopular scientific journals and the scientific abstract indices. The more you can do for yourself, the better; but don't hesitate to ask the reference librarian for needed help. The same applies to calculations: it's nice to do them yourself, but some will probably be beyond you. For those cases, cultivate experts you can ask for help. Universities have them on all kinds of subjects, and many of them are surprisingly willing to help writers who approach them politely and professionally (which means *first* having done all you can on your own). For information dealing specifically with the kinds of background problems commonly encountered by science fiction writers, see the references listed at the end of this essay.

Fundamentals

Does all this mean that you must prove rigorously that everything you write about is possible, and that you must avoid things not covered by present-day science? Not at all. Science has changed radically just in this century; it would be arrogant and unrealistic to assume we're not due for more big surprises. A fundamental breakthrough, by definition, cannot be deduced from existing theories. I use a "negative impossibility" criterion: anything that nobody can currently prove impossible is fair game for science fiction. For example, faster-than-light travel (FTL) is okay *if* you postulate it in a form that doesn't contradict existing theory in any region of experience that has been thoroughly tested experimentally—even though it would surely require radical changes in theory outside the tested range. Several of my own stories, including *Lifeboat Earth*, have used a form of FTL in which objects can "tunnel" to superlight speeds without an increase in energy, while objects traveling below the speed of light act just as Einstein said they do. (The resulting consternation among theoretical physicists becomes part of the story background.) Other writers have used scientific rationales ranging from "hyperspace" (a shortcut through a dimension not normally perceived by humans, as in John W. Campbell's *The Mightiest Machine* and Robert A. Heinlein's *Starman Jones*) to a new kind of force that increases with the mass it is accelerating (as in Norman Spinrad's "Outward Bound").

Psychic talents, like the Bergmann surgery in "A Touch Beyond," are a somewhat special case. Parapsychological phenomena such as telepathy and telekinesis are highly controversial in the scientific community. Some scientists think their existence is well enough established that further research on them is not only worthwhile but important, though the underlying mechanisms are not yet even remotely understood. Others dismiss everything that's been done on the subject as sloppy or fraudulent and deny that there's any real evidence that the phenomena exist at all. For science fiction, if you accept my negative impossibility test, it doesn't matter whether "psi" phenomena have been proved to exist or not. If you portray them as something that *could* exist, in a way that is self-consistent and does not contradict scientific knowledge that *is* well established, they are perfectly legitimate subjects for science fiction. But you do have to put them on a reasonably scientific basis—if not providing a detailed explanation for them, at least making sure they operate according to consistent rules. An occult or "anything goes" approach will not do.

Most speculative ideas are either "extrapolations" (based solidly on known science) or "innovations" (radically new concepts, subject only to the negative impossibility test). With either type of idea, work out as much detail as you can—and include no more in the story than the reader needs in order to understand what's going on. After doing all that work, it's tempting to show it off— but resist the temptation. You don't want to scare off readers who aren't specialists—and even they will sense that you did the work, in a feeling of solidity that the story would otherwise lack. If explanation is *necessary*, slip it in subtly. Readers won't accept large blocks of lecture, even if they're disguised by having characters ask questions they wouldn't really need to ask. A good rule of thumb: *Know as much as you can about your background— and tell no more than you have to.*

From Idea to Story

In its early days, much science fiction was written by scientists or engineers, such as Isaac Asimov, E. E. "Doc" Smith, and George O. Smith, who picked up storytelling as a sideline (and perhaps as an outlet for speculations too far out for the "respectable" journals of their professions). Many early writers, primarily concerned with exploring challenging ideas, did not shape words into stories with the finesse of today's best writers. The "New Wave" of the '60s, associated with such writers as Harlan Ellison,

Thomas M. Disch, and Samuel R. Delany, stressed experimen-
tation with literary forms and techniques, sometimes giving these
aspects greater emphasis than they did to idea content. There is
less avant-gardism now; many editors are leaning toward clear,
straightforward, vivid storytelling—and if it happens also to be
especially evocative or subtle, so much the better. The lasting
heritage of the "New Wave" is a set of standards for *writing* that
are higher than ever before.

Yet, trying to make a story stand out with writing alone, without
fresh and interesting ideas, requires *awfully* impressive writing.
Trying to make it on *ideas* alone requires awfully impressive ideas.
Most stories must be good on *both* counts. "Petals of Rose," for
example, is a story based on an idea so striking that it would have
stood out even with mediocre writing. The Rosans, the aliens
with whom humans must cooperate, live so fast and intensely
that contact with them is dazzling and exhausting. The number
of characters in the story is enormous and each exists for a very
short time, yet the reader must come to know and care about
each one during his brief appearance. That requires vivid, concentrated characterization (for example, the life of Sor Lai Don
Shee lasts less than three pages, and Dor Laff To Lin lives and
dies on a single page). Long-term cooperation between humans
and Rosans is possible only because part of the memory of each
Rosan generation is transmitted chemically to the next—but only
a small part. One human, Cal, is driven over the edge by the
inevitable death of one special Rosan student. He tells a psy-
chologist:

> "I can't stand it. Every day I teach the same thing, again and
> again, and the faces are *different*." The last ended in a howl of
> horror. "Every day different, never the same person twice." He
> whimpered. "Please, let me have just one student twice."

Since a story can almost always be analyzed as one or more
people (or reasonable facsimiles) struggling to solve a problem,
start plotting by trying to imagine the problems that would arise
should your speculation become reality. Don't try to plunge right

into the story; play with the implications of the idea. Consider "Petals of Rose": the Rosans live and die in a single day. How does that affect their concept of life? What do they think about humans, who the Rosans consider immortal? What frustrations and other problems do the humans suffer because of the short lives of their allies? Because of the short individual life spans, generations flash by, and the entire structure of the society can change within a week—how will this "instability" affect the humans?

Think of all the problems that will result from your idea that you can; don't stop with the first one that comes to mind. Thinking of problems will inevitably suggest people who have them—and they will become your characters. When you know them well enough, you will begin to understand how they will react to their problems, and how those reactions create other problems, including conflicts with other characters. At each key point in the story, ask yourself what is the best thing *each* character can do—*from his own point of view*. Then let him do it. All you have to do is write it down.

Perhaps the most important fact a science fiction writer must grasp is that all the changes that make a future or a new world are interdependent. In *Lifeboat Earth*, for example, I started with an almost contemporary Earth, let the aliens make certain changes in it, and then figured out everything I could about what effects those changes had on life. Both individuals and political-economic systems had to react to the physical changes, and some of their actions in turn produced still more changes. And so on.

Building Worlds—And Moving Them

Oddly enough, the first step in the creation of *Lifeboat Earth* focused on an idea that is barely visible in the finished story. I wrote a minor short story based on the realization that an FTL ship could be used to get a second look at an astronomical event seen years ago on Earth. Ben Bova, then editor at *Analog*, quite rightly bounced the story, but added: "The basic idea is good. What can you build on it?"

That kind of question is one of the few things editors are good for. It got me thinking, and when I realized that that idea could combine with a couple of others I had in my "What-do-I-do-with-it?" file, the story ignited and took off. The other two ideas were:

A galactic core explosion, like those seen in other galaxies, could have occurred in ours any time in the last 30,000 years—and we wouldn't know it until the light reached us.

Suppose the Earth were about to become uninhabitable and aliens offered to rescue us, but refused to discuss the reasons for their offer. Should we accept their help?

That last question is the basis of *The Sins of the Fathers*. Before you can start telling such a story, you must recognize and answer key questions. The questions, at this point, are more important than the answers, because knowing the problems that must be solved will lead to your story. In the case of *Sins*, the questions were: *Is such an explosion possible and how would it affect Earth?* That took library research. *How could the aliens move planets, how did they get the ability, and why didn't they want to talk about it?* That required me to invent their civilization in quite a bit of depth, including tracing their history back far enough to provide consistent origins for all their characteristics. I had to invent their methods of travel in enough detail to provide a consistent chronology for the trip and, once the trip was underway, to understand how it would affect the planet being moved.

The central question of *Lifeboat Earth* became: *What happens to human life during the trip?* First I had to know the purely physical effects; that required the calculations I described earlier, which, given the assumed properties of the aliens' innovative technology, was mostly extrapolation. Finally, I had to get to know some of the people affected and watch how they coped with such problems as surviving the loss of the sun, changing apparent gravity, radical changes in political systems to cope with the practical problems of survival, and the psychological problems of underground life and the wholesale extinction of the other species.

Then—and only then—I could write the story.

Writer Poul Anderson once remarked that the best science fiction requires a "unitary" approach, in which "philosophy, love, technology, poetry, and the minutiae of daily living would all play parts concomitant with their roles in real life, but heightened by the imagination of the writer."

To which fellow SF writer James Blish added; "You will note, I think, that this is more than just a prescription for good science fiction. It is a prescription for good fiction of any kind."

Some Useful References

The first group of books listed here deals primarily with *writing* science fiction, though these books also touch on the skills of *scientific imagining* to varying extents. This is not an exhaustive list, but merely a selection of books that are known to have value.

- Barry B. Longyear, *Science Fiction Writer's Workshop I*, Owlswick Press, Philadelphia, Pa., 1980.
- The [former] editors of *Isaac Asimov's Science Fiction Magazine* (George H. Scithers et al.), *On Writing Science Fiction*, Owlswick Press, 1981.
- L. Sprague and Catherine C. de Camp, *Science Fiction Handbook, Revised*, McGraw-Hill, New York, N.Y., 1975.
- Reginald Bretnor (editor), *The Craft of Science Fiction*, Harper & Row, New York, N.Y., 1976.
- Science Fiction Writers of America, *Writing and Selling Science Fiction*, Writer's Digest Books, Cincinnati, Ohio, 1976.

The following books and articles deal specifically with aspects of science especially important to SF writers, in some cases with specific suggestions on how to apply the science to developing SF backgrounds. The books have the added virtue of being rich sources of story ideas (though some of the science is dated).

- I. S. Shklovskii and Carl Sagan, *Intelligent Life in the Universe*, Holden-Day, 1966.

- Poul Anderson, *Is There Life on Other Worlds?* Crowell-Collier, 1963.
- Stephen H. Dole, *Habitable Planets for Man*, Elsevier, 1970.

Only the Shklovskii-Sagan book is still in print at this time. Check your library for the others.

Two of my *Analog* editorials may be of interest in connection with the concepts of extrapolation and innovation: "Extrapolation" (February 1979) and "Nonlogical Processes in Science and Elsewhere" (February 1981). The background development for *Lifeboat Earth* is described in considerably more detail in an article, "How to Move the Earth," *Analog*, May 1976.

The Creation
of Imaginary Worlds
The World Builder's Handbook
and Pocket Companion

POUL ANDERSON

This is an infinitely marvelous and beautiful universe which we are privileged to inhabit. Look inward to the molecules of life and the heart of the atom, or outward to moon, sun, planets, stars, the Orion Nebula where new suns and worlds are coming into being even as you watch, the Andromeda Nebula which is actually a whole sister galaxy: it is all the same cosmos, and every part of it is part of us. The elements of our flesh, blood, bones, and breath were forged out of hydrogen in stars long vanished. The gold in a wedding ring, the uranium burning behind many a triumphantly ordinary flick of an electric light switch, came out of those gigantic upheavals we call supernovas. It is thought that inertia itself, that most fundamental property of matter, would be meaningless—nonexistent—were there no stellar background to define space, time, and motion. Man is not an accident of chaos; nor is he the sum and only significance of creation. We belong here.

Once literature recognized this simple fact. Lightnings blazed around Lear; Ahab sailed an enormous ocean and Huck Finn went down a mighty river; McAndrew saw God in the machinery that man created according to the laws of the universe. But this is seldom true any longer. Barring a few, today's fashionable writers are concerned exclusively with Man, capitalized and isolated—who usually turns out to be a hypersensitive intellectual, capitalized and isolated among his own hangups. This is not necessarily bad, but may it not be a little bit limited?

In science fiction, whatever its faults, we have a medium that still allows exploration of a wider, more varied field. Of course, the story with a highly detailed extraterrestrial background is by no means the sole kind of science fiction. It is not even in the majority. Nor should it be. Too much of any one theme would put the reader right back into the monotony from which he hoped to escape.

However, when a story does take its characters beyond Earth, he is entitled to more than what he so often gets. This is either a world exactly like our own except for having neither geography nor history, or else it is an unbelievable mishmash which merely shows us that still another writer couldn't be bothered to do his homework.

As an example of the latter category, John Campbell once cited the awful example of a planet circling a blue-white sun and possessing an atmosphere of hydrogen and fluorine. This is simply a chemical impossibility. Those two substances, under the impetus of that radiation, would unite promptly and explosively. Another case is that of a world that is nothing but sterile desert, devoid of plant life, yet has animals and air that men can breathe. Where does the food chain begin? What maintains an equilibrium of free oxygen?

At the very least, a well-thought-out setting goes far toward adding artistic verisimilitude to an otherwise bald and unconvincing narrative. By bringing in this detail and that, tightly linked, the writer makes his imaginary globe seem real. Furthermore, the details are interesting in their own right. They may reveal something of the possibilities in their own right. They may reveal something of the possibilities in these light-years that surround us, thereby awakening the much-desired sense of wonder. Finally, many of them will suggest important parts of the plot.

In the most highly developed cases, they practically *become* the story. Hal Clement's *Mission of Gravity* is a classic of this kind. But enchanting though it is, that sort of thing is reserved for writers who have the necessary scientific training.

What I wish to show here is that others can do likewise, in a more modest but nevertheless astonishingly thorough fashion. It doesn't take a degree in physics. It simply takes the basic knowledge of current scientific fact and theory which any person must have before he can properly—in this day and age—call himself educated. In addition, it requires imagination and a willingness to work; but these are qualities that every writer worth his salt already possesses. Anyhow, "work" is the wrong word, if that suggests drudgery. The designing of a planet is fascinating—sheer fun.

Because it is, I believe most readers would also enjoy seeing a few of the principles spelled out.

They involve mathematics, and equations are their natural form of expression. But too many people are unreasonably puzzled, even frightened, by equations. Those who aren't will already know the natural laws I refer to; or they can be trusted to look them up. So instead I shall offer a few graphs. * With their help, and just the tiniest bit of arithmetic, anyone should be able to start world-building on his own.

Needless to say, any serious effort of this kind demands more information than can possibly be squeezed into the present essay. Two reference books that are especially well suited to science fiction purposes and are, in addition, a joy to read are *Intelligent Life in the Universe* by I. S. Shklovskii and Carl Sagan (Holden-Day, 1966) and *Habitable Planets for Man* by Stephen H. Dole

---

*Drafted by Karen Anderson.

(Elsevier, rev. ed., 1970). Of course, there are numerous other good works available.

Like every living science, astronomy today is in a state of continuous revolution. Any book is virtually certain to contain outdated material; and "facts" are always subject to change without notice. (Indeed, as I write, the whole set of methods by which the distances and thus the properties of other galaxies have been obtained is being called into question.) I have no desire to be dogmatic. If I sometimes appear that way in what follows, it is merely to save space. Take for granted that every statement bears a qualifier like: "This is my limited understanding of what the best contemporary thought on the subject seems to be."

Yet let us never forget that it is the best thought available. If we don't use it, we will have no basis whatsoever on which to reason.

Therefore, onward! Mainly we'll consider some of the possibilities regarding planets which, without being copies of Earth, are not as absolutely different from it as are the other members of our own solar system. Anything more exotic, à la Hal Clement, would take us too far afield. Besides, more often than not, a writer wants a world where his humans can survive without overly many artificial aids.

A number of parameters determine what such a globe will be like. They include the kind of sun and orbit it has, the size and mass, axial tilt and rotation, satellites—to name a few of the more obvious. Doubtless there are several more that science has thus far not identified. Our knowledge of these things is less than complete. But simply by varying those parameters we do know about, we can produce a huge variety of environments for stories to happen in. We can also gain, and give to our readers, some feeling for the subtlety and interrelatedness of nature and her laws.

Normally we begin by picking a star, real or imaginary. In earlier days, science fiction customarily put planets around the familiar ones like Sirius, Vega, Antares, or Mira. It was then legitimate enough, if a trifle repetitious. But today we know, or believe we know, that few of the naked-eye stars will serve.

Mostly they are giants, visible to us only because they are so brilliant that we can pick them out across immense gulfs of space. (Sol would no longer be discernible without instruments at a distance of about fifty-five light-years.) Now the red giants like Antares, the variables like Mira, are dying stars, well on their way to the dim, ultra-dense white-dwarf condition. If ever they had planets—their mass makes that unlikely, as we will see in a minute—the inner attendants have been seared or even consumed, as these suns expanded. If outer globes have been warmed up, this won't last long enough to do biological evolution any good.

Probably the majority of stars in the universe are still enjoying health. Their temperatures and luminosities vary enormously. The most important reason for this is the difference in their masses. The more massive a sun is, the more intensely compressed it becomes at its core, and thus the more fierce and rapid are the thermonuclear reactions that cause it to shine. This dependence of output on mass is a highly sensitive one, so that the latter covers a much smaller range than the former.

These stars form a well-defined series, from the largest and brightest to the smallest and dimmest, which is called the main sequence. For historical reasons, spectrographers label the types O, B, A, F, G, K, M. (The mnemonic is "Oh, *be a fine girl, kiss me.*") The series being continuous, a number is added to place each star more exactly on the curve. For example, the F types begin with F_0; then we get F_1, F_2, and so on through F_9, which is followed by G_0. That last, G_0, was formerly the classification of our own sun; but more recent information has gotten Sol to be labeled G_2.

Figure 1 shows a large part of the main sequence. It omits the extremes, because they really are too extreme to diagram very well. That is, the main sequence runs from the hottest Type O blue giants, some as much as a million times the strength of Sol,

on through the yellowish F and G stars, to the red dwarfs of Class
M, the dimmest of which may be less than a thousandth as intense
as our daystar. Types are indicated along the bottom of the graph,
with corresponding masses. Luminosities—necessarily on a log-
arithmic scale—are shown going up the left-hand side.

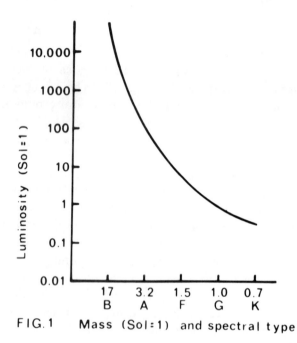

FIG. 1   Mass (Sol:1) and spectral type

From this, you can find the mass corresponding to a given
brightness. It will only be a rough estimate; but then, the real
values don't lie neatly on an infinitely thin curve. They vary by
a fair amount, depending on such factors as the age and exact
chemical composition of the individual star.

More is involved than just the total radiation. As everyone
knows who has ever heated a piece of metal in a fire, temperature
affects color. The hottest stars are called blue giants because they
are not only giants in output, but also their light contains a
distinctly larger proportion of blue than does that of Sol. They

also emit a higher percentage, as well as absolute amount, of ultraviolet and X-ray wavelengths; and no doubt the solar winds streaming from them are something terrific. All these quantities drop off as temperature does, until we get to the cool, ultraviolet-poor red dwarfs. (However, the weaker ones among these last are not mere embers. Sometimes they spit out monstrous flares that may temporarily double the total brightness—a fact which I used in a story once but on which I have no copyright.)

Well, shall we put our imaginary world in orbit around one of the spectacular giants?

Sorry. Because they burn at such a prodigal rate, these great stars are short-lived. Once they have condensed from interstellar dust and gas, Type O suns spend a bare few million years on the main sequence: then they apparently go out in the supernal violence of supernova explosions. Their ultimate fate, and the precise death throes of their somewhat lesser brethren, are too complicated to discuss here. But even an A_0 star like Sirius is good for no more than about four hundred million years of steady shining—not much in terms of geology and evolution.

Furthermore, the evidence is that giants don't have planets in the first place. There is a most suggestive sharp drop in the rotation rate, just about when one gets to the earlier Type Fs. From then on, down through Type M, suns appear to spin so slowly that it is quite reasonable to suppose the "extra" has gone into planets.

Giants are rare, anyway. They are far outnumbered by the less showy yellow dwarfs like Sol—which, in turn, are outnumbered by the inconspicuous red dwarfs. (There are about ten times as many M as G stars.) And this great majority also has the longevity we need. For instance, an F_5 spends a total of six billion years on the main sequence before it begins to swell, redden, and die. Sol, G_2, has a ten-billion-year life expectancy, and is about half-way through it at the present day, making a comfortingly long future. The K stars live for several times that figure, the weakest M stars for hundreds of billions of years. Even if life, in the biological sense, is slow to get generated and slow to evolve on a planet so feebly irradiated, it will have—or will have had—a vast time in which to develop. That may or may not make a significant difference; and thereby hangs many a tale.

So let's take a star of Type F or later. If we want to give it a planet habitable to man, probably it must be somewhere between, say, F_5 and K_5. Earlier in the sequence, the system will presumably be too young for photosynthesis to have started, releasing oxygen into the air. Later, the sun will be too cool, too dull, too niggardly with ultraviolet, to support the kind of ecology on which humans depend.

Granted, a planet of a red dwarf may bear life of another sort than ours. Or it may orbit close enough that the total radiation it gets is sufficient for us. In the latter case, the chances are that it would rotate quite slowly, having been braked by tidal friction. The sun would appear huge and reddish, or even crimson, in the sky; one might be able to gaze straight at it, seeing spots and flares with the naked eye. Colors would look different, and shadows would have blurrier outlines than on Earth. Already, then, we see how many touches of strangeness we can get by changing a single parameter. In the superficially dry data of astronomy and physics is the potential of endless adventure.

But for our concrete example of planet-building, let's go toward the other end of the scale, i.e., choosing a star brighter than Sol. The main reason for doing so is to avoid the kind of complications we have just noticed in connection with a weaker sun. We will have quite enough to think about as is!

The hypothetical planet is one that I recently had occasion to work up for a book to be edited by Roger Elwood, and is used with his kind permission. I named it Cleopatra. While tracing out the course of its construction, we'll look at a few conceivable variations, out of infinitely many.

First, where in the universe is the star? It won't be anywhere in our immediate neighborhood, because those most closely resembling Sol within quite a few light-years are somewhat dimmer—ours being, in fact, rather more luminous than average. (True, Alpha Centauri A is almost a twin, and its closer companion is not much different. However, this is a multiple system.

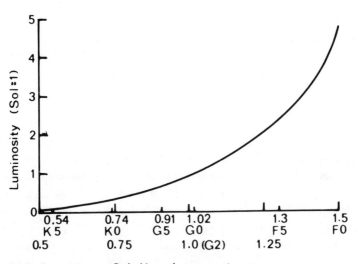

FIG. 2   Mass (Sol=1) and spectral type

That does not necessarily rule out its having planets; but the possibility of this is controversial, and in any event it would complicate things too much for the present essay if we had more than one sun.)

Rather than picking a real star out of an astronomical catalogue, though that is frequently a good idea, I made mine up, and arbitrarily put it about four hundred light-years off in the direction of Ursa Major. This is unspecific enough—it defines such a huge volume of space—that something corresponding is bound to be out there someplace. Seen from that location, the boreal constellations are considerably changed, though most remain recognizable. The austral constellations have suffered the least alteration, the equatorial ones are intermediately affected. But who says the celestial hemispheres of Cleopatra must be identical with those of Earth? For all we know, its axis could be at right angles to ours. Thus a writer can invent picturesque descriptions of the night sky and of the images that people see there.

Arbitrary also is the stellar type, F_7. This means it has 1.2 times the mass of Sol, 20 percent more. As we shall see, the diameter is little greater; but it has 2.05 times the total luminosity.

Numbers this precise cannot be taken off a graph. I computed them on the basis of formulas. But you can get values close enough for most purposes from figure 2. It charts the relevant part of the main sequence on a larger scale than figure 1, and has no need to depict any numbers logarithmically. In other words, with the help of a ruler you can find approximately what mass corresponds to what brightness. Nor is this kind of estimating dishonest. After all, as said before, there is considerable variation in reality. If, say, you guessed that a mass of 1.1 Sol meant an energy output of 1.5, the odds are that some examples of this actually exist. You could go ahead with reasonable confidence. Anyway, it's unlikely that the actual values you picked would get into the story text. But indirectly, by making the writer understand his own creation in detail, they can have an enormous influence for the better.

Returning to Cleopatra: an F_7 is hotter and whiter than Sol. Probably it has more spots, prominences, flares, and winds of charged particles sweeping from it. Certainly the proportion of ultraviolet to visible light is higher, though not extremely so.

It is natural to suppose that it has an entire family of planets; and a writer may well exercise his imagination on various members of the system. Here we shall just be dealing with the habitable one. Bear in mind, however, that its nearer sisters will doubtless from time to time be conspicuous in its heavens, even as Venus, Mars, and others shine upon Earth. What names do they have— what poetic or mystical significance in the minds of natives or of long-established colonists?

For man to find it livable, a planet must be neither too near nor too far from its sun. The total amount of energy it receives in a given time is proportional to the output of that sun and inversely proportional to the square of the distance between.

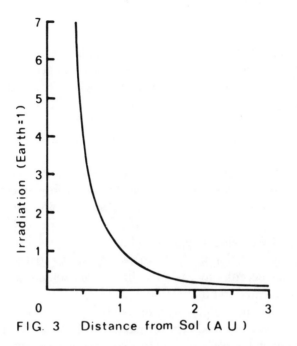

FIG. 3   Distance from Sol (A U)

Figure 3 diagrams this for the inner solar system in terms of the astronomical unit, the average separation of Sol and Earth. Thus we see that Venus, at 0.77 AU, gets about 1.7 times the energy we do, while Mars, at 1.5 AU, gets only about 0.45 the irradiation. The same curve will work for any other star if you multiply its absolute brightness. For example, at its distance of 1.0 AU, Earth gets 1.0 unit of irradiation from Sol; but at this remove from a sun half as bright, it would only get half as much, while at this same distance from our hypothetical sun, it would get 2.05 times as much.

That could turn it into an oven—by human standards, at any rate. We want our planet in a more comfortable orbit. What should that be? If we set it about 1.4 AU out, it would get almost exactly the same total energy that Earth does. No one can say this is impossible. We don't know what laws govern the spacing of orbits in a planetary system. There does appear to be a harmonic rule (associated with the names of Bode and Titius) and there are reasons to suppose this is not coincidental. Otherwise we are ignorant. Yet it would be remarkable if many stars had planets at precisely the distances most convenient for man.

Seeking to vary the parameters as much as reasonable, and assuming that the attendants of larger stars will tend to swing in larger paths, I finally put Cleopatra 1.24 AU out. This means that it gets 1.33 times the total irradiation of Earth—a third again as much.

Now that is an average distance. Planets and moons have elliptical orbits. We know of none that travel in perfect circles. However, some, like Venus, come close to doing so; and few have courses that are very eccentric. For present purposes, we can use a fixed value of separation between star and planet, while bearing in mind that it *is* only an average. The variations due to a moderate eccentricity will affect the seasons somewhat, but not much compared to other factors.

If you do want to play with an oddball orbit, as I have done once or twice, you had better explain how it got to be that way; and to follow the cycle of the year, you will have to use Kepler's equal-areas law, either by means of the calculus or by counting squares on graph paper. In the present exposition, we will assume that Cleopatra has a near-circular track.

Is not an added thirty-three percent of irradiation enough to make it uninhabitable?

This is another of those questions that cannot be answered for sure in the current state of knowledge. But we can make an educated guess. The theoretical ("black body") temperature of an object is proportional to the fourth root—the square root of the square root—of the rate at which it receives energy. Therefore it changes more slowly than one might think. At the same time, the actual mean temperature at the surface of Earth is considerably greater than such calculations make it out to be, largely because the atmosphere maintains a vast reservoir of heat in the well-known greenhouse effect. And air and water together protect us from such day-night extremes as Luna suffers.

The simple fourth-root principle says that our imaginary planet should be about 20°C, or roughly 40°F, warmer on the average than Earth is. That's not too bad. The tropics might not be usable by men, but the higher latitudes and uplands ought to be pretty good. Remember, though, that this bit of arithmetic has taken no account of atmosphere or hydrosphere. I think they would smooth things out considerably. On the one hand, they do trap heat; on the other hand, clouds reflect back a great deal of light, which thus never has a chance to reach the surface; and both gases and liquids blot up, or redistribute, what does get through.

My best guess is, therefore, that while Cleopatra will generally be somewhat warmer than Earth, the difference will be less than an oversimplified calculation suggests. The tropics will usually be hot, but nowhere unendurable; and parts of them, cooled by altitude or sea breezes, may well be quite balmy. There will probably be no polar ice caps, but tall mountains ought to have their eternal snows. Pleasant climates should prevail through higher latitudes than is the case on Earth.

You may disagree, in which case you have quite another story to tell. By all means, go ahead. Varying opinions make science fiction yarns as well as horse races.

Meanwhile, though, let's finish up the astronomy. How long is the planet's year? Alas for ease, this involves two factors, the mass of the sun and the size of the orbit. The year-length is inversely proportional to the square root of the former, and directly proportional to the square root of the cube of the semi-major axis. Horrors.

So here we need two graphs. Figure 4 shows the relationship of period to distance from the sun within our solar system. (The "distance" is actually the semi-major axis; but for purposes of calculations as rough as these, where orbits are supposed to be approximately circular, we can identify it with the mean separation between star and planet.) We see, for instance, that a body

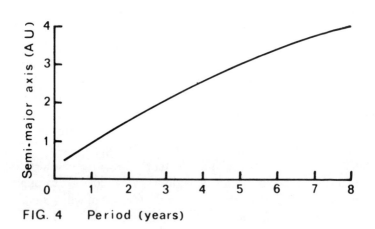

FIG. 4   Period (years)

twice as far out as Earth is takes almost three times as long to complete a circuit. At a remove of 1.24 AU, which we have assigned to Cleopatra, its period would equal 1.38 years.

But our imaginary sun is more massive than Sol. Therefore its gravitational grip is stronger and, other things being equal, it swings its children around faster. Figure 5 charts inverse square roots. For a mass of 1.2 Sol, this quantity is 0.915

If we multiply together the figures taken off these two graphs—1.38 times 0.915—we come up with the number we want, 1.26. That is, our planet takes 1.26 times as long to go around its sun as Earth does to go around Sol. Its year lasts about fifteen of our months.

Again, the diagrams aren't really that exact. I used a slide rule. But for those not inclined to do likewise, the diagrams will furnish numbers that can be used to get at least a general idea of how some fictional planet will behave.

Let me point out afresh that these are nevertheless important numbers, a part of the pseudo-reality the writer hopes to create. Only imagine: a year a fourth again as long as Earth's. What does this do to the seasons, the calendar, the entire rhythm of life? We shall need more information before we can answer

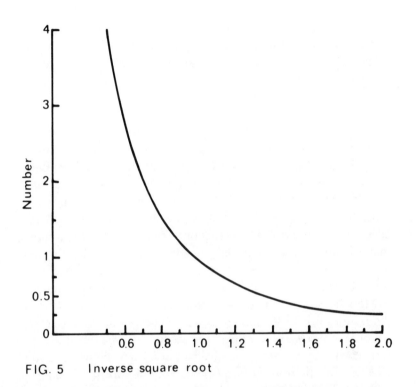

FIG. 5   Inverse square root

such questions, but it is not too early to start thinking about them.

Although more massive than Sol, the sun of Cleopatra is not much bigger. Not only is volume a cube function of radius, which would make the diameter just six percent greater if densities were equal, but densities are not equal. The heavier stars must be more compressed by their own weight than are the lighter ones. Hence we can say that all suns that more or less resemble Sol have more or less the same size.

Now our imaginary planet and its luminary are further apart than our real ones. Therefore the sun must look smaller in the

Cleopatran than in the terrestrial sky. As long as angular diameters are small (and Sol's, seen from Earth, is a mere half a degree) they are closely enough proportional to the linear diameters and inversely proportional to the distance between object and observer. That is, in the present case we have a star whose breadth, in terms of Sol, is 1, while its distance is 1.24 AU. Therefore the apparent width is 1/1.24, or 0.807 what Sol shows to us. In other words, our imaginary sun looks a bit smaller in the heavens than does our real one.

This might be noticeable, even striking, when it was near the horizon, the common optical illusion at such times exaggerating its size. (What might the psychological effects of that be?) Otherwise it would make no particular difference—since no one could safely look near so brilliant a thing without heavy eye protection—except that shadows would tend to be more sharp-edged than on Earth. Those shadows ought also to have a more marked bluish tinge, especially on white surfaces. Indeed, all color values are subtly changed by the light upon Cleopatra. I suspect men would quickly get used to that; but perhaps not.

Most likely, so active a sun produces some auroras that put the terrestrial kind to shame, as well as occasional severe interference with radio, power lines, and the like. (By the time humans can travel that far, they may well be using apparatus that isn't affected. But there is still a possible story or two in this point.) An oxygen-containing atmosphere automatically develops an ozone layer that screens out most of the ultraviolet. Nevertheless, humans would have to be more careful about sunburn than on Earth, especially in the lower latitudes or on the seas.

Now what about the planet itself? If we have been a long time in coming to that, it simply emphasizes the fact that no body— and nobody—exists in isolation from the whole universe.

Were the globe otherwise identical with Earth, we would already have innumerable divergences. Therefore let us play with some further variations. For instance, how big or small can it be? Too small, and it won't be able to hold an adequate atmosphere. Too big, and it will keep most of its primordial hydrogen and helium, as our great outer planets have done; it will be even more alien than are Mars or Luna. On the other hand, Venus—with a mass similar to Earth's—is wrapped in gas whose pressure at the surface approaches a hundred times what we are used to. We don't know why. In such an area of mystery, the science fiction writer is free to guess.

But let us go at the problem from another angle. How much gravity—or how little—can mankind tolerate for an extended period of time? We know that both high weight, such as is experienced in a centrifuge, and zero weight, such as is experienced in an orbiting spacecraft, have harmful effects. We don't know exactly what the limits are, and no doubt they depend on how long one is exposed. However, it seems reasonable to assume that men and women can adjust to some such range as 0.75 to 1.25 Earth gravity. That is, a person who weighs 150 pounds on Earth can safely live where he weighs as little as 110 or as much as 190. Of course, he will undergo somatic changes, for instance in the muscles; but we can suppose these are adaptive, not pathological.

(The reference to women is not there as a concession to militant liberationists. It takes both sexes to keep humanity going. The Spaniards failed to colonize the Peruvian altiplano for the simple reason that, while both they and their wives could learn to breathe the thin air, the wives could not bring babies to term. So the local Indians, with untold generations of natural selection behind them, still dominate that region, racially if not politically. This is one example of the significance of changing a parameter. Science fiction writers should be able to invent many more.)

The pull of a planet at its surface depends on its mass and its size. These two quantities are not independent. Though solid bodies are much less compressible than gaseous ones like stars, still, the larger one of them is, the more it tends to squeeze itself, forming denser allotropes in its interior. Within the man-habitable range, this isn't too important, especially in view of the fact that the mean density is determined by other factors as well. If we assume the planet is perfectly spherical—it won't be, but the difference isn't enough to worry about except under the most extreme conditions—then weight is proportional to the diameter of the globe and to its overall density.

Suppose it has 0.78 the (average) Terrestrial diameter, or about 6,150 miles; and suppose it has 1.10 the (mean) Terrestrial density, or about 6.1 times that of water. Then, although its total mass is only 0.52 that of Earth, about half, its surface gravity is 0.78 times 1.10, or 0.86 that which we are accustomed to here at home. Our person who weighed 150 pounds here, weighs about 130 there.

I use these particular figures because they are the ones I chose for Cleopatra. Considering Mars, it seems most implausible that any world that small could retain a decent atmosphere; but considering Venus, it seems as if many worlds of rather less mass than it or Earth may do so. At least, nobody today can disprove the idea.

But since there is less self-compression, have I given Cleopatra an impossibly high density? No, because I am postulating a higher proportion of heavy elements in its makeup than Earth has. This is not fantastic. Stars, and presumably their planets, do vary in composition.

(Writers can of course play with innumerable other combinations, like that in the very large but very metal-poor world of Jack Vance's *Big Planet*.)

The results of changing the gravity must be far-reaching indeed. Just think how this could influence the gait, the need for systematic exercise, the habit of standing versus sitting (are people in low weight more patient about queues?), the character of sports, architecture, engineering (the lower the weight, the smaller wings your aircraft need under given conditions, but the bigger brakes your ground vehicles), and on and on. In a lesser gravity, it takes a bit longer to fall some certain distance, and one lands a bit less hard; mountains and dunes tend to be steeper; pendulums of a given length, and waves on water, move slower. The air pressure falls of less rapidly with altitude. Thus, here on Earth, at about 18,000 feet the pressure is one half that at sea level; but on Cleopatra, you must go up to 21,000 feet for this. The effects on weather, every kind of flying, and the size of life zones bear thinking about.

A higher gravity reverses these consequences, more or less in proportion.

In our present state of ignorance, we have to postulate many things that suit our story purposes but may not be true—for example, that a planet as small as Cleopatra can actually hold an Earth-type atmosphere. Other postulates—for example, that Cleopatran air is insufficient, or barely sufficient, to sustain human life—are equally legitimate, and lead to quite other stories. But whatever the writer assumes, let him realize that it will make for countless strangenesses, some radical, some subtle, but each of them all-pervasive, in the environment.

(I must admit that certain of them scarcely look important. Thus, the horizon distance—for a man standing on a flat plain— is proportional to the square root of the planet's diameter. On Earth it is about five miles, and for globes not very much bigger or smaller, the change will not be striking. Often mountains, woods, haze, or the like will blot it out entirely. . . . Yet even in this apparent triviality, some skillful writer may see a story.)

If we have a higher proportion of heavy elements, including radioactive ones, than Earth does, then we doubtless get more internal heat; and the lesser size of Cleopatra also helps pass it outward faster. Thus here we should have more than a terrestrial share of volcanoes, quakes, and related phenomena. I guess there would be plenty of high mountains, some overreaching Everest; but we still know too little about how mountains get raised for this to be much more than a guess. In some areas, local concentrations of arsenic or whatever may well make the soil dangerous to man. But on the whole, industry ought to thrive.

Conversely, and other things being equal, a metal-poor world is presumably fairly quiescent; a shortage of copper and iron might cause its natives to linger indefinitely in a Stone Age; colonists might have to emphasize a technology based on lighter elements such as aluminum.

How fast does the planet rotate? This is a crucial question, but once more, not one to which present-day science can give a definitive answer. We know that Earth is being slowed down by Luna, so maybe it once spun around far more quickly than now. *Maybe.* It isn't being braked very fast, and we can't be sure how long that rate of deceleration has prevailed in the past or will in the future. Mars, whose satellites are insignificant, turns at nearly the same angular speed, while Venus, with no satellite whatsoever, is exceedingly slow and goes widdershins to boot.

It does seem likely that big planets will, by and large, spin rapidly—such as Jupiter, with a period of about ten hours. They must pick up a lot of angular momentum as they condense, and they don't easily lose it afterward. But as for the lesser bodies, like Earth, we're still mainly in the realm of speculation.

I assumed Cleopatra has no satellites worth mentioning. Therefore it has been slowed less than Earth, its present rotation taking 17.3 hours. This makes its year equal to 639 of its own days. But I could equally well have dreamed something different.

If it did have a moon, how would that affect things? Well, first, there are certain limitations on the possibilities. A moon can't be too close in, or it will break apart because of unbalanced gravitational forces on its inner and outer sides. This boundary is called Roche's limit, after the astronomer who first examined the matter in detail. For Earthlike planets it is about 2.5 radii from the center, 1.5 from the surface. That is, for Earth itself Roche's limit is roughly six thousand miles straight up. (Of course, it doesn't apply to small bodies like spaceships, only to larger and less compact masses such as Luna.) On the other hand, a moon circling very far out would be too weakly held; in time, the tug of the sun and neighbor planets would cause it to drift elsewhere. At a quarter million miles' removed, Luna is quite solidly held. But one or two million might prove too much in the long run—and in any event, so remote, our companion would not be a very interesting feature of our skies.

(Cleopatra did have a small moon once, which got too near and disintegrated, forming a ring of dust and rocky fragments.

But the calculations about this, to determine what it looks like and how that appearance varies throughout the year, are rather involved.)

Within such bounds, as far as science today can tell, we are free to put almost anything that isn't outrageously big. But if the orbit is really peculiar, the writer should be prepared to explain how this came about. A polar or near-polar track is less stable than one that isn't far off the plane of the primary's equator; it is also much less likely to occur in the first place. That is, through some such freak of nature as the capture of an asteroid under exactly the right circumstances, we might get a moon with a wildly canted orbital plane; but it probably wouldn't stay there for many million years. In general, satellites that don't pass very far north and south of the equators of their planets are more plausible.

Well, so let's take a body of some reasonable size, and set it in motion around our imaginary world at some reasonable average distance. (This is distance from the center of the planet, not its surface. For a nearby companion, the distinction is important.) How long does it take to complete a circuit and how big does it look to someone on the ground?

The same principles we used before will work again here. Take figures 4 and 5. Instead of letting "1.0" stand for quantities like "the mass of Sol," "the mean distance of Earth from Sol," and "the period of Earth around Sol," let it stand for "the mass of Earth," "the mean distance of Luna from Earth," and "the period of Luna around Earth." Thus you find your answer in terms of months rather than years. (This is a rough-and-ready method, but it will serve fairly well provided that the satellite isn't extremely big or extremely near.) Likewise, the apparent size of the object in the sky, compared to Luna, is close-enough equal to its actual diameter compared to Luna, divided by its distance from the surface of the planet, compared to Luna.

But in this case, we aren't done yet. What we have been discussing is the sidereal period, i.e., the time for the satellite to complete an orbit as seen from out among the stars. Now the planet is rotating while the moon revolves around it. Most likely both move in the same direction; retrograde orbits, like polar ones, are improbable though not altogether impossible. Unless the moon is quite remote, this will have a very marked effect. For instance, Luna, as seen from Earth, rises about fifty minutes later every day than on the previous day—while an artificial satellite not far aloft comes up in the west, not the east, and virtually flies through the heavens, undergoing eclipse in the middle of its course.

I would offer you another graph at this point, but unfortunately can't think of any that would be much help. You shall have to subtract revolution from rotation, and visualize how the phases of the moon(s) proceed and how they show in the skies. Bear in mind, too, that very close satellites probably won't be visible everywhere on the planet. Algebra and trigonometry are the best tools for jobs of this kind. But failing them, scale diagrams drawn on graph paper will usually give results sufficiently accurate for storytelling purposes.

The closer and bigger a moon is, the more tidal effect it has. For that matter, the solar tides aren't generally negligible; on Earth they amount to a third of the total. There is no simple formula. We know how tides can vary, from the nearly unmoved Mediterranean to those great bores which come roaring up the Bay of Fundy. Still, the writer can get a rough idea from this fact: that the tide-raising power is proportional to the mass of the moon or sun, and inversely proportional to the *cube* of its distance. That is, if Luna were twice as massive at its present remove, the tides it creates would be roughly twice what they really are. If Luna kept the same mass but were at twice its present distance, its tides would be $1/2^3$ or one-eighth as strong as now, while if it were half as far off as it is, they would be 2^3 or eight times as great. In addition, the theoretical height of a deepwater tide is proportional to the diameter and inversely proportional to the density of the planet being pulled upon. That is, the larger and/ or less dense it happens to be, the higher its oceans are lifted.

As I said, there is such tremendous local variation that these formulas are only good for making an overall estimate of the situation. But it is crucial for the writer to do that much. How do the waters behave? (Two or more moons could make sailing mighty complicated, not to speak of more important things like ocean currents.) Great tides, long continued, will slow down the rotation—though the amount of friction they make depends also on the pattern of land distribution, with most energy being dissipated when narrow channels like the Bering Strait are in existence. We must simply guess at the effects on weather or on life, but they are almost certainly enormous. For instance, if Earth had weaker tides than it does, would life have been delayed in moving from the seas onto dry ground?

One clear-cut, if indirect, influence of tides on weather is through the spin of the planet. The more rapidly it rotates, the stronger the cyclone-breeding Coriolis forces. In the case of Cleopatra, we have not only this factor, but also the more powerful irradiation—and, maybe, the greater distance upward from surface to stratosphere, together with the lesser separation of poles and tropics—to generate more violent and changeable weather than is common on Earth.

Insofar as the matter is understood by contemporary geophysicists, we can predict that Cleopatra, having a hotter molten core and a greater rate of rotation, possesses a respectable magnetic field, quite likely stronger than the Terrestrial. This will have helped preserve its atmosphere, in spite of the higher temperatures and lower gravity. Solar particles, which might otherwise have kicked gas molecules into space, have generally been warded off. To be sure, some get through to the uppermost thin layers of air, creating secondary cosmic rays, electrical disturbances, and showy auroras.

The weather is likewise affected by axial tilt. Earth does not ride upright in its orbit; no member of the Solar System does. Our axis of rotation slants about 23.58 off the vertical. From this we get our seasons, with everything that that implies. We cannot tell how often Earthlike worlds elsewhere have radically different orientations. My guess is that this is a rarity and that, if anything, Earth may lean a bit more rakishly than most. But it's merely another guess. Whatever value the writer chooses, let him ponder how it will determine the course of the year, the size and character of climatic zones, the development of life and civilizations.

If Earth did travel upright, thus having no seasons, we would probably never see migratory birds across the sky. One suspects there would be no clear cycle of the birth and death of vegetation either. Then what form would agriculture have taken? Society? Religion?

It is questions like these that science fiction is uniquely well fitted to ask. Simple permutations of natural law, such as we have been considering here, raise amazingly many of them, and suggest tentative answers.

True, this kind of backgrounding work is the barest beginning. The writer must then go on to topography, living creatures both nonhuman and human, problems and dreams, the story itself— ultimately, to those words that are to appear on a printed page. Yet if he has given some thought and, yes, some love to his setting, that will show in the words. Only by making it real to himself can he make it, and the events that happen within its framework, seem real to the reader.

The undertaking isn't unduly hard. It is mind-expanding in the best sense of that phrase. Or may I end by repeating myself and saying that, for writer and reader alike, it's fun?

The Creation
of Imaginary Beings

HAL CLEMENT

The unheard-of creature and the unhuman character have been part of the storyteller's ammunition since long before the invention of writing, it seems safe to claim. Angel and demon, ghost and vampire, dragon and *rukh*, Homer's Cyclopes and Mandeville's headless men are all part of the basic human heritage. Telling how to create such beings might almost be taken as an insult to normal human imagination.

In science fiction, however, we do try to maintain standards of realism (or at least believability) for a rather more knowledgeable and technically sophisticated audience than Homer faced. This is not to say that we have *higher* standards in these respects; Homer's gods and Sinbad's island-whale were as believable in their day as moon flight and atomic energy are now. Our standards are simply based on a better knowledge of the physical universe.

Also, there is no intended suggestion that the ghost and his nonmaterial kin either have vanished or should vanish from the inventory. It is perfectly possible for a competent, informed, educated materialist of the late twentieth century to enjoy the works of Sheridan le Fanu or Lyman Frank Baum, not only with the full knowledge that they are not true histories but also safely above the need to prove his open-mindedness by saying that such things *might* be possible. However, I am confining my remarks to the rather narrow limits of "hard" science fiction, where I am qualified to hold a professional opinion. It has been charged that in restricting ourselves to "scientific accuracy" my colleagues and I are narrowing the scope of usable story ideas available to us. My answer, mathematically rather horrible but defensible under literary standards, is that the square root of infinity is not really that much smaller than infinity as far as resource material goes. Our main point is that for many modern readers, a violation of the laws of thermodynamics by the author can spoil a story just as effectively as having Abraham Lincoln changing a set of spark plugs in a historical novel.

Therefore, if we travel to Mars in a story, the vehicle must operate either along physical laws we currently think we know, or at least on more or less convincing extrapolations of those laws. Furthermore, when we get there the Martians, not to mention their lapdogs, saddle horses, dinner steaks, and rheumatism, must not strike too jarring a set of notes against the background which author and reader are, it is to be hoped, visualizing together. It is permissible and even desirable to take the reader by surprise with some of these details, of course. However, his reaction to the surprise should be the urge to kick himself for failing to foresee the item, rather than resentment at the author's ringing in a new theme.

It follows that the "hard" science fiction writer must have at least an informed layman's grasp of biochemistry and ecology.

Even in this narrowed realm, there would seem to be two basic lines of procedure for the storyteller who needs nonhuman characters and other extraterrestrial life forms. The two are not mutually exclusive; they overlap heavily in many ways. Nevertheless they represent different directions of attack on the problem, one of which is more useful if the basic story is already well set up in the author's mind, while the other is of more use in creating and developing the story possibilities themselves.

In the first case, the qualities of the various life forms have to a considerable extent already been determined; they are demanded by the story events. Excellent recent examples occur in some of Keith Laumer's "Retief" novels, such as the wheeled metallic natives of Quopp in *Retief's War* and the even more peculiar Lumbagans in *Retief's Ransom*.

In other words, if the savages of Fomalhaut VII are going to kidnap the heroine by air, they must be able to fly with the weight of a human being. If the hero is going to escape from a welded-shut steel safe with the aid of his friend from Regulus IV, the friend must be able either to break or dissolve the steel, or perhaps get into and out of such spaces via the fourth dimension. These are part of the starting situation for the author, who must assume that the creations of his intellect do have the requisite powers. If he is really conscientious (or worries greatly about being laughed at by scientific purists) he will also have in the background an ecological system where these powers are of general use and which contains other creatures whose behavior and abilities fit into the same picture.

Flying must be easier on Fomalhaut VII than on Earth. Perhaps the air is denser, or the gravity weaker, or native muscle more efficient and powerful. Ordinary evolution will have been affected by the fact that flight by larger animals is possible, so there will be a much wider range of large flying organisms than we know on Earth. There will be carnivores, herbivores, and omnivores. There will be a wide range of attack and defense systems among these beings. In short, there will be more ecological niches available to large flyers, and it may be confidently expected that evolution will fill them.

Of course there will be limits, just as on Earth. Vertebrates have been flying for nearly two hundred million years, which for most of the forms involved means about the same number of generations; but we have no supersonic birds on this planet. Even the insects, which have been flying a good deal longer, haven't gotten anywhere near Mach 1; the eight-hundred-mile-per-hour deer-bot fly that appeared in the literature during the 1930s was very definitely a mistaken observation. It would seem that our biochemistry can't handle energy at the rates needed for supersonic flight. It is the evident existence of these limits that forces the author to assume a different set of conditions on the Fomalhaut planet.

Similarly, fourth-dimensional extrusion will have to be general on Regulus IV, and the local ecology will reflect the fact. There will be hide-and-seek techniques among predators and prey essentially incomprehensible to human beings, and therefore a tremendous challenge to the imagination and verbal skill of the writer.

If fourth-dimensional extrusion is not the answer chosen, then the ability to dissolve iron may have developed—which implies that free iron exists on the planet under circumstances that make the ability to dissolve it a useful one. Or . . .

There is, of course, a limit to the time any author can spend working out such details. Even I, a spare-time writer who seldom saddles himself with deadlines, spend some of that spare time writing the story itself. In any kind of story whatever, a certain amount of the background has to be filled in by the reader's/listener's imagination. It is neither possible nor desirable to do everything for him. In this first line of attack, the time and effort to be spent on detail work are reasonably limited.

Even the second line, which is my favored technique, has its limits in this respect. However, it does encourage the author to spend longer in the beginning at the straight slide-rule work. As it happens, I get most of the fun out of working out the physical and chemical nature of a planet or solar system, and then dreaming up life forms that might reasonably evolve under such conditions. The story (obviously, as some critics have been known to remark) comes afterward. My excuse for using this general technique, if one is needed, is twofold.

First, I find it more fun. This will carry smaller weight for the author who is writing for a living.

Second, it is not unusual for the nature of the planet and its life forms, once worked out, to suggest story events or even an entire plot line that would never otherwise have occurred to me. This fact should carry some weight even with the more fantasy-oriented writer, who cares less about "realism."

I do have to admit that realism, or at least consistency, is a prime consideration with me; and as I implied some pages back with the Abraham Lincoln metaphor, even the most fantastic story can jar the most tolerant reader if the inconsistency is crude enough—anachronism is only one form of inconsistency.

This sort of realism in life design has to be on at least two levels: biochemical and mechanical.

It is true that we do not yet know all the details of how even the simplest life forms work. It is still defensible to build for story purposes a creature that drinks hydrazine, and say that no one can prove this impossible. Beyond a certain point, however, I have to dismiss this as ducking out the easy way—sometimes justifiable for storytelling purposes, but jarring on the scientific sensibility. Some facts of life are very well known indeed, and to contradict them, a very good excuse and very convincing logic are needed.

For example, any life form converts energy from one form to another. On our own planet, the strongest and most active creatures use the oxygen in the atmosphere to convert food materials to carbon dioxide and water. The chemical reactions supply the needed energy. Obviously, the available oxygen would be quickly used up if there were not some other set of reactions to break down the water and carbon dioxide (actually it's the water, on this planet) to replace what is exhausted. It takes as much energy (actually more must be supplied, since no reaction is completely efficient) to break up a molecule into its elements as is released by forming it from these elements, and any ecological system must have a long-term energy base. On this planet, as is common knowledge, the base is sunlight. There seems no need here to go into the very complicated details; few people get through high school these days (I'd like to believe) without at least a general idea of photosynthesis.

In passing, some people have the idea that fish violate this basic rule, and are some sort of perpetual motion machine, because they "breathe water." Not so; fish use the elemental O_2 gas supplied as usual by photosynthesis and *dissolved* in water, not the O in the H_2O. Aquarium suppliers are perfectly justified in selling air pumps; they are not exploiting the innocent fish fanciers.

Substitutes for free oxygen in energy-releasing reactions are perfectly possible chemically, and as far as anyone can tell should be possible biologically (indeed, some earthly life forms do use other reactions). There is no chemical need for these substitutes even to be gases; but if the story calls for a nonhuman character to be drowned or strangled, obvious gaseous candidates are fluorine and chlorine. The former can run much more energetic reactions than even oxygen, while chlorine compares favorably with the gas we are *all* hooked on. (That last seems a justified assumption about the present readers. If it is wrong, please come and introduce yourself!)

Neither chlorine nor fluorine occurs free on this planet; but, as pointed out already, neither would oxygen if earthly life were not constantly replenishing it by photosynthesis. It has been pointed out that both these gases are odd-numbered elements and therefore in shorter universal supply than oxygen. This may well be true; but if some mad scientist were to develop a microorganism able to photosynthesize free chlorine from the chloride ion in Earth's ocean, it wouldn't have to do a very complete job to release as much of this gas as we now have of oxygen. Breaking down ten percent or so of the ocean salt would do the trick. Present-day biological engineering is probably not quite up to this job yet, but if you want to use the idea in a story be my guest. I don't plan to use it myself; the crazy-scientist story is old hat now except in frankly political literature, and even the germ-from-space has been pretty well worked to death in the last forty years.

As mentioned, there is no chemical reason why the energy-producing reactants have to include gases at all. Oxidizing a pound of sugar with nitric acid will yield more energy than oxidizing the same pound with oxygen (if this seems improbable at first glance, remember the bond energy of the N_2 molecule that is one of the products of the first reaction). True, raw concentrated nitric acid is rather hard on most if not all terrestrial tissues; but we do handle hydrochloric acid—admittedly in rather dilute form in spite of the antacid-tablet ads—in our own digestive systems. I see little difficulty in dreaming up a being able to store and utilize strong oxidizers in its system. The protective mucus our own stomachs use is only one of the possibilities.

Many chemical sources of energy are therefore possible in principle for our life forms; but one should be reasonably aware of the chemistry involved. Water or iron oxide would not be good fuels under any reasonable circumstances; there are admittedly some energy-yielding reactions involving these, but they call for special and unlikely reactants like sodium or fluorine—and if those reactants are around, we could get much more energy by using them on other substances.

To get more fundamental, sunlight is not the only conceivable energy base for an ecological pyramid. It is, however, by far the most likely, assuming the planet in question has a sun. Remember, the energy source must not only be quantitatively large enough; it must be widely available in both space and time, so that life can originate and evolve to complex forms. Radioactivity and raw volcanic heat are both imaginable, but the first demands rather unusual conditions if much of it is to be on hand. Vulcanism, if Earth is a fair example, tends to be restricted in space at any one time and in time at any one location, a discouraging combination. Also, radioactive energy in its most direct form comes in high-energy quanta, furnishing an additional complication to the molecular architecture problem to be considered next.

It seems pretty certain that life, as well as needing energy, must be of complex structure. It has to do too many things for a simple machine. An organism must be able to absorb the chemicals needed for its energy, and carry out at the desired rate the reactions that they undergo. It must develop and repair its own structure (immortal, invulnerable, specially created beings are conceivable, but definitely outside the realm of this discussion). It must *reproduce* its own structure, and therefore keep on file a complete set of specifications—which must itself be reproducible.

Whatever mystical, symbolic, and figurate resemblances there may be between a candle flame and a living creature, the concrete *differences* between them seem to me to constitute a non-negotiable demand for extreme complexity in the latter.

On Earth, this complexity involves the phosphate-sugar-base polymers called popularly DNA and RNA for specifications, polypeptide and polysaccharide structures for most of the machinery, and—perhaps most fundamentally—the hydrogen bond to provide structural links that can be changed around as needed without the need for temperatures high enough to ruin the main framework.

I see no reason why other carbon compounds could not do the jobs of most of these, though I cannot offhand draw formulas for the alternates. The jobs in general depend on the shapes of the molecules, or perhaps more honestly the shapes of the force fields around them; these could presumably be duplicated closely enough by other substances.

I am rather doubtful that the cruder substitutions suggested by various writers, such as that of silicon for carbon, would actually work, though of course I cannot be sure that they wouldn't. We have the fact that on Earth, with silicon many times more plentiful than carbon, life uses the latter. The explanations that can be advanced for this fact seem to me to be explanations as well of why silicon won't work in life forms. (To be more specific: silicon atoms are large enough to four-coordinate with oxygen, and hence wind up in hard, crystalline, insoluble macromolecular structures—the usual run of silicate minerals. The smaller carbon atom, able to react with not more than three oxygens at once, was left free to form the water-reactive carbon dioxide gas.) True, some earthly life such as scouring rushes, basket sponges, and foraminifera use silicon compounds in skeletal parts; but not, except in trace amounts, in active life machinery.

I also doubt that any other element could do the job of hydrogen, which I am inclined to regard as "the" essential life element, rather than the more popular carbon. Life machinery is complex, but it must have what might be called "moving parts"—structures that have to be altered in shape, or connected now one way and now another. A chemical bond weak enough to be changed without affecting the rest of the machine seems a necessity—a gasoline engine would be hard to design if springs didn't exist and a cutting torch were needed to open the valves each cycle. The hydrogen bond (I don't propose to explain what this is; if you don't know, consult any beginning chemistry text) is the only thing I know of that meets this need on the molecular level.

This, however, is not much of a science fiction problem. Something like 999 out of every 1,000 atoms in the universe are hydrogen atoms; even Earth, which seems to be one of the most thoroughly dehydrogenated objects in the observable part of space, has all its needs for an extensive collection of life forms. I suspect it will generally be easier for an author to use hydrogen in his homemade life forms than to work out a credible substitute.

To finish with the fundamental-structure level, one must admit that very complex electric and magnetic field structures other than those supplied ready-formed by atoms and molecules are conceivable. At this point, it really is necessary to fall back on the "we can't say it's impossible" excuse. Personally I would develop such life forms only if my story demanded of them some ability incompatible with ordinary matter, such as traveling through a telephone wire or existing without protection both in the solar photosphere and a cave on Pluto. At this point, simple scientific realism fades away, and I must bow out as an expert. It's not that I'm above doing it; it's just that practically anyone else could do it equally well.

The other principal basis for believability of life forms lies in the field of simple mechanics, much more common sense than biochemistry. For example, in spite of Edgar Rice Burroughs's calots, a fast-running creature is far more likely to have a few

long legs than a lot of short ones. Whether muscle tissue on
Planet X is stronger or weaker than on Earth, muscular effort
will be more efficiently applied by fewer, longer strokes. Even if
the evolutionary background for some reason started off with the
ten legs (e.g., high gravity), I would expect an organism spe-
cializing in speed to develop two, or perhaps four, of them to
greater length and either have the others degenerate or put them
to other uses as the generations rolled on.

On the same general principle, if the creature lives on grass
or the local ecological equivalent, it will probably not have much
of a brain. If it doesn't have to catch food or climb trees, it will
lack any equivalent of a hand—in short, any anatomical part an
organism has should either be useful to that creature in its current
life, or be the degenerate remnant of something useful to its
remote ancestors. Exceptions to this rule among earthly life forms
are hard to find, and may be only apparent; we simply don't know
the purpose of the organ in question. A former example was the
"sail" on the backs of some Permian reptiles, now believed to be
a temperature control device.

In addition to being useful itself, a structure must have been
at least slightly useful through its early stages of development; it
is hard to believe that a single mutation would produce a completely developed ear, but any ability to sense pressure variations
would clearly be useful to an animal. Creatures must have existed
showing development all the way from a slightly refined sense of
touch to the present organ capable of detecting and recognizing
a tiger's footfall in a windy forest—or an out-of-tune flute in an
orchestra.

Similarly with the eye. There are now alive on Earth creatures
with light-sensitive organs ranging from the simple red spot of
the single-celled euglena, through pinhole cameras with complex
retinas (some cephalopods), to the lens-and-iris-equipped dif-
fraction-limited organ of most mammals and birds, complete with
automatic focusing. There are also examples of parallel evolution
that were good enough to help their owners survive all the way
along the route: the compound mosaic-lens eyes of arthropods

and, I have heard, at least one organism that scans the image of a single lens by moving a single retinal nerve over the field.

But eyes and ears are hardly original enough for a really imaginative science fiction story. What other long-range senses might an organism evolve? Could an intelligent species develop without any such sense? If so, what would be that creature's conception of the universe? How, if at all, could sighted and hearing human beings communicate with it?

The first question at least can be partially answered without recourse to mysticism. Magnetic fields do exist, as do electric ones. Certainly some creatures can sense the latter directly (you can yourself, for that matter; bring your hand close to a highly charged object and feel what happens to the fine hairs on your skin). There is some evidence that certain species of birds can detect the Earth's magnetic field. Sound is already used in accordance with its limitations, as is scent. A gravity-sense other than the one we now use for orientation would probably not be discriminating enough, though I could certainly be wrong (read up on lunar mascons if you don't see what I mean by lack of discrimination).

It is a little hard to envision what could be detected by a magnetic sense, and how its possessor would imagine the universe. Most substances on this planet have practically no effect on a magnetic field, and this is what makes me a little doubtful about the birds mentioned above. I can see the use of such a sense in navigation for a migratory species, but I have trouble thinking through its evolutionary development. Perhaps on a planet with widely distributed ferromagnetic material, the location of which is of life-and-death importance to the life forms, it would happen; maybe our Regulus IV character who can dissolve iron needs it for biochemical reasons.

The important point, from which we may have been wandering a trifle, is not whether I can envision such a situation in detail, but whether the author of the story can do so, and thereby avoid having to invent *ad hoc* a goose that lays golden eggs. If the life form in question has hearing but no sight, all right; but it should not be able to thread a needle with the aid of sonic perception. Sound waves short enough to have that kind of resolving power would demand a good deal of energy to produce, would have very poor range in air, and would incidentally be decidedly dangerous to human explorers. Of course, a story could be built on the unfortunate consequences of the men who were mowed down by what they thought must be a death ray, when the welcoming committee was merely trying to take a good look. . . .

Sound does have the advantage of being able to diffract around obstacles, so that straight-line connection is not needed; light (that is, light visible to human beings) is of such short wavelength that diffraction effects are minor. This means that the precise direction of origin of a sound ray cannot be well determined, while a good eye can measure light's direction to a small fraction of a degree. On Earth, we both eat and keep this particular piece of cake, since we have evolved both sight and hearing.

Scent seems to have all the disadvantages and none of the advantages, as a long-range sense. However, under special circumstances even a modified nose may fill the need. In a story of my own some years ago ("Uncommon Sense," *Astounding Science Fiction*, September 1945), I assumed an airless planet, so that molecules could diffuse in nearly straight lines. The local sense organs were basically pinhole cameras, with the retinal mosaic formed of olfactory cells. Since the beings in question were not intelligent, the question of what sort of universe they believed in did not arise.

Granting the intelligence, it would have been—would still be, indeed—interesting to work out their cosmology. Naturally, the first few hours are spent wondering whether and how they could fill the intellectual gaps imposed by their lack of sight and hearing. Then, of course, the intelligent speculator starts wondering what essential details are missing from *our* concept of the universe, because of our lack of the sense of (you name it). This, for what my opinion is worth, is one of the best philosophical excuses for the practice of science fiction—if an excuse is needed. The molecule-seers presumably lack all astronomical data; what are *we* missing? This question, I hope I needn't add, is not an excuse to go off on a mystical kick, though it is one that the mystics are quite reasonably fond of asking (and then answering with their own version of Truth). The human species has, as a matter of fact, done a rather impressive job of overcoming its sensory limitations, though I see no way of ever being sure when the job is done.

Philosophy aside, there are many more details of shape to be considered for nonhuman beings. Many of the pertinent factors have been pointed out by other writers, such as L. Sprague deCamp ("Design for Life," *Astounding Science Fiction*, May–June, 1939). DeCamp reached the conclusion that an intelligent life form would have to wind up not grossly different in structure from a human being—carrying its sense organs high and close to the brain, having a limited number of limbs with a minimum number of these specialized for locomotion and the others for manipulation, having a rigid skeleton, and being somewhere between an Irish terrier and a grizzly bear in size. The lower size limit was set by the number of cells needed for a good brain, and the upper one by the bulk of body that could be handled by a brain without overspecialization. Sprague admitted both his estimates to be guesses, but I have seen no more convincing ones since. Whenever I have departed greatly from his strictures in my own stories, I have always felt the moral need to supply an excuse, at least to myself.

The need for an internal skeleton stems largely from the nature of muscle tissue, which can exert force only by contracting and is therefore much more effective with a good lever system to work with. I belittle neither the intelligence nor the strength of the octopus; but in spite of Victor Hugo and most other writers of undersea adventure, the creature's boneless tentacles are not all that effective as handling organs. I don't mean that the octopus and his kin are helpless hunks of meat; but if I had my choice of animals I was required to duel to the death, I would pick one of this tribe rather than one of their bonier rivals, the barracuda or the moray eel, even though neither of the latter have any prehensile organs but their jaws. (If any experienced scuba divers wish to dispute this matter of taste, go right ahead. I admit that so far, thank goodness, I am working from theory on this specific matter.)

This leads to a point that should be raised in any science fiction essay. I have made a number of quite definite statements in the preceding pages, and will make several more before finishing this chapter. Anyone with the slightest trace of intelligent critical power can find a way around most of these dicta by setting up appropriate situations. I wouldn't dream of objecting; most of my own stories have developed from attempts to work out situations in which someone who has laid down the law within my hearing would be wrong. The Hunter in *Needle* was a deliberate attempt to get around Sprague's minimum-size rule. *Mission of Gravity* complicated the size and speed issue by variable gravity.

And so on. If no one has the urge, imagination, and knowledge to kick specific holes in the things I say here, my favorite form of relaxation is in danger of going out with a whimper. If someone takes exception to the statement that muscles can only pull, by all means do something about it. We know a good deal about earthly muscle chemistry these days; maybe a pushing cell *could* be worked out. I suspect it would need a very strong cell wall, but why not? Have fun with the idea. If you can make it plausible, you will have destroyed at a stroke many of the currently plausible engineering limitations to the shapes and power of animals. I could list examples for the rest of my available pages, but you should have more fun doing it yourself.

There is a natural temptation to make one's artificial organisms as weird as possible in looks and behavior. Most authors seem to have learned that it is extremely hard to invent anything stranger than some of the life forms already on our planet, and many writers as a result have taken to using either these creatures as they are, or modifying them in size and habit, or mixing them together. The last, in particular, is not a new trick; the sphinx and hippogriff have been with us for some time.

With our present knowledge, though, we have to be careful about the changes and mixtures we make. Pegasus, for example, will have to remain mythological. Even if we could persuade a horse to grow wings (feathered or not), earthly muscle tissue simply won't fly a horse (assuming, of course, that the muscle is going along for the ride). Also, the horse would have to extract a great deal more energy than it does from its hay diet to power the flight muscles even if it could find room for them in an equine anatomy.

Actually, the realization that body engineering and life-style are closely connected is far from new. There is a story about Baron Cuvier, a naturalist of the late eighteenth and early nineteenth centuries. It seems that one night his students decided to play a practical joke, and one of them dressed up in a conglomeration of animal skins, including that of a deer. The disguised youth then crept into the baron's bedroom and aroused him by growling, "Cuvier, wake up! I am going to eat you!"

The baron is supposed to have opened his eyes, looked over his visitor briefly, closed his eyes again and rolled over muttering, "Impossible! You have horns and hooves." A large body of information, it would seem, tends to produce opinions in its possessor's mind, if not always correct ones.

The trick of magnifying a normal creature to menacing size is all too common. The giant amoeba is a familiar example; monster insects (or whole populations of them) even more so. It may pay an author with this particular urge to ask himself why we don't actually have such creatures around. There is likely to be a good reason, and if he doesn't know it perhaps he should do some research.

In the case of both amoeba and insect, the so-called "square-cube" law is the trouble. Things like strength of muscle and rate of chemical and heat exchange with the environment depend on surface or cross-section area, and change with the square of linear size; Swift's Brobdingnagians would therefore have a hundred times the strength and oxygen intake rate of poor Gulliver. Unfortunately the mass of tissue to be supported and fed goes up with the cube of linear dimension, so the giants would have had a thousand times Gulliver's weight. It seems unlikely that they could have stood, much less walked (can *you* support ten times your present weight?). This is why a whale, though an air breather, suffocates if he runs ashore; he lacks the muscular strength to expand his chest cavity against its own weight. An ant magnified to six-foot length would be in even worse trouble, since she doesn't have a mammal's supercharger system in the first place, but merely a set of air pipes running through her system. Even if the mad scientist provided his giant ants with oxygen masks, I wouldn't be afraid of them.

It is only because they are so small, and their weight has decreased even faster than their strength, that insects can perform the "miraculous" feats of carrying dozens of times their own weight or jumping hundreds of times their own length. This would have favored Swift's Lilliputians, who would have been able to make some remarkable athletic records if judged on a strictly linear scale. That is, unless they had to spend too much time in eating to offset their excessive losses of body heat. . . .

Really small creatures, strong as they may seem, either have structures that don't seem to mind change in temperature too much (insects, small reptiles), or are extremely well insulated (small birds), or have to eat something like their own weight in food each day (shrew, hummingbird). There seems reason to believe that at least with earthly biochemistry, the first and last of these weaknesses do not favor intelligence.

A rather similar factor operates against the idea of having a manlike creature get all his energy from sunlight, plant style. This was covered years ago by V. A. Eulach ("Those Impossible Autotrophic Men," *Astounding Science Fiction*, October 1956), who pointed out that a man who tries to live like a tree is going to wind up looking much like one. He will have to increase his sunlight-intercepting area without greatly increasing his mass (in other words, grow leaves), cut down his energy demands to what leaves can supply from sunlight's one-and-a-half-horsepower-per-square-yard (become sessile), and provide himself with mineral nutrients directly from the soil, since he can't catch food any more (grow roots!).

Of course, we can get around some of this by hypothesizing a hotter, closer sun, with all the attendant complications of higher planet temperature. This is fun to work out, and some of us do it, but remember that a really basic change of this sort affects everything in the ecological pyramid sitting on that particular energy base—in other words, *all* the life on the planet.

It may look from all this as though a really careful and conscientious science fiction writer has to be a junior edition of the Almighty. Things are not really this bad. I mentioned one way out a few pages ago in admitting there is a limit to the detail really needed. The limit is set not wholly by time, but by the fact that too much detail results in a Ph.D. thesis—perhaps a fascinating one to some people, but still a thesis rather than a story. I must admit that some of us do have this failing, which has to be sharply controlled by editors.

Perhaps the most nearly happy-medium advice that can be given is this: Work out your world and its creatures as long as it remains fun; then write your story, making use of any of the details you have worked out that *help the story*. Write off the rest of the development work as something that built your own background picture—the stage setting, if you like—whose presence in your mind will tend to save you from the more jarring inconsistencies (I use this word, very carefully, rather than *errors*).

Remember, though, that among your readers there will be some who enjoy carrying your work farther than you did. They will find inconsistencies that you missed; depend on it. Part of human nature is the urge to let the world know how right you were, so you can expect to hear from these people either directly or through fanzine pages. Don't let it worry you.

Even if he is right and you are wrong, he has demonstrated unequivocally that you succeeded as a storyteller. You gave your audience a good time.

How to Build
a Future

JOHN BARNES

Building worlds mathematically is so basic to hard SF that we rarely think about *why* we do it.

I won't presume to say why anyone else does, but I do it because I have too little imagination.

Does that seem a shocking admission from a science fiction writer?

Think about what most fictional planets are like. The writer who doesn't worldbuild usually creates the familiar in drag: a single, excerpted environment. Jungle planets, ice planets, or desert worlds are usually just the Amazon, Antarctica, or the Kalahari without the research or detail a story actually set in those places requires.

Not merely limited in variety, they all seem to be the size of Chicago, or at best Georgia. Jerry Pournelle has aptly described this with the phrase "It was raining on Mongo that morning." Though SF writers claim to explore the wonder and vastness of the Universe, many forget that a planet is *big*. The Earth includes places as diverse as the Grand Canyon, the Black Sea, the Pacific atolls, Greenland, and the Mid-Atlantic Ridge. Yet how often are we told some planet is a "steamy jungle world" or a "polar waste?" (So what's the Earth—a "room temperature world with an oxygen-rich, water-saturated atmosphere?" Tell that to the poor tourist dropped off, wearing only his bathing suit, in the Whichaway Nunataks of Qattara Depression.)

Now compare those bastardized Earth environments with the wonderfully diverse created worlds of Poul Anderson, Larry Niven, or Hal Clement. I think it's exactly because those writers do calculations that they reach as far as they do. The calculations spur them to leap over the usual walls of imagination. The imagination must really stretch to take what the numbers say is plausible and see what that looks like standing on the ground. (The vivid picture Clement gives us of what it's like to *be* on Mesklin is what really makes that a classic piece of wordbuilding.)

It Was Raining That Century . . .

What's true of physical environments is true of social ones. How many versions of the Roman Empire, the high feudal period, or Tokugawa Japan, are there in SF? Just as many SF writers invent familiar environments, they also invent familiar history.

This does have the advantage that everything "goes together"— a first-century polity with a first-century economy and society automatically has some plausibility. (So do crocodile-like reptiles on jungle planets.)

Yet it cheats the reader of the excitement of going somewhere *really* new. How many Star Trek fans would argue that the "set-of-the-week club" episodes in the last year of the original series were as good as the earlier ones?

You also get the social equivalent of it raining on Mongo that morning. Just as we forget that there are a lot of very different places on a planet, we forget that a lot of different things happen in a century. When John D. Rockefeller was born, the last Revolutionary War veterans were still alive; when he died Neil Armstrong was seven years old. Thomas Jefferson lived through one-quarter of the nineteenth century, Thomas Edison more than half of it—that same century contained clipper-ship races, the experimental development of radio, the Romantic movement in music and literature, the birth of modern advertising, Greek Revival and Victorian Gothic, the canal era, Freud's early work, Lewis and Clark, Impressionism, the 1848 revolutions in Europe, the opening of Japan, and the first hints of atomic energy.

Yet many science-fictional future histories have less happening between now and 3000 than actually happened between A.D. 900 and 1200. Often, in SF, social change seems to have arrested anywhere from ten to fifty years after the present, technological change a century at most.

The Same Spur for Another Wall

Just as doing the numbers can drive a planet builder into realms of possibility he wouldn't otherwise enter, calculations that grow out of mathematical social science can help the society builder envision the unprecedented.

I have a fairly extensive background for this (a math-heavy BA in economics and a math-methods-emphasis MA in political science) so my bag of tricks is bigger than will actually fit into any space reasonable for an *Analog* article. What I'm going to do now is take you along as I build a future, with some substantial commentary on why I'm making the choices I am and what other ones you might make. I'll only use a few tools from the kit, but this should at least give you some feel for what can be done.

Let me warn you that this is all just fun. With all respect to other writers (Flynn 1987), I do not believe that the use of math methods in the social sciences will ever lead to social forecasting even on the level of pre-satellite weather forecasts. Sensitive dependence on initial conditions and measurement error are both intrinsically too extreme in social data for that. This stuff can be a good basis for stories, but if you get the feeling that you are forecasting the future, I suggest you lie down until it gets here.

Starting from an Idea

I wanted to do a story about the introduction of instantaneous travel (the transporter booth, if you like) into a civilization that had spanned several solar systems for centuries. Expansion and intensification of contacts between cultures has often caused spectacular events, so I was sure I could find plenty of excitement in such a world.

What kind of future would FTL break into?

If you're going to write about a new way to do something, you first need some understanding of how it was done before. I arbitrarily decided to limit my pre-FTL starships, at least the colony-sized ones, to a velocity of one-half lightspeed—fast enough, with suspended animation limited to one century, to put many nearby stars within reach. At .5c, relativistic time dilation only slightly extends the human crew's range of travel. Additionally, limiting accelerations to 1.5g maximum for any time more than a couple of days put the outer reachable limit for manned expeditions at about forty light-years.

If I were doing a story about the exploration/colonization period, I'd need to do much more elaborate detail work, but with a non-scientist hero in a future where these technologies had been familiar for centuries, I could leave the suspended animation as a given, and needed only cursory work on the propulsion technology.

Again arbitrarily, I decided the starships would be photon rockets with a power-plant that converted mass to energy with perfect or near-perfect efficiency. Allowing for acceleration and deceleration in a one-way trip, a speed limit of .5c could be set by limiting the ratio of propellant mass to total mass to .75 maximum. Whether that limit is imposed by problems in handling antimatter, or the necessary size of the "field generators" (whatever they might be), or the tensile strength of Larry Niven's "balonium," doesn't matter because ship operation won't figure in the story, so again I left the problem for the physicists to play with.

From the Budget for Balonium to the Tea Ceremony

Assuming that interstellar colonization would be a relatively low priority for future civilization (important for prestige or PR, perhaps, but not truly vital), how long before colony ships would be cheap enough to represent little or no strain on the global budget? That would mark the beginning of a plausible colonization era.

Where physical worldbuilding uses equations, social worldbuilding generally must use models. A model, technically, is a "system state vector" (a set of numbers, like population, growth rate, GNP, economic growth, and per capita income, that characterizes the system at one moment in time [say 1989] plus a "transformation rule" for calculating a next vector in the same format ["multiply the growth rate by the population and add it to population to get new population," "divide GNP by population to get per capita income," etc.]). By applying the transformation rule over and over, you can project a set of values indefinitely into the future.

To do modeling, I usually set up a spreadsheet (a columnar pad, for the rare *Analog* reader not yet computer-initiated). Each row is a system state vector, the values for one time period; each column is a social variable of interest. The cell formulas are the transformation rule. The values of social variables are calculated partly from present-day, and partly from lagged (previous period, next row up) values of other social variables. You simply record the initial state of the world in the first row, set up the cell formulas to calculate the next row, and then generate more rows until you reach the desired year. (If you're using pencil, calculator, and columnar pad, you'll be at it a *long* time—probably the major reason this wasn't done much before the early '80s. And be aware, if you're using a computer, that spreadsheet models tend to be huge—one I discuss below eventually took up about 600 kb of hard disk space.)

Initially I just wanted a quick-and-dirty estimate of the earliest quarter century in which a colony starship might reasonably depart Earth, so I set up my spreadsheet with one row equal to twenty-five years.

I started forward from 1985 with the following assumptions:

1. The fully loaded ship, exclusive of fuel, masses about 330 million kg. (60 percent of the size of the biggest present-day oil tankers). Dividing by 25 percent gives 1.33 billion kg of mass at launch, so one billion kg of fuel are required (regardless of destination because the ship travels ballistic most of the time).

2. GWP (gross world product, the annual total value of all production and services worldwide) grows at a conservative 2.5 percent indefinitely. (This and other unattributed specific numbers are either found, or calculated from values found, in the 1989 *World Almanac*. There are better and more esoteric sources of numbers, but you can do just fine with that one simple source.) Working in increments of twenty-five years, that's about 85 percent per iteration.

3. The starship is a government venture. As Earth continues to industrialize, the public/private mix, and the growth of the public sector, will tend to approximate those of the Western democracies of today.

   (If you think that's a whopper of an assumption, you're right. Feel free to play around with drastically different values.)

   Right now the average size of total government budget

among Western democracies is about 37.9 percent of GDP (gross domestic product—GNP without foreign trade, to more accurately reflect the actual size of a national economy) and the public sector claims an additional 7 percent per twenty-five years (Heidenheimer, Heclo, and Adams, page 173). We might simply figure a future date at which the government budget becomes 100 percent of GWP, but I chose to assume that the private sector is actually *losing 10 percent share* per twenty-five years. Thus the private sector dwindles but does not disappear (in fact it continues to grow in absolute terms—just more slowly than government).

4. The first colonizing starships will be built when one of them represents one half of one percent of five years of global government budgets. Modern nations rarely pursue non-vital projects of more than five years' duration, and one half of one percent of total government budget is about two-thirds the proportion of all federal, state, and local outlays going to NASA, and thus a conservative estimate of what the future civilization might find a sustainable funding level.

5. Fuel is the cost bottleneck. A century or more of unmanned or small-crew exploration has developed the necessary technology. This seems especially credible because the fuel converts to five million times present American annual energy production.

6. The price of energy remains constant. Energy price automatically sets a boundary on fuel price because the price of any fuel must lie between the price of the energy it will yield, and the price of the energy it takes to obtain it—below that range, none will be made; above, it will be too valuable to burn. I assumed starship fuel (antimatter or balonium) could be produced from electricity with perfect conversion, so it cost exactly what electricity did—good enough for the one-digit-or-so accuracy needed. For greater precision, I'd have had to specify a fuel-to-energy conversion efficiency and an energy consumption per unit fuel made, and calculated prices based on those.

Given a starship budget and a price of fuel, I just put a column for "starships per year" (annual starship budget divided by the price of 1 billion kg of fuel) on the modeling spreadsheet, and scanned down the sheet to see where it exceeded .2; that date plus five years would be a good figure for the first launch.

Unfortunately, with energy prices at present levels, launch year came to 3165. From past experience, that's much too far into the future to model at all, not to mention being extremely discouraging.

To get out of that situation, I added more balonium to the technology mix. I came up with the "Von Neumann powersat" or "VNP"—a space-borne electric power plant that puts out fifty trillion watts and reproduces itself every eight years. Whether VNPs are solar, nuclear, antimatter generators, or balonium transformers didn't matter to me any more than it usually matters to a mainstream author whether the electric power in his fictional house comes from hydro or coal. If it were relevant to the story, I'd simply work up some specific physical rationale to fit those economic parameters.

So this gave me a new Assumption 6, to replace the one above:

6. Sometime in the early 2000s the first VNP is constructed; within a few decades, their rapidly growing population is virtually the whole electric production for the solar system.

VNPs increase about eightfold every quarter century. GWP increases 1.85-fold in the same time. Demand for electricity is roughly a function of the square of national GNP, so presumably that means demand is going up $(1.85)^2 = 3.24 =$ fold per quarter century at the same time supply is increasing eightfold.

In the very long run—and in twenty-five years you can modify machines, homes, practically anything—you can use an almost infinite amount of electricity if it's cheap enough. Assuming society holds growth in its electric bill at the same proportion of total expenditures, then, every twenty-five years the planet is buying 8 times as much electricity for 3.24 times as much money.

Or, to the one digit of accuracy we needed, the VNP causes price of electricity to halve every twenty-five years.

Under the new assumptions 2285 began the quarter century in which launching was feasible. Humankind's first interstellar colony would be launched in 2290.

Three centuries is still a very long way into the future—think back to 1690—and that's just the beginning of the colonization era. Since the idea I started out to work on pretty much demands that other solar systems have been colonized for some centuries, it takes a while to build and launch hundreds of starships, and it might take as much as eighty-five years travel time to some of the colonies, the date of the story is still further away from the present than any reasonable ability to extrapolate. (My experienced-based rule of thumb is that five-hundred years is the absolute maximum.)

I didn't want the world to get utterly unrecognizable (though that might make another good story), but clearly I would need a reason *why* it wasn't unrecognizable. I decided to add an event to the background: at or around the time the colony ships are leaving, for some reason or other, the global human culture decides change in general is bad, and begins the Inward Turn (a period like the Enlightenment or Renaissance). There will be much refinement but little new development after A.D. 2300.

Such things have happened. The familiar case is Tokugawa Japan, but China, Persia, and India have done similar things at times, and the tendency was clearly there in other cultures (e.g. Dark Ages Ireland, fourth century Rome). So it's a reasonable human possibility.

Of course, after several centuries of the tide running the *other* way in our culture, we're out of sympathy with such a cultural turning, and may think of it as "decadent," as "stagnation" and "degeneracy." But it need not be. The Inward Turn simply means people will value and explore one set of possibilities at the expense of another. It will tend to favor skills, arts, and crafts that require extensive refinement and disciplined training: gymnastics, martial arts, formal or classic styles in the arts, religions requiring elaborate meditative practices, taxonomic or "catalog" sciences, ethics and ontology in philosophy. By the same token, it will devalue that which requires novelty and personal passion: team contact sports, romanticism and subjectivism in arts, religions based on fervor and conversion experiences, theoretical sciences, epistemology. That's a choice—not a moral collapse. They'll have fewer Beethovens and Rimbauds, but more formal gardens and tea ceremonies.

And at the time of the story, centuries later, the Inward Turn will be as automatically accepted, unremarked, and beyond debate as the Renaissance is today.

Cycling Forward

What triggers the Inward Turn? We need to have some major event happen three hundred years from now, give or take fifty. What could it be?

If I already had a clear picture of the society of 2285, I might simply make up a shock to impose. Since I don't, I'll develop the society first. Because good social models tend to be unstable, there may be a big enough shock occurring "naturally" near the desired date.

For this projection, I calculated annual values of the social variables, giving a more elaborate fine structure, because the social event I was looking for would lie somewhere in the rich detail of history. I'll discuss only the seven variables that gave me a result I would use for the story, but I actually modeled more than forty variables. (Like photographers, modelers have to shoot a lot more pictures than they keep.)

We'll start with the economy, taking Woodward and Bernstein's advice—as good in the social sciences as it is in investigative journalism—to "follow the money." It also happens to be a good example of cyclic phenomena.

The major cycles in economic growth are the Kondratiev (54 years), Kuznets (18.3 years), Hansen 1 (8.3 years), and Hansen 2 (3.5 years). The error bars on those times are so wide that you can arbitrarily flex values plus or minus 10 percent.

These are cycles in the rate of growth, not in the actual size of the economy itself. You can take growth in GWP as varying from 1 percent to about 6 percent annually (postwar values for industrial nations except for peculiar cases like Japan and Germany during postwar reconstruction) with the average at around 3.8 percent; or, taking data going much further back in history, you can assume annual economic growth can fluctuate between -3 percent and $+9$ percent, with an average of around 2.7 percent. I chose the smaller range.

The effect of each cycle is about 1.8 times as large as the effect of the next shortest—thus the Hansen 1 is 1.8 times as big, the Kuznets $1.8^2 = 3.24$ times as big, and the Kondratiev $1.8^3 = 5.83$ times as big as the Hansen 2.

I usually just use a sine wave with a period equal to the length of the cycle. First pick a year when the cycle "troughed"—went through a minimum. The year 1795 seems to have been the last four-cycle trough, but all cycles except the Kondratiev seem to "resest" during very deep depressions, so you might arbitrarily pick three years during the 1930s for the Kuznets and Hansen troughs.

The trough will be one quarter cycle before the start of a new cycle, so you add one quarter of the period to that year, and now you have the zero year for that cycle. For the value of each cycle at all future dates, then:

Cycle value $= \sin ((\text{Current date-zero year})/(\text{Period}/2\pi))$.

Total cycle value $=$ sum of all the cycles times their coefficients (those powers of 1.8).

Growth $=$ average growth $+$ k(total cycle value), where k is a normalizing constant, a simple fudge factor to make the results come out within the range of growth you've selected.

The value of GWP in year Y is then simply:

GWPY $=$ GWP Y_{-1} (1 + growth rate).

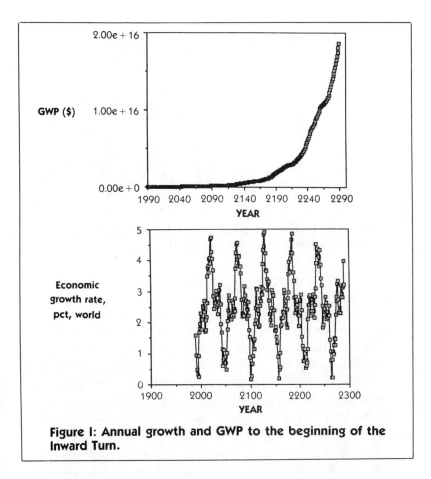

Figure 1: Annual growth and GWP to the beginning of the Inward Turn.

As you can see in figure 1, in the next three centuries the growth rate flexes all over the place, but in the long run of history what we see is simply the same explosive growth that has characterized the last century or so. By the time of the Inward Turn, everyone is a lot richer. But what is available for them to buy?

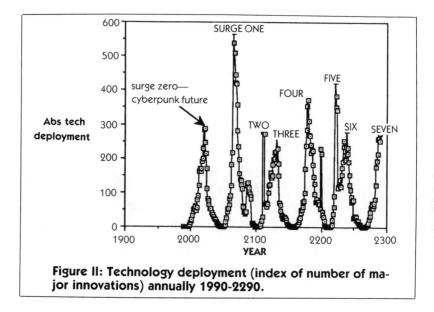

Figure II: Technology deployment (index of number of major innovations) annually 1990-2290.

Half Magic

I need not tell an SF audience that technological advance has dramatic effects. There are a lot of different ways to model it; this time I used the "shopping list" approach—gadgets are invented at a steady rate, but they are economically deployed (that is, come into actual widespread use) in bursts. Schumpeter suggested deployment might correlate with the upswing in the Kondratiev wave; it's also a truism that war brings rapid technical development.

To express this, I simply assume significant new inventions go onto a "shopping list" or "technological backlog" of potential technology, and move off the list and into real deployment at a rate that varies between 0 and 100 percent, depending on the Kondratiev cycle value and the values of warfare indicators (see below).

As you can see in figure 2, this gives a fairly credible situation: technology sometimes stagnates as nothing new is deployed for a long time, and at other times skyrockets, especially after a long hiatus. This gave me as much information as I really wanted: eight major surges of technological innovation between now and the beginning of interstellar colonization. (A "major surge" is something on the order of the highly innovative periods 1900–20 or 1940–65.)

To envision the surges, I use a rule of thumb that has no justification other than gut feeling. Each new surge is 90 percent what you might have expected from the last one, plus 10 percent magic (in its Clarke's Law sense). So from the viewpoint of 1920, 90 percent of the gadgets of the (roughly) Manhattan Project through Apollo Project boom would be imaginable (indeed, some, like TV, were abortively available in the previous boom). But 10 percent (lasers, nuclear power, transistors) would be absolutely incomprehensible—magic.

I further arbitrarily assume that the major discoveries for the next surge have all been made as of today.

The graph shows a major surge in the 2000s and 2010s, Surge Zero, which should deploy everything in SF that seems pretty likely right now. *Everything.*

Does that feel like a real explosion in the brain, like Bruce Sterling or William Gibson at their dazzling best? All the same it's only the start.

Surge One must be an immense extension of everything in Surge Zero, *plus a 10 percent addition of things that work according to as-yet-undiscovered principles.* Surge Two must be extensions on everything (including the 10 percent of magic) plus 10 percent *new* magic. From our viewpoint it's now 19 percent magic.

And Surge Three . . . well, you see where this gets to. Since the Inward Turn starts at the end of Surge Seven, 52 percent of significant new technology in the culture we're imagining must be stuff we currently would not find comprehensible.

Realistically, the world should be half magic. Who'd have thought calculations, the lifeblood of hard SF, could drive us that far into fantasy?

Three Hundred Years of Sex and Violence

Since we've already been through the business of setting up cycles, I'll just mention that there are four prominent cycles in the Index of International Battles, of lengths 142, 57, 22, and 11 years, in battles per year. (Any separable clash of armed forces between competing sovereignties is a "battle.")

The same cycles apply to "battle days per year." Each day contains as many "battle days" as it does battles—so that, for example, if ten distinct battles go on for ten days duration, that's a hundred battle days.

Like the economic cycles, the longer the cycle the bigger its effect, but it's not quite so pronounced, and one-digit accuracy is about as far as I can comfortably go, so I suggest coefficients of 3, 2, 2, and 1 for those cycles.

Estimates on actual numbers of battle days per year vary wildly; all sorts of international, defense, and peace organizations publish estimates, and no two are even remotely close to each other. (The problems include defining when a battle starts and stops, which incidents are big enough to be battles, and how separated things must be to be separate battles.) Thus there's no good guidance on what the numbers actually should be.

Once again flying by the seat of my pants, I simply estimated a range. In all of human history, I doubt there's been a day of peace—somewhere on the Earth, two military forces were probably fighting each other on every day of history. So an absolute minimum would be four hundred battle days per year (one-digit accuracy, again).

On the maximum side, the most battles probably occurred either during the nineteenth-century European colonial conquests or during World War II. There were eight major European colonial conquest powers, and most of them were fighting one insurrection or another most of the time. Add in the American Indian wars, and assume the larger British and French Empires were usually fighting two insurrections at once, and you get eleven battle days/day.

In World War II, counting four Allied fronts against Japan and five against Germany/Italy, plus partisan activities in occupied areas, and counting each front as a battle day every day, we get eleven battle days/day.

Either way it comes to about four thousand battle days per year, which is obligingly one order of magnitude greater.

After about 1900, the percentage of global population killed in war per annum is an exponential function of the number of battle days. (This is just something I've found in playing with UN and various other statistics. It's purely do-it-yourself social science and comes with no institutional pedigrees, so if you don't like it please feel free to cook up your own.)

Again, I set this up as a function that would flex between a minimum and a maximum. According to UN figures, in a very good year only about 1 in 100,000 people worldwide die of something directly war-related.

About the highest figure I can conceive (excluding genuine nuclear wars of annihilation so that there will be a future to write about) is that a twenty-year war might kill half the global population. That's about an order of magnitude worse than World War II, which, if you extend it to include the Sino-Japanese, Ethiopian, Spanish, and Russo-Finnish wars leading into it and the many aftershock wars (Greece, Malaya, Korea, China, Ukraine, Palestine, etc.), killed around 5 percent of the global population between 1931 and 1952. So the global fatality rate varies between .00001 percent and 3.4 percent per annum, as an exponential function of battle days.

Wars are allegedly about something or other. We aren't interested in every little brushfire conflict, of course, and neither will our descendants be—when was the last time you heard anyone refer to the War of the Pacific, Queen Anne's War, or Prusso-Danish War in passing, and expect you to follow the reference? But the two really heavy periods of fighting that appear in the three hundred years should have some global significance.

In the theory of international competition, the classification "great power" comes up frequently. I like a modified version of Kennedy's definition: a great power is, first, a nation that can, if it has the will, militarily enforce its wishes on any other nation not classified as a great power, and on credible alliances of non-great powers; and second, a nation that is able to make conquest by any other great power too painful for the aggressor to contemplate.

If you apply those rules the way I do, there are five great powers in the world today: the United States, Japan, the Soviet Union, China, and the European part of the NATO alliance.

Great powers come into being from sustained periods of economic growth. Major wars against other great powers produce very high death tolls and economically ruin great powers, busting them back to secondary status, sometimes permanently and often for decades.

The great powers normally get and consume the bulk of the world's wealth, so an ambitious secondary power needs a generation—twenty-five years—of fast world growth to rise to great-power status. Success for one rising power precludes anyone else's success. There are finitely many resources, power vacuums, and unclaimed turf in the world, and the secondary power that gets all or most of them is the one that becomes a great power—while shutting out everyone else, so I also allowed only one new great power to emerge per decade.

To express the way wars between great powers quickly knock them down the scale, I assumed that if annual global war deaths exceed 1 percent, twice their WWII value, all the great powers must be involved. I expressed this as a simple fraction—every time war deaths went over 1 percent, I busted three-eighths of the great powers (to the nearest integer) to secondary status. Thus a three- or four-year war at those historically unprecedented levels is enough to break all the great powers in the world.

The numbers of great powers, along with war deaths, are shown in figure 3. There are two truly big wars in this future—World War III and IV, let us cleverly call them—and the starship launches come right when a second power manages to lurch up

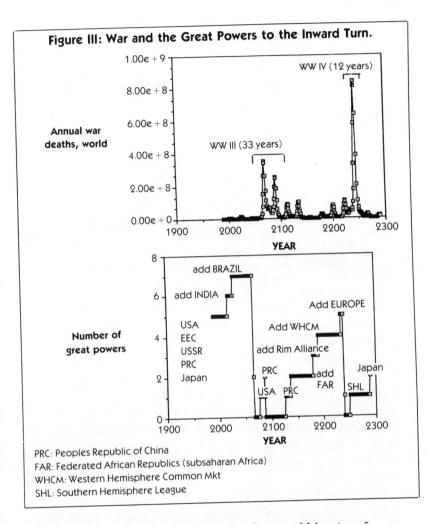

Figure III: War and the Great Powers to the Inward Turn.

PRC: Peoples Republic of China
FAR: Federated African Republics (subsaharan Africa)
WHCM: Western Hemisphere Common Mkt
SHL: Southern Hemisphere League

to great powerhood again. Normally that would be time for another war . . . so why not this time?

Let's look at population statistics. (This stage of the creative process approaches sex, like violence, in terms of its quantitative results, rather than its messy particulars.)

How many people are there in 2290, and where do they live?

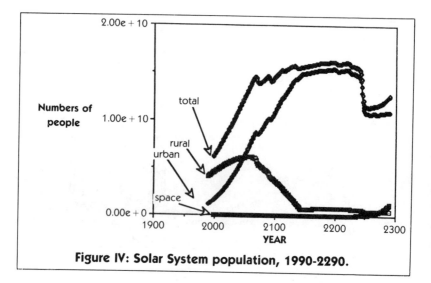

Figure IV: Solar System population, 1990-2290.

The results of the model can be seen in figure 4.

Virtually all the growth of population in the long run comes from rural populations. This is caused by something that always startles elitists: people are not stupid. Agriculture is labor-intensive, and as long as an additional person can produce food in excess of its consumption, it pays to have another baby. (Famines are generally caused by a drastic change from the expected future—war, drought, or land confiscation changes the value of children after they're born.) In most parts of the world, the expected value of children doesn't reach zero right out to the limit of human fertility.

By contrast, life in cities is expensive, and work children can do there is less valuable, so having kids really doesn't pay. Thus over the long run (it takes time to alter perceptions, and peasants who move to the city don't suddenly de-acquire children), city dwellers will have children at or below a replacement rate and rural people will have all they can. "All they can" globally currently corresponds to a global rural population increase of about 2.3 percent per year.

Luckily, practically everyone would rather live in the city. (The American back-to-the-land fetish is an extreme minority taste.) Currently a bit under half of one percent of global population moves from country to city per year. If that continues, by 2056, the growth of rural areas has reversed, and as they decline in population the rate of population growth slows. In fact, World War IV is so big that global population actually peaks at around fifteen billion in 2237 and declines to just under eleven billion by the beginning of the colonization era. Global population is then more than 95 percent urban (as opposed to 22 percent today).

For a quick extrapolation of spaceborne populations, assume a VNP makes work for 100 people and the percentage of space-borne population that would be working in the energy industry declines steadily by 10 percent every twenty-five years. That gives a population growth rate of 6 percent (most of it supplied by immigration at first).

By the beginnings of interstellar colonization, there are 1.256 billion people living permanently in space. Go ahead and gasp—but it's a slower rate than the European population increase in Australia 1788 to 1900, and Australia effectively cost more to get to.

Beyond Megalo

Megalo- is the prefix for "real big." Hence the SF idea of "megalopolis," the giant city.

I won't report full details here—it's another article in its own right—but in playing around with statistics on the world's very largest cities, I've noticed there are roughly three groups: (1) New York and Tokyo, (2) eight industrial centers with populations of ten to fifteen million, and (3) about twenty Third World popu-lation jams.

They seem to group unusually clearly according to what I call a "respiration statistic"—how many dollars worth of goods per year must flow per unit perimeter to keep the city functioning. Tokyo and New York have respiration statistics about an order of magnitude greater than the eight giant industrial centers, which in turn have respiration statistics two orders of magnitude greater than the Third World giant cities. (The one interesting exception is that the respiration statistic for Osaka-Kobe-Kyoto (OKK) is about one-fifth that of New York or Tokyo, so it may be an intermediate case, or one in transition.)

It doesn't take a lot of travel to discover that the fundamental experience of living in these three kinds of places is drastically different, especially that categories 1 and 2 are different from category 3. So I set up a simple system to let categories 1 and 2 grow as population grew. Category 2 I call a "megalopolis"— similar in lifestyle and scale to LA, London, or Moscow today. Category 1, of which New York and Tokyo are the existing representatives, I dubbed a "hyperpolis."

And because in three centuries it didn't seem unreasonable to have at least one more kind come into being, I created the imaginary category of "transpolis" to cover a respiration statistic one order of magnitude greater than that of Category 1. This works out to a city of a hundred million with a population per unit ground area like that of a modern high-rise apartment building. The technology to feed such a thing doesn't exist today, but I see no inherent impossibility.

I simply set up allocations so that some of the world's urbanizing population would flow into megalopoli, some megalopoli would grow into hyperpoli, and a very few hyperpoli would become transpoli. Which cities or areas became which, again, wasn't critical for the time in which I wanted to set my story, so I simply left it as a piece of cultural background to be filled in as necessary.

The Time of the Inward Turn

In A.D. 2290, global population is steady at eleven billion, down 27 percent after World War IV, forty-one years ago. Practically everyone lives in town, and about 17 percent of the population lives in giant high-density towns—the equivalent of twentieth century LA or bigger. Half the technology is, by twentieth-century standards, magic. Global per capita income is about 110 times 1985 American per capita income. World War IV reduced transpoli from seven to five, and hyperpoli from twenty-three to seventeen, well within living memory. There are many veterans, former refugees, and survivors around, and the ruins of the destroyed hyperpoli and transpoli are still in existence, raw scars visible even from the cities on the moon, visited by grieving pilgrims as Auschwitz is today. In the last few years, the hegemony of one superpower has been challenged by the rise of another, and the fear of another war is in the air.

And that seems to me enough to explain the Inward Turn. At such a moment a charismatic leader might successfully move for an effective global sovereignty. The Earth becomes a loose federation, committed to develop internally, refining and integrating its culture, bringing technical, social, and political change to a near stop, letting humanity find time to knit together. (Again, that sounds unattractive to us—but we don't have four billion dead in a landscape of ruins, and a recent scare that it might happen again. People whose world was shattered only forty years ago might feel very differently.)

If they take the Inward Turn, why would they launch colonies at all? Perhaps as a bribe—"your way of life must be assimilated here—but you can perpetuate it in the stars." Any group that can raise the money can launch something the size of a big twentieth-century ship on a one-way trip to a preselected colony site on some other habitable planet. (I assume unmanned probes, and perhaps some manned scientific missions, have thoroughly scouted the feasible worlds.)

Arbitrarily, I've set the colony ship size at ninety-six adults, one million preserved human embryos, plus everything needed to fully establish the colony. I also assume that because our descendants get better information faster, and perhaps have a better way of using it, there are no mistakes on the order of Jamestown or Botany Bay. (You could write a terrific story about such a mistake, though—remember these ships are much more strictly one-way.)

Planets Wholesale

The physics/astronomy/geology side of worldbuilding has been covered extensively and well elsewhere (see Gillett 1989 for a good update and reading list) so I won't deal with it here. When I need a lot of planets in a hurry, I set up a spreadsheet of the basic equations, one row to a planet. I put in randomizing factors that will keep planets within habitable zones and give acceptable mass, surface gravity, etc. In this case I used some real stars (G's, warmer K's, and cooler F's) within forty light years of Sol, so the stellar information was a given and only the planets had to be generated.

For more colorful place names, I assigned habitable planets preferentially to stars that had individual names over stars with constellation names.

This is very unlikely to turn out to be the actual case.

Nearby stars that have individual names are almost invariably red giants, too old to have living worlds; several of the ones that aren't have white dwarf companions so that any living world there was cooked long ago. But for purposes of fiction and romance (and I hold few purposes higher), I preferred to use those star names. So I cooked up a hypothetical process that would cause practically all such stars to have, not living planets, but extremely easy to terraform planets—so easy, in fact, that robot equipment sent at near lightspeed would be able to have them "ready to move in" by the time the colony ships got there. Since the story itself was to be set only a few hundred years after terraformation, this immediately suggested all sorts of interesting local color that wouldn't have been there otherwise. Just such a dialogue between calculation and art is what worldbuilding is all about.

The planet sheet can be as sophisticated as desire or skill can make it, but in practice you'll always end up doing a great deal of further work on each generated planet, drawing maps and so forth.

This time, rather than use a random number table, or the supplied random number generator, for the six randomizing factors that went into each planet, I used the function $y_{n+1} = ky_n(1 - y_n)$, going down the columns of the spreadsheet, with k in its chaotic range between 3 and 4, to make values cluster irregularly, creating just a few kinds of planets plus a few weird outliers.

I did that for several reasons. It fit my basic feeling that the universe is made up of endless variations on just a few themes. There aren't an infinite number of kinds of stars, the gas giant planets we know are all clearly of the same family, and there are just a few common kinds of ecosystem on land on the Earth . . . so why not just a few common kinds of habitable planet, plus occasional "Australias" and "Galapagoses"?

It also created an interesting potential situation in interstellar trade, because the more alike two places are the less they have to trade and the more they compete with each other. If there are just a few types, then most planets will have several serious trade rivals and a finite number of good markets.

Finally, there's only room for a finite number of symbols in any story or collection of stories, and if you intend that the environment mean something, contrasts will work better aesthetically if they're to a small number of alternatives (Arrakis v. Caladan for example). You need enough "normal" planets to establish that one in particular is "weird."

This time my generator gave me three basic categories of planet:

- Six "Wet Mars" planets, smaller and cooler than Earth with big oceans and just scatterings of volcanic islands and some

Greenland or New Guinea sized pieces of continental rock.
Colonies tend to huddle in their tropics.

- Fourteen "Utah" planets, worlds 5- to 15-percent larger than
  Earth with much more extensive continents and 10- to 35-
  percent of their areas covered with dense briny seas (mostly long
  and narrow like the Red, Mediterranean, or Timor seas), intense
  insolation, and high axial tilts. A lot of their surface area is
  fantastically hostile—deserts drier than the Atacama, enormous
  daily and seasonal temperature swings, mountain ranges that
  dwarf the Himalayas—but seacoasts are habitable well into arc-
  tic latitudes.

- Eight "Cold Indonesia" planets—earthlike but cooler, with bigger polar caps, and somewhat less land area broken into many
  smaller pieces. The tropics and lower temperate zones are pleasant.

In addition to these, the sheet also generated five outliers,
mixed or peculiar cases that added variety.

When Do We Get Where?

With the set of destinations worked out, the next question was
timing of colony arrivals. Obviously that depended on when they
were launched.

The simplest assumption is that since economic growth continues, if we leave the starship budget at a fixed five hundredths
of global government budget, starships will be launched at a rate
proportional to cumulative economic growth. There were thirty-
three habitable planets in twenty-five solar systems, presumably
all well-surveyed. Knowing what is available, what does the world
government do?

Trying to think like hypothetical bureaucrats under the circumstances, it seems to me that a system whose overriding concerns are peace and stability would want, first of all, to insure
that there was as little basis as possible for rivalries between col-

onies on any one planet, and that there were no "wild" or "open" frontier worlds out there where dissidents or malcontents might build up strength in isolation. There's going to be a lot of looseness for cultural development, but you don't want to create, or leave, a space for an actual enemy to exist in. In fact, if you're trying to keep social change slow, you don't want anywhere out there undergoing uncontrolled growth—you risk creating a potential Commodore Perry in a few centuries, and a culture that thinks like this one thinks in terms of millennia.

So clearly, to avoid having untended open real estate anywhere, the first priority is to get *some* colony down in every system, and then on every planet. The first twenty-five colonies go one to a solar system, and the next eight go to empty planets in solar systems that have more than one habitable world.

To insure quality, you make sure nobody has to live in the truly nasty parts of the planet. Every colony is granted a land with area, resources, and worst-case climate comparable to France, Texas, or the Ukraine. In the whole set of habitable worlds, 1,240 such spaces were available, four-fifths of them on the 14 Utah-type planets. (For comparison, the sheet gives a value of 46 such spaces for Earth.)

For political stability, you want most of the colonies on any one planet to be close together in age—as we'll see, these colonies grow so fast that in a century or two they might well start grabbing land assigned to somebody else. So you want the last colony to land within one hundred years of the first colony's arrival.

Thus after the "elder" colonies are planted on each planet— three planets don't have good spaces for more than one—you "fill up" each planet rapidly with younger colonies. That way the younger colonies will all be close together in age, and can, if necessary, support each other against the larger elder colonies.

Obviously the fewer colonies assigned to a planet, the faster it can be filled up, especially in the early years when you're still not launching many ships per year. So each successive colonizing mission goes to whichever planet has the *fewest* open slots.

Knowing ships per year launched, order of colonization, and travel time, working up founding dates of every colony is no harder than coming up with a simple bus schedule. The first colony, on a Utah planet circling Alpha Centauri, is planted in 2299; the last colony arrives at another Utah planet, this one circling Theta Ursa Major, in 2475, having left Earth in 2390. (Coincidentally, exactly one hundred years after the first colony left.)

With those missions, the "colonization era" is over. Colony ships can't reach any more systems from Earth, and none of the colonized systems is as yet ready to launch a secondary colony. Of course, colonies could be sent out from Earth to be refueled in distant systems, but remember that this is a century after the Inward Turn began—the interest in reaching out may have dwindled. So the colonies get planted, and grow, and time goes by . . .

The Nuclear Family:
Ten from the Womb, Thirty from the Vat

I gave each ship forty-eight couples of childbearing age and one million frozen embryos. What would that grow into?

This required only a very rough demographic model, because I just wanted to know what the population age profile and size would look like, and from past experience I knew that a "point entry" demographic model would give me the two digits of accuracy needed.

The quick-and-dirty spreadsheet I created is thus extremely crude. A point entry model is one in which all the major demographic life changes are assumed to happen simultaneously for everyone. So in this model:

1. The ship arrives on the nineteenth birthday of all ninety-six adults.

2. Exactly one year later, on their twentieth birthdays, each of the forty-eight couples adds a decanted baby (a former frozen embryo) to the family. In addition, one-third of the mothers give birth on their twentieth birthday.
3. Every birthday thereafter, through the forty-ninth, all adult couples adopt a decanted baby (until the supply runs out) and one-third of them have an additional birth.
4. All children pair off into couples on their nineteenth birthdays and are part of the reproductive pool beginning with their twentieth birthdays.
5. Everyone drops dead on his or her eightieth birthday.

No doubt Lewis Carroll could have a lot of fun with such a society. One can imagine Big Day celebrations every January first, in which the whole family gets together to unbottle a new crowd of babies in the morning, attends a mass wedding at lunch followed by a mass birthing, and then goes out to the cemetery to watch the old people drop into their predug graves before going home to the traditional dinner.

Yet although the results this model yields are different from the real world, for the story I want to tell, four hundred years after landing, they aren't different enough to matter. The demographic profiles for two planets (size of cohort by age) are shown in figure 5.

If you need a more accurate model (e.g., to get accurate effects of baby booms, plagues, or wars in the age profile), you can always improve the precision by cutting down the time represented by one iteration, making deaths or births depend on variable fractions of many age cohorts, and installing more leaks (bachelorhood, early death, individual preference, sterility) into the reproductive pool.

Just one warning—if you do try a more elaborate model, make sure that the total death fractions applied to each cohort add up to 1, as do the total fractions moved out of the reproductive pool. Few things screw up a demographic profile as thoroughly as

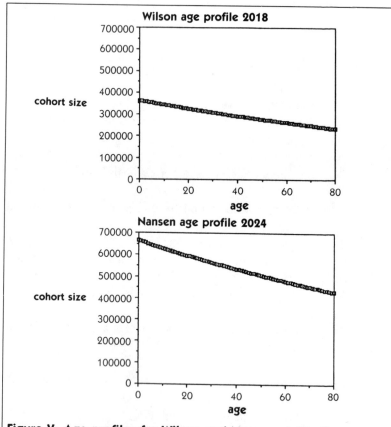

Figure V: Age profiles for Wilson and Nansen at the time they get instantaneous travel.

Wilson was colonized some decades prior to Nansen—notice that the downward slope of the profile is less acute. The downward slope indicates a growing (hence youthening) population.

immortality, negative people, perpetually fertile dead people, or reverse mothers!

By prior assumptions, these would be planets without significant technology gains or wars, so I didn't put those cycles into the process. You could probably do interesting things with diffusing technology via radio from multiple points, and the shopping list model might be very interesting for that, but again, that's another story.

For the economic cycles, I suggest starting the Kondratiev wave with its minimum value on the landing date, the Kuznets cycle whenever you think they'd start putting up buildings, the Hansen 1 cycle at the point where they'd be setting up factories, and the Hansen 2 cycle whenever they'd start making their own goods rather than living on what came in the ship, because the three shorter cycles are traditionally identified with building, physical capital, and inventory investment.

The Student Exchange Economy

Before the introduction of FTL travel, is there anything to trade between planets?

It is a basic principle of transportation economics that, if there's a faster way to get it for the same price, the slower way won't be there at all.

First of all, since a radio transmission can carry instructions on how to make certain goods and gets there in half the time of a ship carrying the goods, given the speed of construction possible with self-replication, it's very hard to see how any finished goods could be involved in trade. Designs will probably travel by radio, and thus money and information might flow between star systems, but cargoes of finished goods won't.

Given the quantities of energy available at the very low prices that make colonization possible at all (presumably every colonized solar system has VNPs), it's equally hard to see what raw materials could be in short enough supply to be a problem. With 50 percent magic technology, even if somehow you had a whole solar system with none of some vital element, I would guess transmutation would be cheaper than transportation.

Works of art can also go by radio, even paintings, sculptures, and dances if the recordings are precise enough holograms. Scientific papers are no problem either, though biological specimens might have to go by ship. Again, though, with our 50 percent magic technology, it's more likely that a full genetic description would be sent by radio, and the lifeform of interest "constructed" on site, and if the technology base also includes really sophisticated computer simulations, rather than doing the traditional random searches for interesting pharmacological materials, biochemical engineers will be constructing specific molecules for specific receptor sites. In that case no one will be interested in exobiotes for potential new drugs or spices—which have traditionally been high-priced for low-shipping-cost goods, and hence great openers of trade routes.

Are we left with nothing but one-way tourism?

Well, almost. Although all kinds of information comes in via radio from thirty-three other worlds, the big problem is that it gets increasingly hard to understand. Other cultures diverge from your own, and it can take up to eighty-five years to get an answer to a question.

Ideally you want someone to talk to about it who won't take decades to reply. So maybe you get the equivalent of interstellar Fulbright scholars, students on life-abroad programs. They might serve as "interpreters" for data from their home system and perhaps from those beyond it (from the standpoint of their adopted system).

They probably do *not* spend all their travel time in suspended animation; instead, they put a lot of time into reading and viewing transmissions from back home and from their destination, so that they'll be fluent in the culture they left (though behind it) and fairly fluent in the one they're joining—thus making good interpreters for some decades afterwards.

On the other hand, the older they are, the less useful life is left in them—so perhaps they spend half their time in the tank. Further, since we've established that suspended animation is risky (remember, after a hundred years, odds are you're dead—which is why the ships can't get much further than their forty light-year limit), a few of them probably die on the way.

Well, then who will go? You can hardly send condemned criminals (usually not the academic type), dissidents (not representative), or desperate poor people (probably no poor people— living standards are likely to be as high as Earth's in short order).

Probably most of them will be self-selected. In a population of millions, you can surely find one hundred or so acceptable people who will have personal reasons for taking a one-way trip to somewhere else entirely, especially if the "somewhere else" is a place where they'll be in a very high-prestige, high-authority position. They will have five major characteristics—they'll be:

1. young enough to be worth sending,
2. smart enough to be able to enjoy the years of study aboard ship,
3. socialized enough to be endurable company for everyone else on board, and
4. abjectly miserable enough in their home culture to leave it forever, but
5. not actually incapable of happiness (if they were, they'd stay home and kill themselves).

One hundred such people confined in a small space for several years . . . that sounds like a story to me. It's still not the one I'm writing, however.

The Network in the Stars

To do this next step, you need to do enough simple trigonometry to figure out how far apart the stars all are. This gives you a "distance matrix," not unlike the mileage charts found in road atlases. Then, given the known performance of the starships, it's fairly trivial to convert the distance matrix to a travel time matrix.

Assuming we don't want people to spend more than fifteen years out of suspended animation (too much aging, since they must leave as educated adults and arrive with some decades of vigorous health still ahead of them), and that they need to spend about half their time awake to keep track of the cultures they're moving between, the practical travel time is about thirty to thirty-five years. Planets will exchange only within that radius, *unless* there are no closer neighbors with which to exchange. In that case, a planet will exchange with its closest neighbor, paying enormous premiums, plus any other planet that is insignificantly further away than that (say less than 10 percent greater travel time).

The acceptable routes by these rules are shown in the "route map," map 1. It shows the major trade routes (those that make economic sense) and the secondary trade routes (those within a few percent of making sense, plus the routes to the nearest neighbors for those planets that don't have any choice in the matter).

Getting Down to Cases

The map immediately drew my attention to the Mufrid and Arcturus systems. Though they exchange easily among themselves, they're quite remote from the hub. That combination of close relationship with each other and being a long way away from the rest of Human Space suggests really deviant subcultures could grow there, more so because there are only two colonies in the Mufrid system and one in the Arcturus—fewer elements in the mix means it will be less homogenized. Cultures there can be both very archaic (i.e., comprehensible to my twentieth-century readers) and truly bizarre to the rest of Human Space. If I chose a protagonist from there, when the transporter booth was invented, I would have a good pair of eyes to go see twenty-ninth-century Human Space through.

I set up a convention to avoid having to do too much thinking about names: habitable planets are named, in order of distance from Earth, after winners of the Nobel Peace Prize, beginning with the oldest. So Alpha Centauri's habitable planets are Dunant and Passy, Arcturus's is Wilson, and Mufrid's is Nansen.

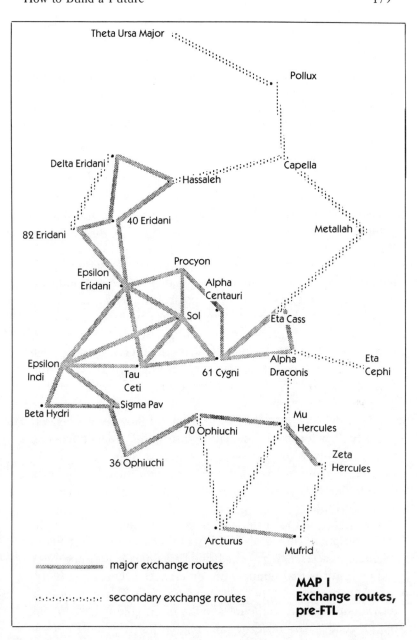

Theta Ursa Major

Pollux

Delta Eridani

Hassaleh

Capella

40 Eridani

Metallah

82 Eridani

Procyon

Epsilon
Eridani

Alpha
Centauri

Sol

Eta Cass

Epsilon
Indi

Alpha
Draconis

Eta
Cephi

Tau
Ceti

61 Cygni

Sigma Pav

Beta Hydri

Mu
Hercules

70 Ophiuchi

Zeta
Hercules

36 Ophiuchi

Arcturus

Mufrid

━━━━━━ major exchange routes

············· secondary exchange routes

MAP I
Exchange routes,
pre-FTL

Circling Mufrid, Nansen has good spaces for only two colonies. This world, one of the five "outliers" (fitting none of the three classifications) is cold, wet, and heavy—oceans almost saturated with salt, just to keep it from freezing (and even then I had to add a great deal of calcium chloride in solution as well), gravity 1.2 Earth's, Antarctic conditions on small continents in its temperate zones, continent-sized rafts of polar ice on which CO_2 snow falls every winter. But at the equator, there are a few islands with year-round weather not too different from that of Seattle in the winter—rainy and cold and nasty, but humanly bearable.

Around Arcturus, a mere 6.5 light years away from Mufrid but some 25 light-years from Earth, Wilson is a Cold Indonesia planet with just one habitable area—an island about the size of Borneo with the climate of Auckland, New Zealand. (There would be room for many more colonies except that Wilson is almost devoid of land around the equator.) Besides the one large equatorial island, there are two polar continents, plus many Greenland-like islands in the temperate zones. Arcturus is much more massive and puts out more heat than Sol, but Wilson orbits so far away it gets only about half the insolation Earth does (much more of it is infrared, though—it's dim but warm). As a result, Wilson circles Arcturus at a distance of 7 AU, with a year of about 12 Earth-years.

Given its steep axial tilt, I created the following deliberately weird ecology for it: continental ice forms on the dark pole every winter but melts completely every summer, watering very fast-growing vegetation. Every fall the whole continent burns down. (This image may have to do with my having spent the last few years in Montana.)

The soot from the burning produces more rapid cooling in the fall hemisphere, but it also darkens the ice in the other hemisphere, thus accelerating the melt and hastening the warming there.

The result is that temperature differences between the hemispheres are large, and they reverse very rapidly. That's a formula for violent weather, so the folks in the single colony have to look out for good-sized hurricanes as a regular thing, a brief "nuclear

fall" every six Terran years, and, about three years after each nuclear fall, spectacular hurricanes on a scale never seen on Earth.

On the other hand, between those, the weather's extremely
nice, and the surfing is probably terrific. People might do a lot
of hiking and camping on the continents or the other islands
during their summer.

Now—what if we amplified the contrast between those two
worlds by setting up cultures that differed drastically emotionally
and psychologically? Suppose, for example, the icy, cloudy tropics of Nansen got a couple of dour, stern, puritanical groups ("we
are not in this world for a good time"), and the warm sunny
island on Wilson got a bunch of free-spirited, fun-loving ro-
mantics ("let the good times roll!")? You might think of it as an
exaggerated version of the difference between traditional New
Hampshire and traditional New Orleans.

Now, what if someone who had long ago fled from one of
Nansen's constricted, cold colonies for the warm tolerance of
Wilson—had the chance to go back instantaneously?

Perhaps it sounds like he'd have to be crazy, but maybe there
is something he really must do. And when people really have to
do something they don't want to—there's the start of a story.

In developing that story, there's a whole other realm of economic and social models to be tackled—the dynamic/chaotic
models that can generate a month by month picture of what
happens on each planet the day after they turn on the transporter
booth. Those are interesting too, but space doesn't allow tackling
them this time out.

And somewhere along the way, of course, I still do have to
write that story.

Suggested Sources and Nifty Reading

A Loose Guide to Finding More Good Tricks

Beenstock, Michael R. *The World Economy in Transition*, Unwin Hyman, 1984. Technical; a lot of good data.

Dewey, Edward R. *Cycles*. New York: Hawthorn, 1971. Out of print. Dewey's theories of the origins of cycles are mystical, and grossly out of date in the light of chaos theory, and he reports the coincidental and the ludicrous side by side with the well established, but there's much that's useful as well. Second edition edited by Og Mandino is even less accurate and useful.

Dunnigan, James F. *How to Make War*. New York: William Morrow, 1983. All the basic information you'd need for near future military simulations.

Flynn, Michael F. "An Introduction to Psychohistory," parts I and II. *Analog*, April and May 1988. Good coverage of many different regularities in social phenomena.

Gillett, Stephen L. "On Building an Earth-Like Planet." *Analog*, July 1989. Readable discussion of physical worldbuilding, plus a solid bibliography.

Goldstein, Joshua, S. "Kondratieff Waves as War Cycles." *International Studies Quarterly*, Spring 1985. Highly technical exploration of possible coupling. Some excellent tables of data.

Heidenheimer, Arnold J., Hugh Heclo, and Carolyn Teich Adams. *Comparative Public Policy: The Politics of Social Choice in Europe and America*, 2d ed., New York: St. Martin's Press, 1983. Many tables of interesting social data hard to find anywhere else. Also an excellent guide to what modern governments actually do and how they actually do it; a good antidote to some of what you'll find in SF.

Kennedy, Paul. *The Rise and Fall of the Great Powers.* New York: Random House, 1987. An excellent, highly readable discussion of many of the basic issues from a historical perspective.

Modelski, George. *Principles of World Politics.* New York: Free Press, 1972. *Long Cycles in World Politics.* Seattle: University of Washington Press, 1986. The basic texts on cyclic phenomena in international power relations. Highly technical. Good data.

Overseas Development Council. *The U.S. and World Development: Agenda for Action.* New York: Praeger. Published annually. The statistical appendix is invaluable.

Rosecrance, Richard. "Long Cycle Theory and International Relations," *International Organization,* Spring 1987. Review article on current issues in the field.

Samuelson, Paul A. *Economics.* New York: McGraw-Hill. So many editions it's hard to keep up, but anything from about the 10th (1976) forward should be fairly accurate. In my opinion, one of the best textbooks ever written on any subject.

Sundquist, James. *Dynamics of the Party System.* Washington, D.C.: Brookings Institution, 1973. The fundamental text on party realignment, the basic dynamic of American political change.

Van Duijn, J. J. *The Long Wave in Economic Life.* Unwin Hyman, 1983. Probably the closest thing to a classic in cyclic theory.

World Almanac. New York: Pharos. Published annually. There's no disgrace in using it; data you get here are usually reliable. Excellent for browsing for ideas if you're doing any statistical work yourself.

Building a Starfaring Age

NORMAN SPINRAD

A few years ago Harry Harrison asked me to contribute an original story to an anthology he was trying to put together, under contract, called *One Million A.D.* Anything I wanted to do, as long as it was set in the far, far future.

Well, the concept was intriguing, but I seldom am able to come up with a story for a theme anthology, even one whose theme was as loosely framed as this one, and I didn't come up with one for *One Million A.D.*, either.

A couple of years after that, I asked Harry what had become of the anthology, which I never had seen published. "Nothing came of it," he told me. "I just couldn't get the stories. You people just weren't capable of writing them."

Including me.

In my first twenty years of writing the stuff, I had only tried to create advanced far-future human societies twice.

Why?

Why, as a science fiction writer, had I pretty much ignored dealing with far-future settings?

Because, as a science fiction *reader*, I had read so little in this vein that I found convincing. Almost all of it assumed a discontinuity of some sort, almost all of it took place on the other side of some kind of cultural amnesia, and the implication of even current information technology is that this simply is not likely to happen.

Even if one does assume a nuclear war, an ecological disaster of monumental proportions, or some other cataclysm, a far-future human civilization, no matter how star-flung, is still likely to have pretty much total access to all previous human history and culture—certainly, at least, as far back as the turn of the twentieth century.

It's a matter of redundancy of information storage. Books printed by the hundreds of thousands of copies, by the millions, reprinted regularly if they have achieved cultural significance. Microfilm storage in large libraries at hundreds or even thousands of locations. Dozens, scores, sometimes hundreds of prints of significant films. And, since the invention of TV and videotape and the VCR, all of ongoing history and culture recorded as it happens with sound and in color, endlessly duplicated. CD-ROMs capable of storing vast amounts of prose, images, sound, data, blueprints, on a single disc, and those discs capable of being stamped out by the millions.

In reality, even an all-out nuclear war, unless it did exterminate human life on the planet (in which case there would be no successor culture to set the story in anyway), is simply not going to be able to create a real historical amnesia. No matter what happens, multiple copies of everything and in a multitude of different media are going to be left lying around in the ruins to be discovered and decoded by any advanced successor civilization.

Our far-future descendants are going to know far more about us than we know about classical Greece and Rome or ancient Egypt or even the Middle Ages, and our knowledge of these predecessor civilizations is not inconsiderable. Our literature still is enriched by references to their history and mythology. Great figures from *our* millennial past, like Alexander, Pericles, Jesus, Buddha, still resonate strongly in our present. Our dream lives, our very consciousness, incorporate archetypes deeply rooted in the distant past. We are even in possession of fairly decent transcriptions of the major works of Homer.

The classical Greeks, the ancient Egyptians, the early Chinese dynasties, still make their heritage felt today, and *they* didn't have high-speed printing presses, videotape, CD-ROMs, or motion picture film to produce thousands or millions of identical copies of everything of any importance.

In other words, the nearly universal literary convention of using a historical amnesia of one sort or another as a device for creating comprehensible far-future humans in a far future culture quite violates the rules of rigorous technological plausibility.

So why do most writers of "hard SF" do it most of the time anyway?

Well, consider the alternative.

If you *don't* use some kind of historical discontinuity—be it a nuclear holocaust, an ecological disaster, a cosmic catastrophe, or the collapse of one or more galactic civilizations into devolved barbarism—to get yourself and the reader to the far future, look at the job of work you've set yourself up for!

Dreaming up a technology even a thousand years in advance of our own may seem like a formidable task, but that's the *easy* part.

Without an intervening breakdown in human civilization, your citizens of A.D. 3000 will long since have elucidated and quantified the total nature of physical reality and will long since have used this knowledge to create a technosphere in which anything that can be done and should be done *has been done*, and plenty of things, no doubt, that shouldn't.

This may seem quite impossible to describe realistically in terms of rigorous extrapolation, but in *literary* terms, it really isn't all that difficult.

Fantasy writers do it all the time by waving their magic wand. Gregory Benford might object to this as "playing tennis with the net down," but it was Arthur C. Clarke, certainly possessed of gilt-edged hard SF credentials, who declared that "any sufficiently advanced technology will seem like magic."

You don't have to know how they do it, nor does the machinery need to be made visible. You can legitimately give any sufficiently advanced technological civilization the magical power to do anything the story requires, as long as you don't egregiously violate what is already known to be plain impossible, such as the violation of the conservation of mass-energy. There even exist some credible magic words from the realm of quantum and particle physics to conjure up faster-than-light travel—tachyons, worm-hole tunnels—in terms that the reader will accept as "scientifically justified" for the sake of the story.

I certainly own up to doing this myself in *The Solarians*, my first novel and my first attempt at a far-future setting, which had giant space battles between fleets of faster-than-light spaceships just because I needed them, and while people may have complained about the primitive prose, and I myself am embarrassed by the blown ending, no one blinked twice at the latest semitraditional space opera. This may not be rigorous science fiction, but even this is a rigorous and useful literary form all its own, a kind of fantasy in science fiction clothing, and when done right, it can produce acknowledged masterpieces like *The Stars My Destination*, where Bester makes you accept even teleportation by act of will as something in the realm of the possible.

On the other hand, even way back here in the boondocks of the twentieth century, what with quantum mechanics, and cosmological physics, and quantum cosmology, we're probably no more than half a unified field theory away from knowing the parameters of the physically possible. And the news isn't all that bad for the science fiction writer. For any sufficiently advanced civilization, meaning any civilization advanced enough to create the technology that even our present knowledge implies, will be able to do magic enough to liberate the imagination *within* the realm of the possible.

In *Riding the Torch*, I wanted to tell the story of a civilization advanced to the point where in a sense it has transcended the universe it evolved in—a dead universe (for the sake of argument) in which this civilization is literally the crown of creation.

Literally speaking, how to get from here to there? And can it be done with the net still in the center of the court?

This was the first time I had really tried to do this, and it was the first time that I proceeded to write myself an entirely self-indulgent monster wad of straight extrapolative exposition outlining the path from here to there. This was a lot of fun to write, a process I highly recommend when approaching the far future, but of course the reason that I could afford to be so self-indulgent was that none of this was going to appear in the finished work.

The short form of the long story I told myself goes something like this: Humans have destroyed the Earth through the standard shitheadedness and all that remains of the species is a refugee fleet cobbled together out of the rubble of a civilization not much more advanced than our own, boat people in leaky tubs searching for a new living world across an infinite sea.

But even this is a sufficiently advanced technology to evolve in an interstellar vacuum. Any civilization sufficiently advanced to cobble together even the most half-assed generational starships is going to at least have fusion technology to power them. Something better may come along in the future, but nothing *less* is going to make it even as far as Centaurus.

Given enough steady acceleration over the years, no matter how minimal, sooner or later your fleet will reach a velocity where the conversion to an interstellar ramscoop drive becomes inevitable. Speed raises the effective density of the interstellar medium to the point where either you let it ablate you to ribbons or you learn how to ride it.

The theory is well known today, and a lot of the technology can be cobbled together out of off-the-shelf hardware. All you need to fudge is some kind of electromagnetic funnel, miles in diameter, scooping the energy-rich relativistic incoming ions and particles down a great big mother of a containment tube, where it ignites to fuel a self-sustaining fusion plasma that converts part of the mass to energy and ejects the considerable remains as high-speed relativistic reaction mass.

The fuel source is unlimited, for all practical purposes, and the faster you go, the more of it your fusion torch devours per unit time, making you go faster still, ad infinitum, or at least asymptotically close to the speed of light. You don't need anything more exotic than this to get up to within an itsy-bitsy decimal place of the speed of light, and, what with the extreme time-dilation effect, even have whole universes die and be reborn within the normal life spans of your characters, as Poul Anderson has done in *Tau Zero*. At these speeds, even time travel of a certain peculiar kind is possible to your sufficiently advanced civilization.

And look what else it implies!

Such a starfaring civilization also would possess what is called a "perfect power source"—one that is unlimited, inexhaustible, and clean.

Not only that, such technology implies unlimited raw materials, winnowed from the interstellar medium itself as the fusion torch plasma breaks down everything that comes in into its constituent atoms, from which plasma stream even *we* probably could collect them selectively by some electromagnetic scheme using their mass differentials.

Indeed, a civilization sufficiently advanced to have a perfect power source will, sooner or later, be able to use that energy to transmute matter on a *particle* level, to assemble atoms of any desired element out of raw basic particles dissociated from anything. The fusion torch is the perfect garbage disposal unit in the bargain, and it literally can turn shit into gold.

That's the good news. And when you think about it, that's about as much science as you need to know to create a credible far-future technology. Any sufficiently advanced civilization will be able to make anything the rules of the universe allow, period. Any such civilization will be much more concerned with what it should or should not create than about enhancing its technological powers. A civilization even half a century in advance of our own will be the perfect masters of the doable, within the rules of our continuum.

Feel free to exercise a pretty unfettered imagination. Your far-future humans certainly will have the freedom to let their internal imagery pretty much determine the style of their environment, and so do you when you create it for them.

All you have to do is put yourself in their place and imagine what *you* would do with this reality-making potential.

That's the bad news.

How *do* you get inside a character whose civilization is thousands of years in advance of your own? How can you realistically portray the intellect and emotional life of a being whose *consciousness* transcends your own?

And it will, you know. A sufficiently advanced civilization implies that, too. It implies the ability to tailor states of consciousness quite finely by altering the physical matrix in which it arises—chemically, electronically, or even by downloading to a more perfect medium via brain implants. It implies the ability to write DNA with off-the-shelf chemicals and to synthesize organisms to whim and fashion, including, perhaps, yourself. It implies instant universal access to all of recorded human history and art via full-sensory internal access to enormous data banks.

Is it really possible to convey the consciousness of a *real* citizen of the thirtieth century?

How could it be? In order to realistically convey a consciousness more advanced than your own, *your* consciousness would have to be capable of containing *theirs*, and explicating it to the reader as well, the psychic equivalent of lifting yourself by your own bootstraps.

Human consciousness thousands of years of continuous upward evolution in our future and with an unoccluded historical perspective of same would have to be portrayed as the end product of that process, a process that the writer would have had to undergo before he or she could convey its spiritual, psychic, and intellectual results.

Science fiction writers who believe they have attained such satori either go on to found religions or end up in the rubber room.

But despair not. For while you cannot really create a fictional consciousness that transcends your own, you certainly can use certain literary techniques to create the *illusion* that you've brought such a personage onstage.

If any sufficiently advanced civilization will be able to synthesize anything it wants to out of the quantum soup itself, what will it do with this power? Any civilization that has managed to evolve to the point where it can handle even a tenth of all of this without destroying itself is not going to pursue imperialist adventures. All of the scientific questions that are answerable will have long since been answered. Everyone will have all of the matter and energy they want to play with.

What else can such a civilization do to keep from falling asleep but pursue *novelty*, the delightful shock of the new, be it a raw planet, contact with other races, or the self-created synthetic realities of art?

Is this beginning to sound familiar? Yes indeed, such a civilization must have a cultural core not unlike the aesthetic core of science fiction itself, the pursuit of wonder in the real world and its consequent intellectual and spiritual self-enhancement.

How convenient for those of us trying to write about it!

Science fiction writers can use *themselves* as templates for the creation of a Weltanschauung for a far-future culture. Anything you can fantasize that does not violate a few universal fundamentals *they* can create.

What they create then becomes something you can just let bubble up out of your own subconscious creative processes, because that's precisely what they'll be doing. Where else can such imagery come from? We science fiction writers dream this stuff up and write it, they will dream it up and call it into being, and from the point of view of writing about it, where's the effective difference?

In a sufficiently advanced culture in which most inner fantasies can become realities, most fantasy becomes the legitimate content of science fiction, and a character living in such a future will bear some usable resemblance to the character writing it and to the reader.

In *Riding the Torch*, the viewpoint character is a creator of full-sensory "movies," and how different is that, really, from what the science fiction writer does with prose?

This is a nice little trick adapted from method acting. Conceptualize your far-future story so that it forces you into the skin of your viewpoint character, or, from another point of view, set him up so that he legitimately can have some psychic congruence with the writer and the reader.

That's what you're doing in a much less interesting way when you drop a contemporary viewpoint character into a far-future setting, when you have the quantum tornado plunk down your Dorothy in star-flung Oz.

Of course, in *Riding the Torch*, I used the special trick of making my far-future consciousness a kind of science fiction creator in his own culture, something I really couldn't get away with more than once, which may be why it was my only serious attempt at depicting a far-future culture through the viewpoint of one of its citizens for the first twenty years of my writing career.

That was really the only kind of far-future science fiction I wanted to write or read; very little of it was being written and less still seemed successful; my only attempt seemed based on a technique that didn't seem generally applicable, which is to say, if it wasn't being done successfully by others, and I couldn't see how to do it myself, maybe it just couldn't be written as a general rule.

But maybe not.

Here and there it had been done successfully, most notably in the work of Cordwainer Smith. Smith's huge "Instrumentality" cycle resonated with a truly strange and yet palpably believable future culture, and the stories were told from entirely within the viewpoints of that culture's truly strange people.

So it had been done, and done masterfully, too, meaning that it could be done. But how had Smith done it?

Unfortunately, by no means capable of being generally emulated.

Cordwainer Smith was the pseudonym of one Paul Linebarger, a kind of American Lawrence of Arabia during the Chinese Civil War, and what made his future magic was that it was the future not of Western technological civilization triumphant but a future heavily molded by the consciousness of Chinese civilization and all that its millennial history implies.

But if this was the product of one man's unusual life history rather than a general solution to the problem, it did get me thinking.

Will the consensus reality we presently regard as world civilization be the only one to evolve a far future? What about the vast billions of the Asian mainland, what about the millennial civilizations of India and China and their zen-cyberpunk mutation in Japan? What about the whirling dervishes in Tehran? What do you mean *the* future, white man?

The citizen of A.D. 3000 is going to be the psychic product of a cross-cultural bouillabaisse, not the Epcot Center, and there's nothing like confrontation with consciousness extrapolated from a melange of cultures exotic to their own consensus reality to convince the readers that they're just met someone who definitely isn't from Kansas.

Maybe you can never really get inside the head of a character whose consciousness has evolved beyond our own or really create a far-future culture whose glories can lucidly be seen to have evolved continuously out of our own, but maybe there are *literary* techniques to create the *illusion* that you have.

You can use the whole wide present-day world as your extrapolative pallet, to start with, rather than just *your own* here and now. You *can* at least write about characters whose cultural matrix is greater and richer than your own by fusing together elements from other cultures that have produced plenty of literature for your education.

And you can create the illusion that there is much more to your future universe than you are describing and depths to your future characters beyond the reader's understanding by the simple literary techniques of piling on description and detail while limiting its sphere of operation and giving your characters less than total understanding of *themselves*.

The Void Captain's Tale was my first attempt to deal with the far future after this satori. In *Riding the Torch*, my far-future culture exists only aboard a fleet of starships endlessly roaming the great dead Void; in *The Void Captain's Tale*, my far-future Second Starfaring Age encompasses hundreds of planets, a true golden age of interstellar cultural evolution.

How do you cope with conveying all of that?

Easy. Set the whole story aboard an interstellar Void ship.

This made creating the *illusion* of a vast, complex culture out there beyond the spatial and temporal bounds of the novel much more manageable.

To finesse the advanced-consciousness paradox, I told the whole story from a single first-person viewpoint, that of the Void Captain, who himself is writing it in what he imagines "captain's log style" to have been in his own millennial past.

But how to convey the consciousness of my Second Starfaring Age Void Captain's attempts to explain his actions to himself in his diary?

How else?

Through language. Through *his* language, not my own.

This, of course, is what a lot of fiction tries to do a lot of the time, tell the story in a prose that mirrors the style of the viewpoint character's consciousness. It can be as basic as having Quakers think in thee and thou and street thugs in crude unprintables, as dumb as a long, boring dialect joke or as subtle as *Flowers for Algernon* or as raygun-blasting sheer powerful as William Burroughs.

This is ordinarily a matter of writing talent and perhaps the current evolutionary state of one's craft; this is the art of it, over which you have little volitional control. You either find the voice you need for the story or you go write something else until you do.

In the case of *The Void Captain's Tale*, it took me about ten years to find the form and voice for the story I wanted to tell, so don't get discouraged by concepts beyond your current ability to handle. Let them age a bit in your mental wine cellar.

The reason I couldn't turn this obsessively interesting concept-constellation into a story for so long was that I literally couldn't even begin to write it until I had found an appropriate style to write it in.

If you're trying to extrapolate seriously and portray the results realistically, this is a formidable problem.

Most science fiction simply chooses to knowingly ignore it. Most science fiction set in the far future has the characters speaking and thinking in more or less conventional contemporary or standard English, and it is written in so-called transparent prose crafted to efface itself from the forefront of the reader's consciousness and create full-sensory brain movies.

But, of course, in realistic terms this is nonsense. The language or languages of a millennial future will be as different from contemporary English as English is from archaic German or French is from Latin, and then some.

So I postulated the evolution of a generalized human language called "Lingo." Lingo speakers, humans, would more or less understand one another throughout the far-flung worlds of men and women. More or less. For Lingo has evolved out of all human languages, and the rule is to have no rules; any speaker can choose any word from any language in his data base, and the rules of grammar are anything that can make you understood.

In a sense, then, everyone would speak his or her own personal dialect, or "sprach," of the universal Lingo, sharply or dimly comprehensible to one another depending upon linguistic congruence.

Of course, any novel *really* written in such a made-up language would be entirely incomprehensible to anyone but the writer. James Joyce confined himself to his concept of the Ur-linguistic *present*, but *Finnegans Wake* is still probably the least-comprehensible work of fiction in the literary canon.

Ah, but I had set up Lingo so that I could choose a first-person narrator who spoke an "anglish sprach of Lingo," which is to say, English merely spiced with words and phrases from other languages and using a rather Germanic syntax. The illusion could be completed by having other characters spout bits and pieces of other sprachs that were not in English but were comprehensible just the same.

Pas problem mit that, amigos, beaucoup auslander cognates in packrat íngles!

Sure, I was flattered when certain critics praised the novel for being written in the actual language of the future culture, but I was laughing up my sleeve all the time.

All I had done was create the literary *illusion* that the book was really written in "Lingo."

Smoke and mirrors. A legitimate literary technique.

Could I find literary techniques to do another Second Starfaring Age novel with a broader panoramic vision? In *Child of Fortune*, I chose another first-person narrator who "happened" to speak "an anglish sprach of Lingo" (of course), but since I wanted more geographic scope, I needed a different restricting device within which to contain the illusion.

Instead of confining the action to a single starship, I chose as the viewpoint character a young girl on a voyage of discovery, a somewhat naïve consciousness moving through her extremely sophisticated culture.

Instead of a sophisticated adult viewpoint, I used a highly evolved and educated teenage ingenue from the galactic sticks, Holden Caulfield in outer space, as it were, a bright young initiate into the wider realms of her own culture with as much to learn about it and herself as the writer and reader.

Literary technique. Smoke and mirrors.

Many readers and certain critics spoke of the lead character's travels to a profuse diversity of planets. But actually the action is confined to two starships, three cities, a small town, and an alien forest.

This low-budget literary special effect was borrowed from film; montage, it's called there, using a few selected and fairly easily rendered or affordable locales to suggest a culture and a universe far more diverse than what is actually described or depicted. Much beyond five, and the human mind can be convinced that it's experiencing "many," the reader's imagination collaborates wonderfully in filling the implied gaps and in artful cutting if you let it.

So, too, with creating the illusion of historical connection between the Second Starfaring Age, our present, and the centuries of imaginary history between.

As contemporary fiction is often larded with references—historical, literary, and mythic—to the past in order to give it depth and resonance, so did I use this time-honored technique of literary and mythic reference to lard the speech patterns, tales told by the characters, artforms, architecture, and so forth, of the Second Starfaring Age with references to both real past human history and the imaginary history of the back story.

By jumbling references that resonate in the contemporary reader's consciousness together with references to vague back history I was laying in, I created the literary illusion that the latter existed on the same reality level as the former.

The great lesson of all of this is that portraying a far-future society is strictly a matter of literary technique.

Real accuracy, true realism, is, after all, plain impossible. The science fiction writer of today has about as much chance of accurately predicting the *real* future of even a thousand years from now as Homer did of describing rock and roll, interactive video games, genetic engineering, or the Nielsen system for rating network TV shows.

You're just making all this up, remember?

The far future doesn't really exist for you to describe.

"Accuracy" cannot be a criterion here any more than "realism" can.

What counts is *verisimilitude*.

And what a deconstruction of the word reveals is that it means "appearing to be like reality," or "creating the psychological illusion of reality."

If you faithfully transcribed a real dinner table conversation into prose, the reader would doze off long before dessert. The insides of our ongoing stream of consciousness is not realistically described in *Finnegans Wake* any more than *Child of Fortune* or *The Void Captain's Tale* are really written in Lingo.

Which comes perilously close to saying that writing science fiction set in the far future is, at least in terms of using literary techniques to create verisimilitude, indistinguishable from writing fantasy.

In the far future, where almost anything can be technologically plausible, the success of a piece of science fiction, no less than a piece of fantasy, is dependent on the resonance of the story, the fascination of the characters, and the ability of the writer to use much the same bag of literary techniques to create the literary illusion of verisimilitude, to con the readers into believing the fictional universe is in some way continuous with their own.

No doubt this reeks of heresy to the devotees of hard science fiction, who would insist that I'm talking about science fantasy here, not the real stuff, which, as Gregory Benford puts it, plays the game "with the net up," meaning that, unlike fantasy, it eschews any violation of the presently known laws of the continuum.

But this, too, is a literary convention, an arbitrary assumption made for literary purposes and generally accepted by the reader, just as the reader may accept the reality of magic for the duration of a fantasy.

Namely that we already know everything there is to know about the nature of the net and that we can fix its position precisely in the center of the court in space and time. And by stretching a scientific metaphor a tad, one can even argue that this assumption is inherently paradoxical, violating as it does the Heisenberg Uncertainty Principle, a central maxim of the hard science game itself.

Nevertheless, accepting this restriction can be a legitimate literary device, and indeed a useful and powerful one. It adds a certain unique intellectual interest to a piece of science fiction and it also helps create the literary illusion that the future imagined universe is continuous with our own.

But it *is* a literary device, and the farther out you go along the timeline, the more obvious that becomes. Best current cosmological physics still has black holes in it, singularities beyond which the theories of quantum reality declare themselves inapplicable. So, too, does informed scientific opinion believe that there were eras in the deep past when the so-called immutable natural laws were different and in inherently unknowable ways.

All of this being so, how can we even really place the intrusion of other sets of natural law into our continuum in the far *future* outside the realm of legitimate possibility?

Only by making an arbitrary literary assumption if it suits our aesthetic purpose.

From a hard SF purist viewpoint, maybe the editors chose the wrong person to write this chapter. Then again, maybe not, since the assignment was to offer some advice about *writing* about the far future, not predicting it.

Yet, paradoxically enough, the more you ponder the shape of the far future, the more you reach the conclusion that a sufficiently advanced civilization, far from being defined by scientific limits, will be defined by the scientific liberation of the almost-infinitely possible, and therefore will be centrally engaged with the *creation* of realities, with actualizing its own internal landscape.

Just as you are when you boot up your word processor and open up a new file, or put a clean white piece of paper in the typewriter.

The Ideas
that Wouldn't Die

STANLEY SCHMIDT

Science fiction, it has often been said, is a "literature of ideas."
The more original the ideas a story is based on, the more likely
it is to make an editor sit up and take notice. Editors recognize,
of course, that it's hard—and rare—to come up with a *completely*
original idea, and that some ideas (such as robots and faster-than-
light travel) are so *useful* that many writers will find new things
to do with them. Still, some ideas have been so overworked that
editors tend to groan when they see them yet again.

A couple of years ago I wrote an *Analog* editorial dedicated to
the proposition that both writers and editors would benefit from
writers being aware of which ideas had achieved that unenviably
venerable status. I listed several of them, and soon after it was
published, I got a letter from the fiction editor of another well-
known magazine chiding me for failing to mention talking fish
stories, which she said she seemed to get more of than anything
else. "Actually," I said, "I don't get all that many talking fish
stories—but I did buy one once." ("Downeast Encounter," by
Thomas A. Easton.)

That example proves that it is *possible* to sell a story based on
an old, overworked idea. They don't come much older than that

one; you probably remember it as a fairy tale read to you when you were too young to read it yourself. But it's not *easy* to sell a story based on such an idea. Easton got away with it by making the fish an alien in disguise and setting the story in rural Maine—and capturing the *flavor* of that time and place most engagingly. As you read the following list of popular offenders, you will no doubt recognize others of my "favorite clichés" from familiar and sometimes prize-winning stories—but when that's true, I hope you will also recognize that the stories you remember feature truly exceptional writing. In general, the more familiar the idea, the more outstanding the execution must be to resurrect it. You should, of course, strive for excellence in everything you write—but why make it harder on yourself by making your story's impact depend *entirely* on that?

One more comment before I get into my list. Some of these you may *not* recognize as old and tired. That's because some ideas occur to lots of people but don't really have much substance—so they are often written but seldom published.

And now, without further ado, my list.

Surprise Endings That Aren't

1. *"But it was only a dream."*
2. *"And it was all just a game!"*
3. *"And the computer game turned out not to be a game after all!"*
4. *"The planet's inhabitants called it Earth."*
5. *"And his name was Adam and hers was Eve."*
6. *"And so, after great and protracted agony, the traveler finally emerged into the frightening new world. . . . And the doctor said, 'Congratulations, Mrs. Johnson, you have a fine baby boy!' "*

O. Henry handled twist endings so strikingly that they are commonly identified with his name. Unfortunately, few of his imitators have done nearly as well. The basic trouble with "surprise" endings is that even the best ones will fail to surprise some readers—so if you do use one, it's generally best to treat it as frosting on the cake, and make sure there's enough substance to the story otherwise so that even the reader who guesses the surprise will not feel cheated. The ones in my list will be guessed well in advance by many readers and all editors—few editors, in fact, will need more than one paragraph to recognize any one of them. "Only a dream" was probably old long before I was young—and I imagine my great-great-grandparents were as disappointed as I always am to find that the matters they had been convinced were of monumental importance were really of no importance whatsoever. The two "game" variants became appallingly popular about the time that home computer games did, but mercifully that fad seems to have largely subsided. So does "Adam and Eve," though both that and others like it still crop up often enough that *Analog*'s standard suggestion sheet includes a warning against "scientific retellings of Biblical tales." The planet that turns out to be Earth remains an old standby and usually gives itself away quite early by a reference to "the third planet of a mediocre yellow star," just as the mysterious traveler usually gives himself away by his dramatically alien ordeal and the curious lack of names in his narrative.

Babies and mediocre yellow stars lead us naturally into another class of clichés, these with the added vice of being *wrong*.

Scientific Misconceptions

7. "*She suffered terrible prejudice and persecution because she was a clone instead of a real person. . . .*"
8. "*Jeb rocked on his front porch, squinting out at the steamy jungles that covered Vega V. . . .*"

A clone of a person *is* a person, genetically related to the original in *exactly* the same way as an identical twin. It may well be that some future societies will treat clones as nonhuman (the number of writers who make that mistake makes that seem sadly likely), but that prejudice will be based on a misconception, not scientific fact. The author should not share the misconception with his subjects.

Example #8 offers two misconception/clichés for the price of one. An entire planet covered by a steamy jungle is most unlikely, for purely physical reasons. Think of the enormous variety of habitats and climates Earth has; almost any real world will have comparable variety. Furthermore, worlds suitable for humans to rock on front porches are most unlikely to be found around Vega or any of the other very well-known, distinctively named stars. If you don't see why, and you want to write about other stars and planets, you should first learn something about their true natures and relationships—including such basics as how far apart they are and in what direction. It's bad enough to place your colonies around stars where they wouldn't work; it's worse yet to have people jaunting casually from one to another in directions and at speeds completely inconsistent with reality—but some writers still do it. To avoid being one of them, be advised that the facts you need are available in books. Use them!

Stock Plots

From here on, instead of giving a representative quote, I'll give capsule summaries or descriptions:

9. *"Helen O'Loy" clones.* Not clones in the literal sense, this time, but robots in the form of attractive humans whose owners fall in love with them—just like the one Lester del Rey wrote about in 1938.

10. *The world after a holocaust (usually nuclear) has destroyed civilization*—typically populated by people who spend most of their time moaning about how terrible things are, and

occasionally lecturing each other on how their ancestors brought this upon them.

11. *Totalitarian societies that look just like hundreds of other fictitious totalitarian societies*—but probably not very much like any real one.

12. *Couples applying for state permission to have a baby.*

13. *Individuals applying for state permission to live another year.*

14. *Time travel stories that add nothing new to venerable formulas,* such as killing—or unsuccessfully attempting to kill—one's own grandfather. (The version featuring time travelers involved in the assassination of John F. Kennedy may have added something new the first couple of times it was tried, but seldom, if ever, since 1970 or so—despite far too many attempts.)

15. *Psi stories that add nothing new.* Stories of telepathy, telekinesis, clairvoyance, etc., can be fun, regardless of what you think about the scientific evidence for or against their actual existence. Unfortunately, people had so much fun with them in decades gone by that readers aren't eager to see more—unless you can come up with a really novel variation on the theme.

16. *UFOs, the Bermuda Triangle, vampires, astral projection.* In general, these are so far out on the fringes of science that they are more the stuff of fantasy than of science fiction. If you're clever enough, you may still be able to give one enough scientific basis to sell it to an editor who makes a distinction between science fiction and fantasy—but bear in mind that he's read an *awful* lot of unsuccessful attempts!

17. *Cryogenically preserved patients awakening in Strange New Futures.* True, this is an awfully convenient way to get a contemporary observer into a future society. But those "wake-up" scenes look so much alike that sometimes I think there's a piece of bootleg software out there that generates them at the touch of a key!

18. *Aliens evaluating* Homo sapiens *and/or Earth as a candidate for extermination, admission to a galactic federation, etc.*

19. *Deals with the Devil*. They weren't even new when Goethe wrote *Faust*. They certainly haven't been since—though it seems everybody has to try for a new twist on them, and occasionally someone even succeeds. (But in general, please note, these are fantasy rather than science fiction.)

20. *The frustrated science fiction writer using a time machine to find a more congenial market for his work*. (Okay, I confess: I wrote one, too. But I didn't sell it.)

21. *Obvious take-offs on current events*, such as aliens finding Pioneer 10 and trying to read the plaque it carried. (Or occasionally not so obvious: I never did track down the reason for the rash of "kudzu vine taking over the world" stories I saw a few years ago.) News items can be good sources of ideas—but remember that if an item suggests a story to you, it's likely to suggest it to lots of other people, too. So you have to try to look beyond the *obvious* possibilities.

Narrative Devices and Stock Ingredients

Finally, I lump together some items where the cliché lies more in the kind of story or the method of telling it than in its content.

22. *Unnecessary, pointless, and often tedious sex and violence*. Sometimes stories *need* sex and violence as essential and integral parts of their development. Far more often, a writer seems to think he can sell a story by titillating the editor. It doesn't work, if only because so many others are trying it, too.

23. *Feghoots*. A "Feghoot" is a literary form named after a series of very short stories by Grendel Briarton, about one Ferdinand Feghoot. In general, it's a story with a plot contrived to set up a punch line built around a (usually complex) pun. Unfortunatly, most of the ones attempted by people other than Briarton are much *too* contrived—especially those in which the final puns are on terms invented solely for use therein,

rather than words that would have been used in the normal course of telling a real story.

24. *Hard-boiled private eyes.* These were beginning to get a little weary even before they crept into science fiction.

25. *"Lady or the Tiger" endings.* The story that gave this form its name left the reader uncertain which of two dramatically different endings actually occurred. It worked effectively— because the whole story was constructed to produce that effect. In most of the ambiguous endings I see but don't publish, the ambiguity seems to be more a matter of the author's being too lazy to work his story through to a real conclusion. It is, in a word, a cop-out.

26. *The last-minute gender switch.* This is something that apparently everybody has to try once: cagily avoiding specifying the protagonist's gender, but encouraging the reader to make one guess and then telling him, at or near the end, that he was wrong. Unfortunately, I've seen it work only once. Like it or not, a character's gender is an important part of the *picture* a reader builds up of a character—and if you tell a reader who's already built up a picture that it's wrong, the entire illusion of the story tends to collapse. That, in general, is the last thing you want.

As I said at the beginning, almost any of these clichés can, in the hands of a sufficiently skilled writer, be the basis of a successful story. You may recognize Orson Scott Card's Hugo- and Nebula-winning *Ender's Game* as #3 on my list. David R. Palmer's *Emergence* is unarguably a post-holocaust story—but the unforgettable heroine (who does *not* just moan about how terrible things are) makes it far more than *just* a post-holocaust story. I once bought a story called "Floodtide" from Ben Bova, who preceded me as *Analog* editor, and wrote that warning against retelling Biblical tales. I couldn't resist pointing out the irony of the fact that "Floodtide" *was* such a retelling. Timothy Zahn, now successful and popular, launched his career a few years ago with a series of stories that breathed life into the whole psi business by looking at characters with *very limited* paranormal abilities.

But in every such case where a tired old idea led to a lively new story, it did so through the magic of a writer who could add something special to it. In no case did the mere novelty of the idea justify the story; these ideas haven't had that for a long time. As an editor, I'd like every writer's writing to be so inspired that it *can* revivify an old cliché—but realistically, I know that's not likely. So I would instead advise all who would write science fiction to read as much as they can of what has already been written—not so they can imitate it, but so they can avoid repeating it.

And if you can write well enough that you *could* revive an old idea, but apply that skill to something really new—that will be even better.

Part III

THE BUSINESS
OF WRITING

The Mechanics
of Submission

SHEILA WILLIAMS

This chapter may come as a relief to those who are just beginning to learn about the craft of writing science fiction and fantasy. Unlike more abstract qualities of fiction—such as plotting, characterization, and comedy, and the creation of believable far futures, aliens, and alien worlds—the professional presentation of a manuscript is a skill that is not too difficult to acquire.

Although this skill is an essential part of any professional author's repertoire, it frequently is undervalued by the beginner. The need for a professional-looking manuscript should not be perceived as an idle whim. Such a manuscript fulfills a multitude of purposes.

When purchasing fiction, an editor must keep the typesetter's needs in mind. Manuscripts must be formatted in a way that accommodates the editor's corrections and the typesetter's codes. This is why everything meant for publication, including letters to the editor, must be double-spaced. A typesetter will have a very difficult time setting a heavily marked up story, and no typesetter will set a handwritten text.

A clean and professional manuscript also shows the editor that the author is serious about his or her work. It implies that the writer is willing to take the time to do whatever research is required to get things right. By extension, it implies that the author is willing to take the time to work on the more important elements of fiction writing. The sale of even the finest-looking manuscript depends on the tale itself. But careful preparation will ensure that the story receives the consideration it deserves.

Know Your Market

The first step in the process is to find out as much as you can about your market. Presumably you've read some science fiction and fantasy and are certain your story fits in somewhere. Now, if you are a short-story writer, it's time to look at the magazines and anthologies to determine which ones might be interested in the story you want to write. To contact these outlets, you may have to do a little research. Some of these places are listed along with their addresses and the names of the editors to contact in "Market Listings" on page 250. Other listings may be found in such magazines as *Writer's Digest* and *The Writer* and in trade magazines about science fiction, such as *Locus* and *Science Fiction Chronicle*. These magazines also are listed in the "Market Listings," and they can be found at some libraries and local newsstands.

Before you submit your tale to a magazine, you should familiarize yourself with that publication and obtain a set of its manuscript guidelines. If you cannot find a copy of the magazine locally, you can usually purchase a sample copy directly from the publisher.

Once you have a copy of the magazine or anthology, be sure to read it thoroughly. Your own story should not be imitative or derivative of the tales in these publications. From the contents of these works, though, you should be able to determine whether your story seems to be, on a very general basis, the sort of tale the editor is looking for. A magazine whose emphasis is on hard science fiction may not be the place to send a pastoral fantasy or a supernatural horror story. If a story opens with three pages of sex scenes, it may not be right for the magazine that seems to be looking for family entertainment. Remember, though, that we are discussing *types* of stories. Don't despair if you find you've written a fantasy unlike any you have seen in a magazine that caters to fantasy. The editor is on the lookout for refreshingly new tales, and yours just may be the next one she or he purchases. If, after looking at the magazine, you cannot decide whether your tale is right for it, go ahead and send it in. It is up to the editor, not the writer, to ultimately accept or reject the story.

When you know where you want to send your manuscript, write and request the publication's manuscript guidelines. Unless instructed otherwise, be sure to send along a self-addressed, stamped number ten business envelope (that is, a standard 9½-by-4⅛-inch white envelope). These guidelines will briefly discuss manuscript format, the rate of pay, the rights that will be purchased, and the kinds of stories the publication is looking for. To avoid making any serious mistakes, be sure to procure guidelines from each of the publications you are considering. The requirements at one magazine may differ slightly from the next, and in some instances they actually may contradict one another.

These guidelines will let you know whether a magazine or anthology is interested in simultaneous submissions. For a number of reasons, many science fiction publications do not want to see this type of submission. Magazine editors must consider hundreds of manuscripts in a short period of time. Once they have spent time on a story and have decided to purchase it, it can be irritating to discover that the story has been sold elsewhere on a simultaneous submission. Since these editors usually operate within the confines of strict editorial budgets, with standard payment rates set and advertised, it is unlikely that they will have room to negotiate for the tale. If a magazine's payment rate is your first consideration, you should tailor your submission schedule accordingly—send your work first to the highest-paying market and proceed from there.

If your manuscript is a photocopy of the original or has been generated via computer, you may want to make its status clear. Either write NOT A SIMULTANEOUS SUBMISSION on the first page of the manuscript or state it in your cover letter.

Manuscript guidelines also will indicate whether the publication is interested in query letters. Most magazines prefer to make their decision about a story after they have read the entire tale and not on the basis of a query letter. A brief synopsis of the story will not reveal if the tale is publishable, and the time spent responding to the query letter will only detract from the time available for reading your stories carefully. However, if you are thinking of writing a piece of nonfiction or have written a novel that you think the editor may be interested in serializing, it is advisable to query first.

The procedure determining where to send a novel, though, differs from that mentioned above. Visit your library first and look for a current copy of *LMP (Literary Market Place)* or *Writers' Market*. These excellent reference books provide addresses and telephone numbers for virtually every book publisher in the United States. In addition, they each include a section that classifies book publishers by the subject matter they publish. Contact each publisher to determine the name of the editor who purchases science fiction or fantasy, whether he or she is interested in nonagented fiction, and what is the preferable form of submission. Many publishers want to see a sample chapter and outline of a novel before deciding whether to consider the entire book.

Manuscript Preparation

Manuscripts should be neatly typed on one side of white sixteen- to twenty-pound paper. Do not use erasable, onionskin, or any other type of paper that is subject to smearing. Try to avoid smudges, cross outs, and handwritten corrections. Be sure your ribbon is fresh and the type is dark. If you use a computer and have a dot-matrix printer, make certain that it generates letters that are dark and legible. A sloppy manuscript is both difficult to read and dangerous to submit to a typesetter. Remember, the typesetter will reinterpret your notations and, if your type cannot be read clearly, it will be easy to get it wrong.

A professional short-story manuscript does not need a folder or a cover sheet. Since these must be separated from a story before it is readied for the typesetter, they often are lost or filed away. As you will see below, these pages usually are redundant anyway. Any important information must appear on the first page of the manuscript.

The first page of a manuscript should begin with the author's real name and mailing address in the upper left-hand corner. This name is the one that will appear on the check that will be issued if the story is purchased. It does not have to be the same as the name the author chooses to write under. You may also want to include your telephone number beneath your address. While preparing your manuscript for publication, an editor may suddenly have an urgent question that requires he or she reach you by phone. This information is optional, though, because most questions and transactions are handled easily and more appropriately through the mail.

The upper-right-hand corner should contain the manuscript's approximate word count. The easiest way to determine a word count is to count the number of words on an average long line and multiply this number by the number of lines appearing on a full page of your story. This number should then be multiplied by the number of full pages in your manuscript. Partial pages should be added up next and then added to your total. One reason you should never justify your right margin—that is, add extra space to a line so that the right margin is as even as the left—is that by doing so, you will throw off this word count completely. You will find that editors may use a slightly more complicated procedure to determine the actual word count, and in fact, their procedures are not all alike. This formula, however,

will give you a fairly accurate approximation of the number of
words in the manuscript.

Next, you should center your title and byline one-third of the
way to halfway down the first page. The byline is the name you
want to appear with the story. Thus, while your check may go
to Robert F. Newcomb, your story may be by Bob Newcomb,
R. F. Newcomb, Frederick Roberts, or nearly any other name
of your choosing (Robert A. Heinlein or Arthur C. Clarke may
not go over too well with most editors, though). Apart from the
top margin on the first page, all four margins on each page should
be one inch wide. Subsequent pages should carry your last name
and the page number in the upper-right-hand corner.

```
Sheila Williams                          3000 words
380 Lexington Avenue
New York, NY  10017
```

```
                  THE MECHANICS OF SUBMISSION

                       by Sheila Williams


        This chapter may come as a relief to those who are just

   beginning to learn about the craft of writing science

   fiction and fantasy.  Unlike more abstract qualities of

   fiction--such as plotting, characterization, and comedy, and

   the creation of believable far futures, aliens, and alien

   worlds--the professional presentation of a manuscript is a

   skill that is not too difficult to acquire.

        Although this skill is an essential part of any

   professional author's repertoire, it is frequently

   undervalued by the beginner.  The need for a professional-

   looking manuscript should not be perceived as an idle whim.
```

Your story should start about four line spaces beneath the byline. Paragraphs should be indented, and all manuscripts should be double-spaced. Do not put extra spaces between paragraphs. An example of a properly prepared first page appears opposite.

Remember that what you are trying to achieve here is the highest degree of legibility possible. Reading hundreds of manuscripts each month is not an easy task, and it is often complicated by improperly prepared manuscripts. Editors sometimes get stories submitted on reams of unseparated computer paper. Other stories have been typed with ribbons so old that the letters seem to fade away as they are read. And manuscripts have been typed on just about every color of paper available. Even a superficial look at a manuscript of this sort will make any experienced editor leery about the fiction it contains.

The most professional-looking manuscript, however, will not mask an author's poor grasp of spelling, grammar, and punctuation. These skills are essential, and they cannot be stressed too often or too emphatically. They take time to develop. A brief essay such as this one can only offer the aspiring writer some modest tips on this subject.

If you are not comfortable with your spelling, be sure to check everything. Leave nothing to chance. A dictionary is an author's friend. Keep one at your side whenever you are at work. Reference material on the use of language—especially Strunk and White's *Elements of Style*—should be part of any author's library.

Read alertly. You can learn a lot simply by paying attention to the way the English language is employed in books and magazines. These works are usually proofread carefully before they are published, and while they are rarely entirely free of errors, they can be helpful guides to proper usage. Since newspapers tend to follow their own styles for spelling and punctuation, though, it is probably best not to rely on them as a source for this information.

You may want to ask a friend with a diligent eye to take a look at your work and point out your errors. If you doubt her or his accuracy, though, be sure to double-check your reference books before you make the suggested corrections.

Do not let yourself become dependent on a computer spell-checking program. Many manuscripts that do not contain a single misspelling are full of misused words and typographical errors that resulted in real, but improper, words. The person who has to read a pile of unsolicited manuscripts will have a hard time getting past the phrase "he was coping with undo influences" or the sentence "There cat sat over their." Basic errors of this sort seem to reveal a lack of sincerity and effort on the part of the author.

Manuscript Submission

Once your manuscript is written, neatly typed, and ready to go, there are a few other matters to keep in mind. Your story must be accompanied by a self-addressed envelope. This envelope must be stamped with enough postage to ensure that, should your tale be rejected, it can be returned to you. The envelope should accommodate your manuscript comfortably. An eight-page manuscript crammed into a typical business-size return envelope will result in a wrinkled and unsightly looking story.

Always keep a copy of the story on hand. This will avoid an irreparable disaster should your manuscript be lost in the mail. It also will mean that you will have the story available should the editor need to contact you about it. If you intend to send out a new copy of the story each time you submit it, mark your manuscript DISPOSABLE. When doing so, enclose a small envelope with enough postage to cover the mailing costs of a letter of acceptance or rejection. If you are sending your story to a foreign country and do not want to pay too much extra for the return postage, you may find this method to be quite useful. When corresponding with an editor in a foreign country, be sure to include enough International Reply Coupons to cover the cost of a return manuscript or letter. These coupons can be purchased at the post office.

As long as a returned manuscript still looks neat, there is nothing wrong with resubmitting the same manuscript elsewhere. This is part of a time-honored tradition, and it helps cut down on the waste of our natural resources.

You may want to include a cover letter along with your story, but doing so is not essential. If you do send a letter, keep it short. Do not synopsize the tale or send a lengthy biography. You may mention your writing credentials, though, and you may include any experience you have had that is relevant to the tale. If, once the story is purchased, the editor needs additional information for your biographical note, he or she will ask you for it.

Most short-story publishers accept unsolicited manuscripts. You can determine which magazines, anthologies, and anthology series do not from the market listings and the manuscript guidelines. The short-story editor who accepts both agented and non-agented fiction will give equal consideration to both types of submissions. Indeed, agents frequently prefer to let their authors take care of their short stories themselves. This means that the aspiring author does not need an agent to break into short fiction. Once an author has published a few short stories, it usually isn't too hard to find an agent.

Follow Up

Response time will vary from magazine to magazine and from situation to situation. Sometimes it will even differ from what is stated in the market report. If the manuscript is rejected and it seems to come back too quickly, don't despair. To find new material, editors must take a look at every single story that comes in. On rare occasions, they are all caught up and can take a look at a manuscript on the day it arrives. At other times, they may be delayed because of deadlines, illness, holidays, and vacations.

Some stories are delayed in the mail and other delays are due to the need to ponder the fate of a particular tale. An author probably should assume that it may take two months for a story to travel to and from an editorial office. She or he may want to throw in a third month for "unforeseen circumstances." After that it would be wise to write and ask whether the story arrived at the office.

If your story is rejected, do not be discouraged by a form letter. There simply is not enough time to respond personally to every story submission. While your story may not have worked for one editor, it may well work for another. It's important to keep sending it out and to keep on writing new ones.

Be sure to keep a record of every story you have on submission. Record where it has been and where it is going so that you do not resubmit it to an editor.

If you sell your story, you will receive a contract from the publisher. Most publications will be interested in first North American serial rights. This means that that magazine or anthology will be the first to publish your story. The contract may offer additional payments for foreign and anthology rights. Take a careful look at the document to determine whether you are prepared to accept all of its terms. If you have any questions, you should not hesitate to get in touch with the editor or the company's contracts manager.

Mastering the skills described in this chapter brings you one step closer to becoming a professional author. A beautifully prepared manuscript will not sell a story, but a poorly prepared manuscript undermines the effort to market your work.

In the end, it is the finely drawn characters and intriguing ideas that sell a piece of fiction. A properly prepared and submitted manuscript helps ensure that the editor discovers these qualities.

Revisions

ISAAC ASIMOV

When it comes to writing, I am a "primitive." I had had no instruction when I began to write, or even by the time I had begun to publish. I took no courses. I read no books on the subject.

This was not bravado on my part, or any sense of arrogance. I just didn't know that there *were* courses or books on the subject. In all innocence, I just thought you sat down and wrote. Naturally, I have picked up a great deal about writing in the days since I began, but in certain important respects, my early habits imprinted me and I find I can't change.

Some of these imprinted habits are trivial. For instance, I cannot leave a decent margin. Editors have tried begging and they've tried ordering, and my only response is a firm "Never!"

When I was a kid, you see, getting typewriting paper was a hard thing to do, for it required m-o-n-e-y, of which I had none. Therefore what paper I had, I saved—single-spaced, both sides, and typing to the very edge of the page, all four edges. Well, I learned that one could not submit a manuscript unless it was double-spaced and on one side of the page only, and I was *forced*, unwillingly, to adopt that wasteful procedure. I also learned about margins and established them—but not wide enough. Nor could I ever make them wide enough. My sense of economy had gone as far as it would go and it would go no further.

More important was the fact that I had never learned about revisions. My routine was (and still is) to write a story in first draft as fast as I can. Then I go over it and correct errors in spelling, grammar, and word order. Then I prepare my second draft, making minor changes as I go and as they occur to me. My second draft is my final draft. No more changes except under direct editorial order and then with rebellion in my heart.

I didn't know there was anything wrong with this. I thought it was the way you were *supposed* to write. In fact, when Bob Heinlein and I were working together at the Navy yard in Philadelphia during World War II, Bob asked me how I went about writing a story and I told him. He said, "You type it *twice*? Why don't you type it correctly the first time?"

I felt bitterly ashamed, and the very next story I wrote, I tried my level best to get it right the first time. I failed. No matter how carefully I wrote, there were always things that had to be changed. I decided I just wasn't as good as Heinlein.

But then, in 1950, I attended the Breadloaf Writers' Conference at the invitation of Fletcher Pratt. There I listened in astonishment to some of the things said by the lecturers. "The secret of writing," said one of them, "is rewriting."

Fletcher Pratt himself said, "If you ever write a paragraph that seems to you to *sing*, to be the best thing you've ever written, to be full of wonder and poetry and greatness—cross it out, it stinks!"

Over and over again, we were told about the importance of polishing, of revising, of tearing up, and rewriting. I got the bewildered notion that, far from being expected to type it right the first time, as Heinlein had advised me, I was expected to type it all wrong and get it right only by the thirty-second time, if at all.

I went home immersed in gloom and the very next time I wrote a story, I tried to tear it up. I couldn't make myself do it. So I went over it to see all the terrible things I had done, in order to revise them. To my chagrin, everything sounded great to me. (My own writing always sounds great to me.) Eventually, after wasting hours and hours—to say nothing of suffering spiritual agony—I gave it up. My stories would have to be written the way they always were—and still are.

What is it I am saying, then? That it is wrong to revise? No, of course not—anymore than it is wrong not to revise.

You don't do *anything* automatically, simply because some "authority" (including me) says you should. Each writer is an individual, with his or her own way of thinking, and doing, and writing. Some writers are not happy unless they polish and polish—unless they try a paragraph this way and that way and the other way.

Once, Oscar Wilde, coming down to lunch, was asked how he had spent his morning. "I was hard at work," he said.

"Oh?" he was asked. "Did you accomplish much?"

"Yes, indeed," said Wilde. "I inserted a comma."

At dinner, he was asked how he had spent the afternoon. "More work," he said.

"Inserted another comma?" was the rather sardonic question.

"No," said Wilde, unperturbed. "I removed the one I had inserted in the morning."

Well, if you're Oscar Wilde, or some other great stylist, polishing may succeed in imparting an ever higher gloss to your writing and you *should* revise and revise. If, on the other hand, you're not much of a stylist (like me, for instance) and are only interested in clarity and straightforward storytelling, then a small amount of revision is probably all you need. Beyond that small amount you may merely be shaking up the rubble.

I was told last night, for instance, that Daniel Keyes (author of the classic "Flowers for Algernon") is supposed to have said, "The author's best friend is the person who shoots him just before he makes one change too many."

Let's try the other extreme. William Shakespeare is reported by Ben Jonson to have boasted that he "never blotted a word." The Bard of Avon, in other words, would have us believe that, like Heinlein, he got it right the first time, and that what he handed in to the producers at the Globe Theatre was first draft.

(He may have been twisting the truth a bit. Prolific writers tend to exaggerate the amount of nonrevision they do.)

Well, if you happen to be another Will Shakespeare, or another Bob Heinlein, maybe you can get away without revising at all. But if you're just an ordinary writer (like me) maybe you'd better do *some*. (As a matter of fact, Ben Jonson commented that he wished Will had "blotted out a thousand," and there are indeed places where Will might have been—ssh!—improved on.)

Let's pass on to a slightly different topic.

I am sometimes asked if I prepare an outline first before writing a story or a book.

The answer is: no, I don't.

To begin with, this was another one of those cases of initial ignorance. I didn't know at the start of my career that such things as outlines existed. I just wrote a story and stopped when I finished and if it happened to be one length it was a short story and if it happened to be another it was a novelette.

When I wrote my first novel, Doubleday told me to make it seventy thousand words long. So I wrote until I had seventy thousand words and then stopped—and by the greatest good luck, it turned out to be the end of the novel.

When I began my second novel, I realized that such an amazing coincidence was not likely to happen twice in a row, so I prepared an outline. I quickly discovered two things. One, an outline constricted me so that I could not breathe. Two, there was no way I could force my characters to adhere to the outline; even if I wanted to do so, they refused. I never tried an outline again. In even my most complicated novels, I merely fix the ending firmly in my mind, decide on a beginning, and then, from that beginning, charge toward the ending, making up the details as I go along.

On the other hand, P. G. Wodehouse, for whose writings I have an idolatrous admiration, always prepared outlines, spending more time on them than on the book and getting every event, however small, firmly in place before beginning.

There's something to be said on both sides, of course.

If you are a structured and rigid person who likes everything under control, you will be uneasy without an outline. Then, too, if you are an undisciplined person with a tendency to wander all over the landscape, you will be better off with an outline even if you feel you wouldn't like one.

On the other hand, if you are quick-thinking and ingenious, but with a strong sense of the whole, you will be better off without an outline.

How do you decide which you are? Well, try an outline, or try writing without one, and find out for yourself.

The thing is: don't feel that any rule of writing must be hard and fast, and handed down from Sinai. By all means try them all out but, in the last analysis, stick to that which makes you comfortable. You are, after all, an individual.

Writing for
Young People

ISAAC ASIMOV

There is an exceedingly useful volume entitled *The Science Fiction Encyclopedia* edited by Peter Nicholls (Doubleday, 1979) to which I frequently refer. Recently, as I leafed through its pages en route to looking up something, I came across the following passage:

". . . the intellectual level of a book is not necessarily expressed by a marketing label. Much adult sf, the works of . . . Isaac Asimov, for example, is of great appeal to older children, and is to some extent directed at them."

The second line of three dots in the above quotation signals the omission of a few words in which the writer specifies two other science fiction writers. I omit them because they may resent the original statement and may not feel I ought to give the remark further circulation.

As for me, I don't object to the comment because, for one thing, I consider it true. I write my "adult" novels for adults, but I have no objection whatever to young people reading them, and I try to write in such a way that my novels are accessible to them.

Why?

First, it is the way I like to write. I like to have the ideas in my novels sufficiently interesting and subtle to catch at the attention and thinking of intelligent adults, and, at the same time, to have the writing clear enough so as to raise no difficulties for the intelligent youngster. To manage the combination I consider a challenge, and I like challenges.

Second, it is good business. Attract an adult and you may well have someone who is here today and gone tomorrow. Attract a youngster and you have a faithful reader for life.

Mind you, I don't write as I do with the second reason in mind; I write as I do for the first reason I gave you. Nevertheless, I have discovered that the second reason exists, and I have long lost count of the number of people who tell me they have an astronomical number of my books and that they "were at once hooked after reading my book, so-and-so, when they were ten years old."

But if the same books can be read by both adults and youngsters, what is the distinction between truly adult books (ones that the writer of the item in *The Science Fiction Encyclopedia* would judge as possessing a high "intellectual level") and truly juvenile books?

Let's see. Can it be vocabulary? Do adult books have "hard words" while juvenile books have "easy words"?

To some extent, I suppose that might be so. If an author makes a fetish of using unusual words, as William Buckley does (or Clark Ashton Smith, to mention someone in our own line), then the writing grows opaque for youngsters and adults alike, for it is my experience that the average adult does not have a vocabulary much larger, if any, than a bright youngster does.

On the other hand, if an author uses the *correct* words, hard or easy, then the bright youngster will guess the meaning from the context or look it up in a dictionary. I think the bright youngster enjoys having his mind stretched and welcomes the chance of learning a new word. I don't worry about my vocabulary, for that reason, even when I am writing my science books for grade school youngsters. I may give the pronunciation of scientific terms they are not likely to have encountered before, and I sometimes define them, but I don't avoid them, and after having given pronunciation and definition I use them freely.

Well, then, is it the difference between long sentences and short sentences?

That is true only in this sense: It is more difficult to make a long sentence clear than it is to make a short one clear. If, then, you are a poor writer and want to make sure that youngsters understand you, stick to short sentences. Unfortunately, a long series of short sentences, like a long stretch of writing with no "hard" words, is irritating to anyone intelligent, young or old. A youngster is particularly offended because he thinks (sometimes with justice) that the writer thinks that because the youngster is young, he is therefore stupid. The book is at once discarded. (This is called "writing down," by the way, something I try never to do.)

The trick is to write clearly. If you write clearly enough, a long sentence will hold no terrors. If you hit the proper mix of long and short, and hard and easy, and make everything clear, then, believe me, the youngster will have no trouble. Of course, he has to be an intelligent youngster, but there are a larger percentage of those than of intelligent oldsters, for life hasn't had a chance yet to dull the youngsters' wits.

Is it a matter of subject matter? Do adult novels deal with death and torture and mayhem and sex (natural and unnatural) and all kinds of unpleasantness, while juvenile novels deal with sweetness and niceness?

You *know* that's not so. Think of the current rash of "horror" films, which fill the screen with blood and murder and torture and are designed to frighten. Youngsters flock to them, and the gorier they are, the more they enjoy them.

Even censors don't seem to mind the mayhem. When there are loud squawks from the righteous who want to kick books out of school libraries, the objections are most often to the use of "dirty" words and to sex. However, I have, in my time, lived half a block from a junior high school and listened to the young-sters going there and coming back. I picked up a lot of colorful obscenity, both sexual and scatological, in that way, for I had forgotten some of what I had learned as a youngster. I think the youngsters themselves would have no objection to books con-taining gutter language and sexual detail—or fail to understand them, either. *That* distinction between adult books and juvenile books is not a natural one but is enforced by adult fiat.

(I admit that I use no gutter language or sex in my juvenile books, but then I use no gutter language and very little sex in my adult books.)

How about action, then? Adult books can pause for sensitive description of all kinds, or for a skillful and painstaking dissection of motivation, and so on. Juvenile books tend to deal entirely with action. Is that right?

Actually, the distinction is not between adults and juveniles, but between a few people (both adult and juvenile) and most people (both adult and juvenile). Most people, of whatever age, are impatient with anything but action. Watch the popular ad-venture programs on television, subtract the action, and find out what you have left, and then remember that it is adults, for the most part, who are watching them.

On the other hand, my books contain very little "action" (hence no movie sales) and deal largely with the interplay of ideas in rather cerebral dialogue (as many critics point out, sometimes with irritation) and yet, says the *Encyclopedia*, I appeal to young-sters. Clarity, not action, is the key.

Can it be a question of style? Are adult books written in a complicated and experimental style, while juvenile books are not? To be sure, a juvenile book written in a complicated and exper-imental style is more apt to be a commercial failure than one written in a straightforward style. On the other hand, this is also true of adult books. The difference is that tortuous style is fre-quently admired by critics in adult books, but never in juvenile books. This means that many adults, who are guided by critics, or who merely wish to appear chic, buy opaque and experimental books, and then, possibly, don't read them, aside from any "dirty parts" they might have. Proust's *Remembrance of Things Past* springs to mind. My dear wife, Janet, is reading it, every word, for the *second* time but there are moments when I see the perspiration standing out, in great drops, on her forehead.

How about rhetorical tricks? Metaphors, allusions, and all the rest of it, depend upon experience, and youngsters, however bright they are, have not yet had time to gather experience.

For instance, my "George and Azazel" stories are pure fluff, but they are the most nearly adult stories I write. I use my full vocabulary, together with involved sentence structure, and never hesitate to rely on the reader to fill in what I leave out. I can refer to "the elusive promise of nocturnal Elysium" without any indication of what I mean. I can speak of the Eiffel Tower as a "stupid building still under construction" and depend on the reader to know what the Tower looks like and therefore see why the remark is wrong, but apt. Nevertheless, the stories are meant to be humorous and all the rhetorical devices contribute to that. The young person who misses some of the allusions nevertheless should get much of the humor and enjoy the story anyway.

In short, I maintain there is no hard and fast distinction between "adult" writing and "juvenile" writing. A good book is a good book and can be enjoyed by both adults and youngsters. If my books appeal to both, that is to my credit.

New Writers

ISAAC ASIMOV

Max Planck first introduced the quantum theory in 1900. The quantum theory was so revolutionary, involved such a reorganization of mental attitude as far as physics was concerned, that it divides the science into two sections. Physics before 1900 is called "classical physics"; physics after 1900 is "modern physics."

Nevertheless, quantum theory was not immediately or enthusiastically accepted. Most physicists (especially those who were advanced in years and experience and renown) found it impossible to abandon their classical mind-set. Even Planck himself had trouble thinking of quantum theory as anything but a mathematical trick. It was not until 1905, when Albert Einstein, then twenty-six years old, showed how quantum theory could explain the photoelectric effect when classical physics could not, that quantum theory was forced into acceptance.

Even so, Planck is reported to have said, in a moment of despondency, that the only way in which a new scientific theory can be accepted is to wait patiently for all the old scientists to die.

This is not entirely true, of course, but one can easily find examples of first-class, top-notch scientists who reach a mental stage of immobility as they grow old. Lord Kelvin, an absolutely brilliant physicist, found himself, in the last decade of his life, unable to accept the exciting discovery of radioactivity. Ernest

231

Rutherford, probably the greatest nuclear experimentalist who ever lived, was quite certain toward the end of his life that all talk of usable nuclear power was "moonshine."

I like to call this "the principle of the immobility of success." (Others call it "Clarke's Law," because someone named Arthur C. Clarke—whoever he might be—once said, "When a distinguished but elderly scientist states that something is possible, he is almost certainly right. When he states that something is impossible, he is very probably wrong.")

Whatever you call it, this principle of the immobility of success probably holds for all human endeavors to some extent. Thus, it is my contention that a science fiction writer tends to cling to the style of writing and the type of story he (or she—please consider my references as applying to either sex even when, for convenience, I make use of the masculine pronoun) developed as a youngster. His very success seems to make it impossible for him to budge from the spot.

This is not always completely true, of course. Sometimes a writer of some decades of experience is influenced by the changing atmosphere of the field to alter the nature of his own work (perhaps unconsciously, rather than deliberately). If so, the change may be helpful to his continuing career but it is usually comparatively small and the writer's traditional style shines clearly through.

It is also possible that a writer, sensing change about him, deliberately tries to write in a radically new fashion. This (it seems to me) can be disastrous, for it may produce the same effect we get when a sexagenarian decides to dress in the new teen-age styles.

I might as well use myself as an example. My formative decades as a writer were in the 1940s and 1950s. In the 1940s, I wrote my Foundation stories. In the 1950s, I wrote my robot novels. In the 1960s and 1970s, the field changed radically and, since I had no intention of trying to attempt to fit the square peg of my writing into the round hole of the "new wave," I began to turn most of my attention to non-fiction.

When, in the 1980s, I was persuaded to return to science fiction in a massive way, I knowingly and deliberately continued the type of writing I did in the 1940s and 1950s. I was perfectly aware that it would be derided as "old-fashioned" or "passé"—and some critics have used even more forcefully derogatory adjectives—but I felt I had no real choice. Fortunately, the readers (even those who weren't born till well after I had written and published the stories and novels of my youth) flocked to my books with enthusiasm. That greatly relieved me, for I suffer from the immobility of success. I lack the ability, and I *certainly* lack the desire, to budge from the literary style of my earlier youth.

But if writers such as I persist in writing "classical science fiction" rather than "modern science fiction," how is science fiction going to advance? Following Planck's dictum, must we wait for all the old writers to die?

That takes too long, actually. I can think of several leading lights in the field (including me) who have been writing for a long, long time, and who cavalierly dismiss any suggestion that they either die or retire.

Then what about the other side of the coin? Why not concentrate on the young writers, the new writers, those who have radically novel styles and fashions that are being forged in the stress and heat of the 1990s? It is they, after all, who will be at the cutting edge of the field, right?

Right!—But there are problems.

Every once in a while I get a letter from an aspiring science fiction writer who wants to know if I have any hints that can put him on the proper course. I don't have any of the hints he wants, of course, for he probably expects me to tell him to make a certain incantation over the manuscript before he mails it off and that it will then surely be accepted.

I am always reminded, on such occasions, of the tale of Wolfgang Amadeus Mozart, who was asked by a young would-be composer for hints on symphony writing. Mozart said, "You are young. Start with something very simple and work your way up to symphonies."

"But, Herr Mozart," said the youngster, "you wrote symphonies when you were considerably younger than I am now."

"Ah," said Mozart, "but I didn't ask anybody for hints."

Well, I can't quite bring myself to say anything like that, so I generally give those who ask me something I call "the three hints of Asimov."

1. Read as much contemporary science fiction as possible so that you will learn what science fiction is all about right now.
2. Write as much science fiction as possible because you need the practice.
3. Cultivate a very thick skin so that you will survive the disappointment and frustration you will undoubtedly have to cope with.

That's the way I managed, and let no one think that I was "lucky" and that I "had it easy." After I sold my first science fiction story it took exactly twenty years of constant reading and writing before I could actually make a good living as a science fiction writer.

Why is this?

Well, some of the reasons are obvious. For instance, it isn't at all likely that a new writer is going to write a publishable story. Even if a new writer is copiously talented, talent is not enough. One also has to have technique and judgment, and such things come only with experience. It takes time.

Yes, but suppose the talent shines through. Suppose the technique is a bit crude, the plotting a bit obvious, the characters a bit cardboard, but suppose it is obvious that, with time, the writer is going to develop into a major influence in the field.

The sad fact is, though, that editors don't always recognize the fact that talent is shining through.—And even if they do, they're in business to make money, and few editors are willing to lose money on a book by a worthy new writer just to encourage him, when it is so much safer to publish a book by an established writer (such as me) that is so sure to sell that it is money in the bank for everyone.

What is needed then is a flourishing world of science fiction magazines. One story among many per issue is a smaller investment than an entire book. It is easier for a magazine to risk supporting a new writer who shows plenty of talent, and give him a chance to gather experience as well.

It's a gamble, of course, but a science fiction magazine like *Asimov's* (to choose one at random) often presents the maiden efforts of future greats.

Authors vs. Editors

STANLEY SCHMIDT

A fan at a science fiction convention once told John W. Campbell, one of my predecessors as editor of *Analog*, that he occasionally tried his hand at writing stories. Campbell asked the young man whether he had submitted any of them to *Analog*, and he replied modestly, "Oh, no; they're not good enough." Whereupon Campbell drew himself up and demanded indignantly, "How dare you reject stories for my magazine?"

Which illustrates a good point for both aspiring and experienced writers to bear in mind: if in doubt about whether a story or article is right for a particular market, let the editor decide. Yet the idea of submitting your brainchild to an editor is something many writers quite understandably find rather intimidating. Many writers, especially new ones who have never actually *met* an editor face to face, tend to think of editors as The Enemy. Not only does he (or she) exercise considerable power over what happens to the writer's work, but it is all too easy to imagine all manner of dreadful things he *could* do—even if he *buys* your piece.

What is the author-editor relationship really like? Are writers and editors antagonists—or partners? As with any other kind of relationship, the answer depends very much on the individuals involved. Editors really can do some very unpleasant things to writers, and very occasionally, they do. It doesn't happen often, but it's certainly worthwhile for writers to know what to watch out for—and what isn't worth worrying about. On the other hand, editors can be extremely helpful to writers trying to learn or exercise their craft, and it's also worthwhile to know how to encourage that kind of interaction. Similarly, writers can do things that are extremely irritating to editors—but they also do those things which, more than any others, make being an editor worthwhile.

I've been both a writer and an editor long enough to have seen many of the things that can make the author-editor relationship good or bad—from both points of view. I hope the insights I've gained from that "stereoscopic" perspective might be helpful to both writers and editors.

The Editor as Enemy: What Writers Fear and Dislike in Editors

The most basic (and probably commonest) complaint writers have about editors is one for which I can offer no easy cure: "He doesn't appreciate my talent or my work." What this really means is: "He doesn't buy my stuff." One of the first things a beginning writer must do is develop a realistic understanding of the various reasons why work is not bought. Basic principle number one: What an editor buys is in all cases at least partly a matter of *taste*—and this does not mean "good taste" or "bad taste" so much as *taste*, like whether you like fish or not. An editor is *not* a divinely appointed arbiter of what's Good and Bad. He is an individual human being with individual preferences as quirky as those of any other individual. The fact that he doesn't buy your story or article may simply mean that it wasn't his cup of tea— but some other editor may love it. Sometimes an editor may even turn down a piece he personally likes very much because he thinks his readers won't like it in his magazine. For example, *Analog* is a magazine of science fact and science fiction; many of its readers also like fantasy, but they want to get that somewhere else.

Basic principle number two: Most editors receive far more submissions than they can use. At *Analog*, for example, I may get a hundred manuscripts in a typical week; but, on average, I can only buy one or two. Many stories are sent home not because they are conspicuously *bad*, but simply because they don't stand out as *special* from 98 percent of the competition, which is quite literally what they must do to make it. New writers who think they don't have a chance because they're new, while Established Writers have it made and sell everything easily, should note that even the old pros are up against those numbers and get turned down oftener than you might think. *Everybody* has to make his or her work stand out that strongly, and anybody who does it, new or old, is likely to get noticed. The fact remains, though, that what stands out as special depends on the individual editor and what kind of audience he's working for. If a suitable market doesn't exist, you may have to wait until one opens up. My personal record is about twenty years: a "quintessentially 'Twilight Zone'" story that I didn't even know where to submit until a magazine called *Rod Serling's "The Twilight Zone"* started up— and bought it immediately. Never give up on a piece just because one editor turned it down. Try it on every other editor you can find who might be interested—and remember that every time an editor moves from one house to another, that gives you at least one and often two new markets to try.

Of course, many stories do have clearly identifiable and fixable faults, and another complaint writers often have about editors is that they don't provide individual criticism. This, too, is unfortunate but unavoidable; those numbers tell you why. I wish I could critique every story I get, but since I personally *read* every story I get, and sometimes spend large amounts of time critiquing the ones that are almost what I want, those are usually the only ones I have time to critique.

A more justifiable complaint concerns manuscripts being held too long with no response. This can be a real problem, but it's one you'll probably have to live with, to some extent. As an editor, I set myself deadlines and try to make sure you have an answer within a month. As a writer, I wish all editors did that, but some very good ones don't, for one reason or another. I'd rather wait three or four months for a contract, or even useful criticism, than get an unceremonious turndown by return mail. Certainly it's reasonable to write a polite inquiry about a manuscript you haven't heard anything on in a month (but not much sooner). If the wait stretches out so long you decide you'd rather forget that market and try another, it's reasonable to send a registered letter stating that if you've heard nothing by a specified date—say, three weeks off—you're withdrawing the submission. I can only recall having had to do that once, but there was a time when an editor had a manuscript of mine for well over a year, ignored three letters asking about it, and finally returned it (without even a printed rejection slip!) only after I complained to the Grievance Committee of a writers' organization I belonged to. I think it's fair to say that no writer can reasonably be expected to consider that acceptable performance—and I certainly wouldn't advise any editor to emulate it.

Writers sometimes worry about their ideas being stolen while their manuscripts are in an editor's possession. I can recall few, if any, cases where this has actually happened. Most editors and writers have such huge backlogs of their own ideas that it's hard to interest them in working on somebody else's. What's more likely to happen, if an editor sees an idea that he likes in your work, is that he'll be so delighted that he'll want to help you develop it into publishable form. Remember also that truly new, completely original ideas are really very rare. Some are so overworked that I can count on seeing them many times every month (for some examples, see "The Ideas that Wouldn't Die," page 200). But even the most memorable stories often get that way just by bringing some fresh insight to an old basic idea—though if you *can* come up with a genuinely brand-new and striking idea, it's one of the best ways I know to make your work stand out from the crowd.

I have had a very few writers complain, apparently seriously, about *paperclips* being stolen by editors. I will not deny that paperclips sometimes disappear around the office or in transit— not because editors are so hard up they have to steal them, but simply because they fall off easily. If you consider this a serious problem, I suspect that you are far too thin-skinned for a writing career—which will surely and routinely bring you far worse frustrations than that.

Suppose an editor *buys* your manuscript. What dreadful things might he do then? The commonest legitimate fears in this area concern changes made in the manuscript, which could change the meaning or undermine the artistic integrity of the author's work. Let's break those changes down into two classes: those made by the editor, and those requested or suggested by the editor to the author.

I'm told that there are editors who routinely make sweeping rewrites without the author's prior knowledge or approval. I guess I've been lucky; I've had very little experience with them. I did have one unpleasant experience with a book which had already been serialized with only the most minimal copyediting and to considerable reader acclaim, but when it came out in paperback fell victim to a heavy-handed copy editor who made pointless little changes right and left. Fortunately I saw proofs, so I was able to undo most of the damage before it was too late. That's your best protection against this sort of thing: always try to insist on the chance to check and correct proofs—and, if at all possible, the copyedited manuscript—before things get that far. In the case of a book, you or your agent can probably write that requirement into your contract. With magazines, you may have less control— but if you have a choice between a publisher who lets you read proofs and one who doesn't, there's a lot to be said for the former.

What if an editor asks *you* to make changes and you don't agree with them? Then don't make them—but do think about them first. My philosophy as a writer has always been to listen carefully to what an editor had to say, and act on it if I could agree with it. If I couldn't agree with it, or at least agree that his version was no worse than mine, I would try to find a new editor for that piece and write a new one for the first editor. As an editor, I recommend the same approach to everyone who writes for me. By following it, I've probably lost a few sales I might have been able to make. But when I *have* revised in response to editorial suggestions, *I've* almost always liked the result better, too. Humbling as it is to admit, sometimes a good editor can be a very useful critter to have around. Which brings us to . . .

How Editors Can Help Writers

What is a good editor? Probably no editor is good for all writers, but let me define a good editor *for you* as one who can help you do better what you're trying to do on your own. The most important way he or she does this is by serving as a "third eye" that can see your work from a different viewpoint than you can—in particular, a more objective viewpoint. As the author of a piece, you inevitably see it from a viewpoint rather like that of any one of the blind men in the old folk tale about the elephant. You're standing too close to it to be able to see what it looks like to somebody approaching it from a distance with his eyes open. That's what your readers will do; your editor can do it first and point out problems that they would see that you missed. He may even be able to suggest ways to fix them. Many times I have sent a manuscript off with the vague feeling that something about it hadn't worked quite the way I wanted it to, but without being able to put a finger on what was wrong. Sometimes an editor could put into a few words what was bothering me; and once I knew what it was, I could do something about it.

Sometimes an editor's suggestions will be quite specific, such as suggesting a new title or a revised wording for a sentence. When appropriate, I tend to prefer the technique I used to grumble about when John Campbell used it on me: not changing your work, but telling you what bothers me and challenging you to find a way to fix it. In the short run, that makes more work for the writer. In the long run, you learn a lot more from figuring out your own solution than from rubber-stamping mine—and that benefits us both because it makes you more likely to do it right on the first try next time. Finding your own solution also makes it more likely that you'll find one that *you* really like— and since it's your byline on the story, you'd probably prefer that the content be as completely yours as possible.

Another function of an editor is to goad writers into pursuing the consequences of their ideas as far as possible. A great many unsolicited short stories end just when they're really getting started, because the writer has mistaken a good *setup* for a good *story*. My job is to point that out and insist that he finish the job before I buy it. This, too, makes more work for the writer, in the short run—but in the long run is better for his career because the readers see a more memorable piece of work under his name. And just in case you think I only appreciate this philosophy from the viewpoint of an editor making other writers do extra work, let me tell you why my novel *Lifeboat Earth* is dedicated to Ben Bova. He ran five segments of it as novellas when he was editing *Analog*—and he made me rewrite the last two from the ground up before he would take them. That was close to forty thousand words of rewriting, but I'm very grateful that he made me do it— because the book is much stronger than it would have been if he hadn't. Frankly, I find it a little scary to think that some editors might have accepted them in their first incarnation just because I had a contract for the book.

Finally, a thing you can't *expect* an editor to do, but some will, is literally to inspire you—either by outright suggesting ideas (and letting you take full credit for them), or by asking key questions that lead you to think of them on your own. My first cover story in *Analog* was directly suggested by an imaginary situation that John Campbell described in considerable detail in a four-page rejection letter; he claimed it was suggested to him by something in the story he was rejecting. Isaac Asimov's classic story "Nightfall" was a direct result of Campbell's quoting a line of

Emerson's about what would happen if men only saw the stars once every thousand years, and asking Asimov, "What do you think would *really* happen?"

Sometimes an editor's best work of this sort is almost accidental. Once, during a lull in a science fiction convention, I went for a walk in downtown Chicago and ran into two authors I'd been cultivating. I introduced them and a conversation ensued in which one mentioned a story he'd been wanting to write but shying away from because it required a detailed knowledge of both computers (which he knew) and law (which he didn't). The other's eyes lit up. "I've been wanting to write that same story," he said, "but haven't because I don't know enough about computers. But I *am* a lawyer. . . ." The result was a collaboration that wound up a nominee for the prestigious Hugo Award.

What Editors Dread About Writers

Most of the things writers do that irk editors seem to be more the result of inexperience than of malicious intent. It's true that, once in a great while, a well-established writer will prove exasperatingly uncooperative about meeting deadlines or considering changes, or will become shrill and abusive if even a trivial mistake is made in the publication of his work. But what I see far more of is simple but irritating quirks in the *submission* of manuscripts—and most of those come from new writers, presumably because they don't know any better.

It has long been standard practice, for example, that any manuscript submitted for publication should be typed in black ink on one side only of $8\frac{1}{2} \times 11$-inch white paper, with the author's name and address on the first page and *some* kind of identification on every page. It is standard practice that the manuscript be accompanied by a return envelope capable of holding it, preaddressed to the author and stamped with sufficient postage (or, in the case of foreign authors, accompanied by sufficient Interna-

tional Reply Coupons). There are good reasons why all these
things have become standard practice, but they may be more
readily apparent to editors than to writers. Editors spend a huge
portion of their time reading and they only get one set of eyes
each, so they want that reading to be as easy and painless as
possible. Black ink deposited by clean type and a fresh ribbon on
white paper, with lots of space between the lines, fills the bill
quite nicely. If the manuscript is bought, that space is also needed
for writing detailed technical instructions to the typesetter. A
standard paper size makes it easier to handle the towering piles
of manuscripts that fill our offices. "One side only" reduces the
danger of an editor or typesetter becoming confused about which
side he or she should be working on, and makes it easier to
compare pages side by side. Self-addressed, stamped envelopes
(SASEs) are necessary because most manuscripts do get sent back,
and most publishers can afford neither the postage nor the time
required to stamp and address the numbers they receive.

All of these things being as they are, no editor I know appre-
ciates receiving manuscripts scrawled in blotchy red ink on both
sides of yellow legal paper or hotel notepads, or even typed single-
spaced on erasable paper on a typewriter that should have had
its type cleaned and its ribbon changed three years ago. Yet we
all do receive them, and I can't imagine that their authors really
want our first impression to be what it is in such cases. Nor are
we fond of manuscripts that arrive without return postage in three-
foot cardboard mailing tubes—though we occasionally get a submission packaged *so* outrageously that we get a good chuckle from
it before rejecting it. The novel that arrived in a bright-red suit-
case, preceded by several postcards heralding its imminent en-
trance, was pretty good. But my all-time favorite was the short
story that came in a large pizza box—duly accompanied by a
self-addressed, stamped, small pizza box. (I was tempted to return
that one with an anchovy clipped to the front page.)

The last few years have brought a few changes in acceptable
forms of submission—and along with them, new sources of irritation. I refer, of course, to computers. Probably more writers

use word processors than typewriters now, and good printout is quite generally accepted. But a feeble ribbon is no more welcome on a printer than on a typewriter, and most editors prefer output that looks more like printing than a connect-the-dots puzzle. *Please* separate the sheets of tractor feed paper! And while you may reasonably ask not to have a manuscript returned because it's cheaper to print a new one, you'll still need a business-size SASE for the editor's reply.

Then there are cover letters. Actually, cover letters are seldom necessary unless there's something the editor needs to know about the story that isn't obvious from the manuscript itself—for example, that it's a rewrite of one he expressed an interest in three months earlier. A cover letter addressed to "Dear Editor," or to an editor who left eight years ago, or even one who has never been with your magazine, instantly tells the present editor that you haven't bothered to learn anything about your market. Belligerent, boastful, or defensive cover letters—like the one telling me that I would surely publish this article if I had "any guts at all," which the author suspected I did not—do you no possible good. If your work is any good, by the standards the editor is using, he'll notice. If it isn't, no amount of hype by you will conceal that fact. Let your story speak for itself—and try to make sure it speaks *well* for itself.

Cover letters warning the editor of all the elaborate measures the author has taken to protect himself against plagiarism have little effect beyond making the editor not want to be accused of having ever even *seen* the manuscript—so you can imagine how eagerly he's going to read it. I got one of these that included a second paragraph telling me in great detail how intelligent and well-educated the author was, and warning me that parts of the article might be over my head and I should use a dictionary for the hard words. Of course, cover letters aren't the only way to deliver gratuitous and counterproductive insults. An old favorite is the trick of sticking a page in upside down to see whether the editor read that far. I usually leave the page as it is, but attach a note saying THIS SIDE UP or DON'T DO THIS.

There is one kind of request we often see that most of us sympathize with, but seeing it in yet another letter just makes us feel bad about the sheer impossibility of complying. Most of us would *like* to give personal, detailed criticism on every manuscript we see. But, for the reasons I've already explained, we can't. Some writers try to make it easier by providing checklists of things that they think might be wrong and asking us to take "just a couple of minutes" to use the list. What they don't realize is that it takes a lot more extra time than they think to decide where to put the checkmarks. Consider this analogy: Often you can decide very quickly that you're not interested in buying a particular car, but it might take quite a long time to analyze exactly why it doesn't appeal to you, much less figure out what would have to be done to fix it so you would want to buy it. As long as you have a reasonable hope of finding a car that you want to buy as is or with relatively minor repairs, you can't justify spending that time. In the case of stories, even if I did take time to decide where to put a checkmark, very often it would be at best an oversimplified and misleading sort of critique. The problems with almost-publishable stories are often subtle and hard to pin down. I recall one case where I read a revised draft of a novella by a professional with a solid track record and liked everything except the ending—but it was six hours before I could put into words *why* I didn't like the ending.

Being a teacher is an important and rewarding part of an editor's job—but it's not his *primary* responsibility. He is not employed to give writing instruction to all who ask for it but to find and acquire good material to publish in magazines or books. He can afford to spend time giving instruction only to those who show good promise of contributing to that goal in the rather near future. If you want to be one of the few students he can work with individually, you, like the rest of us, will have to get far enough on your own to attract his attention. Otherwise, to get criticism on everything you write, you'll have to go to someone who *is* employed to do that—and pay for his services. Whining to a busy editor that "new writers have no chance" merely convinces him that you're one of them and don't yet understand how the business really works.

What Editors Like About Writers

After all that, you may wonder whether there's anything editors *like* about writers. The answer is a most emphatic *yes:* I've saved the best for last. For me, and I think for most editors, one of the most rewarding aspects of the job is the chance to work with some of the brightest, most interesting people we have ever met. Writers are a highly diversified lot, but almost all I've met are stimulating and likable—and no two are alike. They are what make editing worthwhile.

Even, you may ask, the new ones? *Especially* the new ones. Oh, it's true that sometimes there are long dry spells when I read hundreds of manuscripts and none of them jump out at me as *special,* and a discouraging number do the exasperating things I talked about above. But then, once in awhile after a long period of that, I suddenly discover that I'm about to miss my train because my attention is completely absorbed by a writer nobody else has heard of—yet. It doesn't happen often, but when it does, that thrill of discovery, followed by the satisfaction of watching that "unknown" blossom into somebody readers watch and wait for, is the single biggest reward of editing.

I know how discouraging it can be to keep sending off story after story and getting them back with no real feedback because you haven't yet reached that point. I've been there. But now that I've been on the other side of the desk, I can assure you that your stories are being read. Every time I pick up your latest story, I'm really hoping that it will almost make me miss my train. And if someday you do, you'll have my gratitude and active interest for a long time thereafter.

Who Needs Editors? A Closing Note for the Future

At a recent convention, a young man raised the question: why have editors at all? In his view, art is self-expression and editing is interference with that self-expression—something embarrassingly close to censorship. My reply is that you are certainly free to express whatever you like, however you like—but if you want somebody else to spend his time and money to publish it, you have to expect him to take an active interest in what it is that he's publishing. Nobody can publish everything; anyone who goes into publishing has to make choices. Some of us think that a highly valid criterion for choice is: is there an audience that would like to read this? In our view, art isn't art until it *communicates*. An editor is a matchmaker: he tries to match people who like to write a certain kind of thing and people who like to read that kind of thing. And then he tries to make sure that a smooth connection is established between them.

Nevertheless, I can see a certain validity in the young man's point. What about the writer who's writing things that would appeal to some people, but not very many, and there's no editor currently acting as a bridge to connect that writer to those readers? Are not all other editors acting as a barrier between them? In a sense, yes. So far that has been an unavoidable side effect of the editor's role as a filter, going through a hundred stories that *might* appeal to his readers to find one or two that *will*. But it may no longer be unavoidable. Modern communications technology, with all the capabilities opened up by things like computers and modems, is beginning to make it possible for anybody to publish anything. It will become increasingly possible for a writer who hasn't been able to find an editor to send his work out on its own to seek readers.

But as that movement spreads, I predict a strange side effect: a renewed and increased demand for editors, coming from readers. We are already bombarded by so much information that readers need editors to wade through some particular part of the flood and find things most likely to interest them, because very few would have the time, ability, or patience to do all that wading ourselves. When the flood becomes bigger, people to sort through it will be needed more than ever.

Yet the new option, for publishing even things missed by editors, will be there, too, and once in a while readers will discover somebody who builds a following by word of mouth. The overall result will be a wider range of options for readers: more editors sorting through more material, but at the same time an increased opportunity for writers to be discovered and read *without* editorial intervention.

That, I think, will be a very healthy development for readers. And readers, not writers *or* editors, are ultimately who writing is all about.

Market Resources

IAN RANDAL STROCK

Since the original publication of this book, almost every listing we originally included has changed at least once, and some have changed so many times that we no longer feel we can provide a listing that will be relevant by the time you read this book. However, we can direct your attention to some periodicals and resources that have reliably provided valuable market information.

Two magazines concentrating exclusively on SF/F are *Locus* and *Science Fiction Chronicle*. In addition, there are *Writer's Digest* and *The Writer*, for generic freelance writing. You might also want to check out the *Writer's Market*, published annually by Writer's Digest Books, as well as their biannual volume, *Science Fiction Writer's Marketplace and Sourcebook*.

A number of editors make the comment, "We read your stories, please read our magazine." Find out what the magazine publishes before you submit to it. Also, a magazine's guidelines often will tell you if your work is *not* right for the magazine and saves you the time and expense of buying a copy. *All* magazines emphasize the need for an SASE of sufficient size and postage. Even if you don't want the manuscript back, send a business-size SASE for their response. Submissions to foreign countries must be accompanied by International Reply Coupons (IRCs), since domestic stamps are no good for mailing from foreign countries.

Locus, Locus Publications, PO Box 13305, Oakland, CA 94661. Single copy: $4.50. Yearly subscription: 2d class—$43.00 U.S./$48.00 Canada; 1st class—$53.00 U.S./Canada

Science Fiction Chronicle, PO Box 022730, Brooklyn, NY 11202-0056. Single copy: $2.95. Yearly subscription: $35.00 U.S./$42.00 Canada.

Writer's Digest, Box 2123, Harlan, IA 51593. Single copy: $2.99 U.S./$3.99 Canada. Yearly subscription: $27.00.

The Writer, The Writer, Inc., 120 Boylston Street, Boston, MA 02116-4615. Single copy: $2.50. Yearly subscription: $28.00 U.S./$36.00 Canada.

Scavenger's Newsletter, 519 Ellinwood, Osage City, KS 66523-1329. Single Copy: $2.50. Yearly subscription: $17.00 (bulk mail) or $21.00 (first class).

The Gila Queen's Guide to Markets, P.O. Box 97, Newton, NJ 07860. Sample issue $5.00. One-year subscription $34.00/$38.00 Canada.

Part IV

APPENDIX
Guidelines
(Analog and Asimov's)

ANALOG
SCIENCE FICTION AND FACT

1270 Avenue of the Americas, 10th Floor
New York, NY 10020

Analog will consider material submitted by any writer, and consider it solely on the basis of merit. We are definitely anxious to find and develop new, capable writers.

We have no hard-and-fast editorial guidelines, because science fiction is such a broad field that I don't want to inhibit a new writer's thinking by imposing Thou Shalt Nots. Besides, a really good story can make an editor swallow his preconceived taboos.

Basically, we publish *science* fiction stories. That is, stories in which some aspect of future science or technology is so integral to the plot that, if that aspect were removed, the story would collapse. Try to picture Mary Shelley's *Frankenstein* without the science and you'll see what I mean. No story!

The science can be physical, sociological, psychological. The technology can be anything from electronic engineering to bio-genetic engineering. But the stories must be strong and realistic, with believable people (who needn't be human) doing believable things—no matter how fantastic the background might be.

Manuscripts must be typed, double-spaced, on white typewriter paper, one side of the sheet only. *Good* quality computer printout with these characteristics is fine, but please separate the sheets.

Indent paragraphs but do not leave extra space between them. Please do not put manuscripts in binders or folders.

Author's name and address should be on the first page of the manuscript. No material submitted can be returned unless accompanied by sufficient postage, a stamped, addressed envelope, or International Reply Coupons.

Analog pays 6–8 cents per word for short stories up to 7,500 words, $450–600 for stories between 7,500 and 10,000 words, and 5–6 cents per word for longer material. We prefer lengths between 2,000 and 7,000 words for shorts, 10,000–20,000 words for novelettes, and 40,000–80,000 for serials.

Please query first on serials *only*. A complete manuscript is strongly preferred for all shorter lengths.

The entire contents of each issue is copyrighted at the time of publication. Payment is on acceptance.

Good luck!

Stanley Schmidt
Editor

1270 Avenue of the Americas, 10th Floor
New York, NY 10020

Asimov's Science Fiction is an established market for science fiction stories. We pay on acceptance. Beginners get 6.0 cents a word to 7,500 words, 5.0 cents a word for stories longer than 12,500, and $450 for stories between those lengths. We pay $1 a line for poetry. Poems should not exceed 40 lines. We buy first North American serial rights plus certain nonexclusive rights, which are explained in our contract. The contract also sets forth the additional money we pay you if a story is picked up in one of our anthologies. We very seldom buy stories longer than 15,000 words, and we don't serialize novels. We do not publish reprints, and we don't want to see "simultaneous submissions" (stories sent at the same time to a publication other than *Asimov's*). *Asimov's* will consider material submitted by any writer, previously published or not. We've bought some of our best stories from people who have never sold a story before.

In general, we're looking for "character-oriented" stories, those in which the characters, rather than the science, provide the main focus for the reader's interest. Serious, thoughtful, yet accessible fiction will constitute the majority of our purchases, but of course there's always room for the humorous as well. (No puns, please!) Fantasy is fine, but no Sword & Sorcery or cute little elves, trolls, or dragons. Neither are we interested in explicit sex or violence. A good overview would be to consider that all fiction is written to examine or illuminate some aspect of human existence, but that in science fiction the backdrop you work against is the size of the universe.

Manuscripts submitted to *Asimov's* must be neatly typed, double-spaced on one side of the sheet only, with one-inch margins, on bond paper (no erasable paper, please). Any manuscript longer than 5 pages should be mailed to us flat. Please do NOT send us submissions on disk. When using a word processor, please do not justify the right-hand margin. If sending a printout, separate the sheets first. The title page should include the title of your story, your name and address, and the number of words in your story. Enclose a cover letter if you like. All manuscripts *must* be accompanied by a self-addressed, stamped envelope large enough and carrying enough postage to return the manuscript. If you wish to save on postage, you may submit a clear copy of your story along with a standard long (number 10) envelope, also self-addressed and stamped. If you mark your copy "DISPOSABLE," you will receive our reply (but not your manuscript) in the small envelope. We do not suggest that you have us dispose of your original typescript. If you live overseas or in Canada, use International Reply Coupons for return postage.

Finally, we regret that it has become necessary for us to use form letters for rejecting manuscripts, but time limitations are such that we have no choice. Unfortunately, we are unable to provide specific criticism of each story. Our response time runs from two to five weeks. If you have not heard from us within three months, you can assume your manuscript was lost in the mail, and are welcome to resubmit it to us. We do not keep a record of submissions, but if you would like to know if we received your submission, include a self-addressed stamped postcard.

Thank you for your interest in *Asimov's* and good luck!

Gardner Dozois
Editor

ALSO AVAILABLE FROM ST. MARTIN'S PRESS

	QUANTITY	PRICE
Those Who Can: A Science Fiction Reader edited by Robin Wilson ($13.95) **ISBN: 0-312-14139-4** (trade paperback)	_____	____
Paragons: Twelve SF Writers Ply Their Craft edited by Robin Wilson ($14.95) **ISBN: 0-312-15623-5** (trade paperback)	_____	____
Creating Short Fiction: Third Edition by Damon Knight ($13.95) **ISBN: 0-312-15094-6** (trade paperback)	_____	____
Modern Classics of Science Fiction edited by Gardner Dozois ($16.95) **ISBN: 0-312-08847-7** (trade paperback)	_____	____
Modern Classic Short Novels of Science Fiction edited by Gardner Dozois ($15.95) **ISBN: 0-312-11317-X** (trade paperback)	_____	____
The Encyclopedia of Science Fiction by John Clute and Peter Nicholls ($29.95) **ISBN: 0-312-13486-X** (trade paperback)	_____	____

POSTAGE & HANDLING
(Books up to $12.00 - add $3.00;
books up to $15.00 - add $3.50;
books above $15.00 - add $4.00 —
plus $1.00 for each additional book)   _____

8% Sales Tax (New York State residents only)   _____

Amount enclosed: _____

Name _____

Address _____

City _____ State _____ Zip _____

Send this form (or a copy) with payment to:
Publishers Book & Audio, P.O. Box 070059, 5448 Arthur Kill Road, Staten Island, NY 10307.
Telephone (800) 288-2131. Please allow three weeks for delivery.
For bulk orders (10 copies or more) please contact the St. Martin's Press Special Sales Department
toll free at 800-221-7945 ext. 645 for information. In New York State call 212-674-5151.